Decade of Discontent

Decade of Discontent
The Changing British Economy since 1973

NICK GARDNER

Basil Blackwell

Copyright © Nick Gardner, 1987

First published 1987

Basil Blackwell Ltd
108 Cowley Road, Oxford, OX4 1JF, UK

Basil Blackwell Inc.
432 Park Avenue South, Suite 1503
New York, NY 10016, USA

British Library Cataloguing in Publication Data

Gardner, Nick,
    Decade of discontent : the changing
    British economy since 1973.
    1. Great Britain——Economic conditions——1945–
    I. Title
    330.941'0857   HC256.6

    ISBN 0-631-15307-1
    ISBN 0-631-15308-X Pbk

Library of Congress Cataloging-in-Publication Data

Gardner, Nick,
    Decade of discontent.

    Bibliography: p.
    Includes index.
    1. Great Britain — Economic policy — 1945–
    2. Great Britain — Economic conditions — 1945–
    I. Title
    HC256.6.G36 1987 338.941 86–30949
    ISBN 0-631-15307-1
    ISBN 0-631-15308-X (pbk.)

Typeset in Plantin 10 on 12pt by Alan Sutton Publishing Ltd., Gloucester
Printed in Great Britain by Billing and Sons Ltd., Worcester

Contents

To My Wife

Preface

In a speech made in 1983, the then Governor of the Bank of England referred to the preceding ten years as 'our decade of discontent'. This book retells the story of the economic ideas, policies, and events of that period. It is told from an economist's standpoint, but it is intended to be comprehensible to readers with little or no training in economics.

For those who lived in Britain during that period, there may seem little point in reading about events that they could as well recollect. For them, as for others, the book will contain some surprises. Events will frequently turn out to be not as they recollect – even for those with excellent memories. Many of the statistics which were presented to them at the time have since been revised. Some of the, apparently reasonable, interpretations which were put upon them – especially by interested parties – have since proved to have been mistaken. Memory is in any case, for most of us, a distorting mirror.

The story is in many ways a depressing one. Nevertheless, it encompasses one of the most eventful periods in the history of the formulation and testing of economic ideas, and it may well be that eventually more will be learned from 'the decade of discontent' than from any previous period.

The facts presented in this book are drawn from published sources. The views expressed are mine and not those of any government department in which I have served.

Nick Gardner

1

Background to the Decade

I INTRODUCTION

A traveller returning home after a ten-year absence is inevitably impressed by the changes which occurred during his absence. For a British traveller returning in 1983, the experience would have been exceptional. Many of the changes which he would have found were without parallel in previous peacetime experience. Littered streets, dilapidated buildings and congested traffic might have been among his early impressions, and he would soon have learned of big increases in unemployment and in crimes of violence and of many other changes for better and for worse. The purpose of this book is to tell the story of those changes and of the events and ideas which gave rise to them.

Some of the principal changes which occurred between 1973 and 1983 are reviewed in chapter 6. The intervening chapters are concerned with how those changes came about. Three of them – chapters 2, 4 and 5 – tell the story of events as they occurred. The fourth – chapter 3 – interrupts the narrative to give an account of the crucial changes in attitudes and ideas which occurred in the mid-1970s. The concluding chapter is a postscript on events since 1983 and on prospects for the future. The remainder of this present chapter offers some background information to help the reader to place the events of the decade in a broader historical context.

The story of the period 1973–83 is littered with first-time occurrences and broken trends, and yet the origins of much that happened during that period can be traced to developments in earlier years. Section II of this chapter gives a brief account of some of the major trends in the pattern of life in post-war Britain up to 1973. In later chapters, as the story unfolds, some of those trends will be found to persist, and others to be broken. (A break in the trends of inflation and unemployment did in fact occur before 1973, but consideration of this is postponed until the end of this chapter.)

What people did in the period 1973 to 1983 was strongly influenced by ideas and attitudes which had been formed well before that period. Section

III of this chapter deals with post-war attitudes and ideas in general, and this is followed in section IV with an account of the revolution in economic thinking brought about by the teachings of John Maynard Keynes.

The British experience during that period and before, differed noticeably from what happened in other countries. The differences owed something to the peculiarities of the British political system, and these are the subject of section V below. Section VI deals briefly with the policies adopted by post-war British governments up to 1972. Section VII compares British economic performance over the post-war years to 1968 with the performance of other industrial economies, and section VIII deals with the upsurge of inflation which occurred during the period 1968 to 1972.

II THE CHANGING PATTERN OF LIFE

The standard of living of the British people probably improved more rapidly in the period 1948–73 than in any previous period. The improvement showed itself in shorter working hours, longer holidays and better housing and education, as well as higher incomes.

Table 1.1 Growth rates, 1856–1937 and 1951–73 (average annual percentage rates)

Period	Output growth	Growth of output per employee
1856–1937 (excluding wartime years)	2.0	1.0
1951–73	2.8	2.4

Source: R. C. O. Matthews, C. H. Feinstein and J. C. Odling-Smee, *British Economic Growth 1856–1973*, (Clarendon Press, 1982).

Output and productivity

As the first column of table 1.1 shows, output grew between 1951 and 1973 at an average rate which was some 40 per cent faster than the average rate during the previous peacetime years since 1856. This was despite a reduced rate of growth of the number of people at work; and as the second column shows, the growth rate of output per person employed was well over twice the 1856–1937 average.

Population, employment and leisure

Table 1.2 shows that the population grew less rapidly on average between 1951 and 1973 than between 1856 and 1973 as a whole, and hours worked per head of the population fell more rapidly. The third column of the table shows that the total number of hours worked fell between 1951 and 1973, compared with a rise for the total period between 1856 and 1973.

Table 1.2 Population and labour input growth 1856–1973 and 1951–73 (average annual percentage growth rates)

	Population	Hours worked per head of population	Total hours worked
1856–1973	+0.7	−0.5	+0.2
1951–73	+0.5	−1.0	−0.5

Source: Matthews, et al., *British Economic Growth*.

The fall in the total number of hours worked between 1951 and 1973 was made up of an increase in the number employed, offset by a substantial fall in the average number of hours worked per employee. The benefits of increased prosperity were increasingly taken in the form of more leisure. The normal working week, which averaged 44.5 hours in the 1950s, fell to 40 hours by 1966; and actual hours worked (including overtime) fell from 48 in the 1950s to 44.5 by 1971. Paid holidays also increased: in 1961, 97 per cent of manual workers had an annual entitlement of two weeks; by 1970, over half of them were getting three weeks or more. The combined effect of these developments is shown in table 1.3.

Table 1.3 The fall in working hours 1951–73

Year	Hours worked per week	Weeks worked per year	Hours worked per year
1951	44.6	46.4	2070
1973	38.1	45.9	1750

Source: Matthews et al., *British Economic Growth*.

Although the total number of people employed increased between 1951 and 1973, the number of male employees did not increase. As table 1.4

Table 1.4 Employment changes 1951–73

| | *Employees in employment*[a] *GB millions* | | | |
| | Males | Females | | |
		Full-time	Part-time	Total
1951	13.5	5.75	0.75	6.5
1973	13.5	5.4	3.3	8.7

[a] Excludes the self-employed.

Source: Estimated from *Dept of Employment Gazettes*.

indicates, all of the increase was in female employment, and nearly all of that increase was in part-time workers. There was a persistent upward trend in the numbers of married women going to or looking for work. The proportion of women in this category rose from 26 per cent in 1951 to 41 per cent in 1971 – a rate which was much higher than in most other European countries. This was associated with earlier marriage, improved contraceptives and falling family sizes, and cheaper household equipment, such as washing machines. It was made possible by the fact that employers were prepared to make arrangements for work to be done at times which married women found convenient.

Over the period as a whole, there was a declining trend in the numbers employed in agriculture, mining and manufacture, but a more than offsetting increase in those employed in the service sector; especially in insurance and finance, in professional and scientific occupations, and in the public service.

Investment and technical progress

Investment over the period 1952–73 amounted to nearly 19 per cent of GDP, compared with 9–10 per cent in the period 1857–1937. The capital stock of British industry, in particular, was increased more rapidly than in earlier periods. Table 1.5 gives estimates of the rates of growth of three categories of capital.

Advances in technology were made in many directions. The most spectacular advances were in the fields of electronics and communications. The transistor came into mass production in the 1950s, and was incor-

Table 1.5 Growth rates of gross domestic fixed capital (annual percentage rates)

	1873–1913	1913–37	1937–73
Industry and commerce	2.2	1.2	3.1
Infrastructure	2.4	1.2	2.1
Dwellings	1.9	2.3	2.0

Source: Matthews et al., *British Economic Growth*.

porated with other devices into integrated circuits containing hundreds of components in the 1960s, rising to tens of thousands in the 1970s. Prices fell precipitately, typically to less than a tenth of their level of a decade previously, and electronic equipment became vastly more compact. The impact which these and other developments had upon the availability of computing power is illustrated by the development of cheap pocket calculators, capable by the 1970s of what in the 1940s had required a computer weighing many tons, and costing millions. More important for industry and commerce were modestly priced computers capable of rapidly processing hundreds of thousands of items of data, which soon came to revolutionize manufacturing and service sector processes. Other developments in electronics made high quality communication widely accessible, and with the introduction of telecommunication satellites in the 1960s, live pictures of events 10,000 miles away could be transmitted to homes throughout the country, and large quantities of business inform-ation or of instructions could be transferred almost instantaneously to any part of the world.

Elsewhere there were advances which were less spectacular, but which also had a strong influence upon the pattern of living. The use of standardized freight containers revolutionized sea and land transport. Improved production techniques were introduced into farming. Nuclear reactors were developed to produce cheaper electricity. Plastics replaced conventional materials in a wide range of applications. The jet engine revolutionized international travel. Above all, the processes used for the manufacture of goods of all sorts were improved by learning from experience as well as by the introduction of new technology.

Patterns of expenditure

The changes which occurred in technology and in the general level of prosperity were reflected in changes in patterns of spending. In table 1.6,

Table 1.6 Growth of the main categories of expenditure (annual percentage rates)

	1873–1913	1924–37	1951–73
Consumers' expenditure:	1.7	1.9	2.8
Public current expenditure:	3.3	3.5	1.9
Gross domestic fixed capital formation:	1.5	3.8	4.9
Exports:	2.6	–1.0	4.3
Imports:	2.7	–1.2	4.6
GDP (constant market prices):	1.8	1.9	2.9

Source: Matthews et al., *British Economic Growth.*

the third row of figures points again to the rapid growth of capital expenditure compared with earlier periods. It is also noticeable from the fourth and fifth rows that imports and exports grew faster than before; and comparison with the final row shows that they grew some 50 per cent faster than total expenditure. The British economy was rapidly increasing its dependence upon international trade.

Comparison between the first and last rows of table 1.6 shows that between 1951 and 1973, consumers' expenditure grew at about the same rate as total expenditure. As table 1.7 indicates, there were some changes in its composition over the period, the most noticeable of which was the increased proportion which went on transport and housing.

Other marks of increasing prosperity included a widening ownership of

Table 1.7 Percentages of total family expenditure in various categories

	1953/4	1970	1975
Housing	8.8	12.6	13.1
Fuel, light, power	5.2	6.3	5.5
Food, alcohol	36.7	30.2	29.9
Clothing, footwear	11.8	9.2	8.7
Other goods	13.8	13.9	15.0
Transport, vehicles	7.0	13.7	13.8
Services	9.5	9.0	9.9
Miscellaneous	0.6	0.3	0.5
Total	100	100	100

Source: *Family Expenditure Survey* (CSO, 1982).

durable goods: by 1973, 78 per cent of households had a refrigerator, 67 per cent a washing machine, 45 per cent a telephone, 54 per cent a car, 39 per cent had central heating, and 94 per cent a television set.

Housing and education

A considerable amount of public as well as private expenditure went into increasing the stock of housing and improving its quality. Between 1951 and 1971 the number of houses was increased by 5 million – 1 million more than the increase in the number of households – and by 1971 there were a half million more houses than households. The proportion of households owning their own houses continued its upward trend: 10 per cent of all houses were owner-occupied in 1914, 30 per cent in 1951, and over 50 per cent in 1973. As table 1.8 shows, there was a large reduction in

Table 1.8 Stock of dwellings 1951/60 to 1973 (millions at the end of period)

	1951/60	1961/65	1973
Owner-occupied:	7.0	9.2	10.5
Council housing:	4.4	5.0	6.1
Private rented:	5.2	3.6	3.4
Total:	16.6	17.8	20.1

Source: Social Trends (CSO, 1982).

private rented accommodation (this was associated with the legal restrictions placed upon renting during and after the war), but there was an offsetting increase in low-rent housing provided by local councils.

Housing shortages persisted in particular areas and some of the housing stock continued to be of low quality. But, as table 1.9 suggests, there were substantial quality improvements in some important respects.

Table 1.9 Housing quality

	1951	1961	1971
Percentage of households without bath:	37.6	22.4	9.1

Source: Social Trends (CSO, 1982).

There was also a major advance in numbers receiving Higher Education, with student numbers at universities rising from 83,000 in 1953/4 to 251,000 in 1973/4, and the number of first degrees or diplomas awarded rising from 20,000 in 1953/4 to 54,000 in 1972/3.

Marriage

Under the earlier heading, Population, employment and leisure, there were strong indications of a change in the role of women in the economy. In view of this, it is interesting to note the indications in table 1.10 that, although divorce was on the increase, there was no decline in the popularity of marriage.

Table 1.10 Percentages in the different marital states

		1921	1951	1961	1971
Men:					
	single:	55.0	44.1	43.8	43.6
	married:	41.4	52.0	52.7	52.5
	widowed:	3.6	3.5	3.0	2.8
	divorced:	0	0.4	0.5	0.8
Women:					
	single:	53.5	40.5	38.9	38.0
	married:	38.3	48.7	49.7	49.7
	widowed:	8.2	10.2	10.6	11.1
	divorced:	0	0.6	0.8	1.2

Source: Marriage and Death Statistics (HMSO, 1981).

Growth expectations

In terms of real spending power, the average Briton in the early 1970s was roughly twice as well off as the average Briton in the early 1950s. Prosperity had grown faster in many other countries, as noted in section VII of this chapter. The economy had suffered its ups and downs, but the post-war years in Britain had generally been characterized by low unemployment and moderate inflation – at least until 1968. This long experience of relative stability and growing prosperity was one of the major influences upon the attitudes of Britons in the 1970s. Other influences are discussed below.

III ATTITUDES AND IDEAS

The changes in the pattern of life in the period 1948–73 occurred partly in response to increased prosperity and to technical progress, but they were also the result of choices, made individually or collectively, by the British people. Collective choices, in particular, were influenced by theories or assumptions concerning the consequences of different courses of action. The attitudes and ideas which prevailed at the time also help to explain what happened in the years after 1973.

Planning and the welfare state

A vital feature of the post-war political mood was a conviction that real choices were available, and that they could be tailored purposefully to social aims. In domestic matters, at least, there was confidence that past mistakes could be avoided, and that a better world could be created. (On international matters, the mood was less confident, and there was an undercurrent of apprehension about the prospects of a nuclear holocaust.) The prevailing 'folk-memories' were of the mass unemployment and the associated poverty and humiliation of the inter-war years, and the exploitation and Dickensian squalor experienced by ordinary people during the Victorian era; but there was a conviction, as well as a determination, that these nightmares would not recur.

Despite a resolve that matters would henceforth be ordered differently, there was, however, little support for any contention that this would require extensive institutional change. On the contrary, there was a general belief that Britain's institutions – Parliament, the judiciary, the police and the education system – were the best in the world. Adaptation of some of these institutions might be necessary, but what mainly was required was their more effective and more humane management.

Two ideas which were heard much of in the early post-war years were typified by the terms 'planning' and 'social security'. In pursuit of the latter, a great deal of thought and effort went into the development of what was to become known as 'the welfare state', which was to include extended unemployment insurance, improved state pensions and a free National Health Service. The new system also provided selective support for low-income families, but – to avoid any possibility of a repetition of the humiliations suffered under the pre-war 'means test' – all other benefits were free to all. There was also free compulsory education for all up to the age of fifteen, and extended access to education beyond the compulsory school age. It soon became apparent, however, that the practical effectiveness of these changes was being limited by lack of resources. The health service, for example, developed long queues for treatment, and entry to higher education had to be rationed by the setting of high entry standards.

But faster economic growth came to be seen as the solution to these problems, and 'planning' the means of achieving it. It was taken for granted that it was within the power of government to bring these things about: an assumption which the politicians of the day did nothing to discourage. Explicitly and implicitly, people were led to expect far more of government than in the event it was able to deliver.

The quality of life and the class structure

Subsequent disappointment with the country's rate of material progress – especially by comparison with what was being achieved abroad – was to some extent mitigated by the consideration that in other respects, British society seemed to be comparatively successful. Visitors from abroad tended to see it as tolerant, peaceful and civilized; readily achieving consensus and order without undue social or other pressures upon those whose beliefs or behaviour differed from the social norm. And yet it was generally regarded by overseas observers as unusually class-ridden. Surveys done at the time suggest that in some senses this was true, though in the sense of a hierarchy of occupational classes rather than of the Marxist dichotomy between capitalists and proletariat.[1] Differences in parental attitudes seem to have been particularly apparent, with a persistence of the role of father as a remote and authoritarian figure persisting among working-class families for much longer than among those further up the social scale, and with a more rigid distinction between the roles of husband and wife.[2] Analysts speculated that the greater willingness of middle-class parents to inform their children of the reasons for a command, and to listen to their children's counter-arguments tended to perpetuate the divisions by better fitting children of middle-class origin for positions of responsibility.[3] (For those seeking 'hard' evidence from published statistics that class differences were real rather than imagined, there was the finding that in 1971, the mortality rate among unskilled manual workers was two and a half times that among those in professional occupations). However, parentage was by no means a rigid determinant of occupational class: a 1972 survey using a schedule of seven occupational classes had 72 per cent of its sample in occupational classes different from their fathers, with more moving 'up' than moving 'down'.[4]

Labour relations

The 'managerial revolution' which effectively transferred power from owners to senior managers, was, by 1948, virtually complete and the attitudes of managers had become central to industrial decision-making. There were indications that in the post-war period, British managers were more than usually conscious of their status, taking attitudes to manual workers that can be described as paternalist, but ill-informed. Studies which had shown that large gains were obtainable, both in motivation and in work-design, from involving manual workers in workplace management,[5] had had little influence upon these attitudes,[6] and little was then known of this aspect of the more successful Japanese management style. Communication between senior management and the workforce was largely restricted to the formalized procedures of 'industrial relations', whose agenda was restricted to pay and narrowly-defined conditions of work. The rigidity of the class division at the workplace was symbolized by the almost universal practice of separate canteens and lavatories, segregating manual workers from 'white-collar' workers. The resulting tendency of workers and management to perceive the others' motivation by introspection and stereotyping rather than by communication was to result in numerous misunderstandings, especially when it came to the introduction of new technology.

Occupational class differences were reflected broadly in income differentials. In the 1972 survey, for example, the average income for those in class I (professional) was over twice as much as for class VII (unskilled manual). But routine clerical work (rated as class III) did not pay as well as skilled manual work (class VI), although it attracted privileges not available to any class of manual worker. Differences of occupational class were not the only source of income differences, however. On a crude statistical comparison, average pay was lower for women than for men,[7] and lower for those with black skins than for those with white.[8] On closer analysis, a substantial part of those differences in averages can be attributed to differences in the quantity or the quality of their labour inputs – to the prevalence of part-time working among women, and to lower qualifications in the case of blacks. But differences remained after these factors have been allowed for, and they persisted after anti-discrimination laws had been passed. The explanation lay mainly in the more restricted access, for women and for blacks, to the higher-paid occupational levels.

The practical uses of welfare economics

In the sphere of economic theory, problems were being tackled which had seemed of little relevance in the pre-war days of *laissez-faire*, but which now assumed some urgency. On behalf of the public at large, government was now expected to act to promote the production of wealth and its equitable distribution. Stated in these terms, social objectives may seem to be well defined, but their practical interpretation posed many questions. Production of what? From what resources? For whom? The answers to these questions – in principle, at least – were sought in the already well-developed study of welfare economics. This branch of economics attempts to set out a logic of choice for a society which is independent of that society's institutions: which has equal validity whether choices are regulated centrally, or whether they are taken individually and co-ordinated by a system of markets. Its theorems can be summarized in terms of rules governing how resources should be combined to produce a particular output, what combination of outputs should be produced, and how they should then be distributed. But there are difficulties. The practical application of the rules required knowledge which often was not available, and which would be hard to acquire. More seriously even than that, they depended upon the assumption that objective comparisons could be made between the 'utility' of a particular item – that is to say its contribution to personal well-being – as between different recipients. On examination, this turns out to be a conceptually impossible task.[9] Nevertheless, in spite of its conceptually shaky foundations, welfare economics did play a part in the formulation of reasonably consistent principles governing the behaviour of state-owned institutions and the regulation of private-sector institutions, especially where those institutions had an unusual degree of market power or where they were in a position to impose costs upon others. Probably its best-known and most effective application was to the 'cost-benefit analysis' of public-sector projects such as roads and power stations.

The implicit assumption of welfare economics is that available resources are fully employed: that the economy is so regulated that the bouts of mass unemployment, which had occurred from time to time in post-war years, can be avoided. Welfare economics in itself had nothing to contribute on this matter, however, and the major influence upon thinking came from the revolution which had occurred in the relatively new study of 'macro-economics'.

IV   THE KEYNESIAN REVOLUTION

For those concerned with economic policy, the most important influences were the 'Keynesian revolution' of the 1930s and the 'monetarist counter-revolution' of the 1970s. The controversy which developed between those competing theories is described later, in chapter 3. In the post-war period up to 1973 – and for some years after – it was the Keynesian theory which dominated policy. What follows in this section is a brief resumé of the essential features of Keynesian thinking. For those already familiar with that theory, it may serve as a reminder. For others, a broad appreciation of the gist of the argument – omitting, perhaps, the paragraphs on the IS/LM diagram (p. 15) – should make it easier to understand the thinking behind some of the economic policy decisions which are described later.

'Classical' economic theory

Economic theory before Keynes was mainly concerned with the behaviour of individual producers and consumers, and with buying and selling transactions between them. A central concept was that of a well-informed 'market' in which transactions are made by bargaining. In such markets, demand is brought into line with supply by price adjustments, so that everything offered for sale is in fact sold. The patterns of prices emerging from such markets serve as signals to producers concerning the preferences of consumers, in response to which producers make any necessary adjustments to the pattern of production. Surpluses or shortages could occur when tastes changed or the harvest was bad, but these would be temporary effects which would disappear in due course as a result of the normal working of markets. This was of course no more than an idealized description of the sort of behaviour which could be observed in the markets for internationally-traded commodities such as metals, wheat and coffee.

The next – and crucial – step was the assumption that what was true of the supply and demand for individual products, would also be true of the total levels of supply and demand in the economy as a whole: namely that there could be no persistent shortages or surpluses. On this assumption, the explanation for any departure from this theoretical conclusion – the occurrence, for example, of mass unemployment – must lie in deficiencies in the market mechanisms, and the remedy must be the correction of such deficiencies.

Keynesian macroeconomics – saving and investment

The study of 'macroeconomics', to which Keynes made his major contribution, takes an entirely different approach. Instead of inferring the behaviour of the economy as a whole from what could be observed about individual behaviour, it deals directly with what can be observed about economy-wide totals.

The ultimate economy-wide total in macroeconomics is national income, which can be defined either as the total of the incomes of all the households in the country, or – equivalently – as the total of the output of all of its producers. The incomes of households are thought of as going either into consumption or into savings; and the output of producers is thought of as being either for consumption or for investment. Since total income must be the same as total output, total saving must, on these definitions, be equal to total investment.

Taken thus far, macroeconomics is no more than a system of classification, in which the equality of saving and investment emerges directly from the definitions which have been adopted. The principal departure from conventional (or 'classical') thinking introduced by Keynes concerned the actual mechanism by which savings are brought into line with investment. In an industrialized economy, savings plans and investment plans are usually made independently by different groups of people, so there is no reason to assume that planned saving will be consistent with planned investment. There must, therefore, be a mechanism by which these initially inconsistent plans are so modified as to bring actual saving into line with actual investment.

Classical theory envisaged that mechanism as being a market in which the demand for savings is brought into line with the supply of savings by price adjustments: the price in question being the market rate of interest. This explanation was rejected by Keynes. He accepted that investment – and hence the demand for savings – would be influenced by interest rates. But he did not accept that interest rates were the main influence upon the supply of savings. He thought it more reasonable to assume that the supply of savings would be determined mainly by the level of household incomes. This change in assumption made a crucial difference to the way the economy is seen to work. In Keynes's scheme of things, an excess of planned saving over planned investment would lead, not to an equalizing fall in interest rates, but to a progressive fall in national income, until that proportion of income which constitutes planned savings, came into line with planned investment. On his assumption, the economy does not have the 'self-righting' property attributed to it by classical economic theory: on the contrary, a disturbance to it could cause the economy to settle down at a level of national income which could leave a substantial proportion of the country's productive capacity unused.

Keynes's theory brought about a revolution in economics because it offered an explanation of economic recessions, but also because it suggested action to avoid them. To correct any tendency for economic activity to fall below the level necessary for full employment, all that would be necessary was that the government should make good the shortfall by reducing taxes or increasing its own spending. The government would need to borrow to make this possible, but it could do so by drawing upon the excess of savings which had been part of the process. Recessions and their accompanying unemployment could thus be avoided – or, at worst – alleviated.

The Keynesian labour market

A second departure from the assumptions of classical economic theory was, however, implicit in Keynes's prescription. In classical theory, government action would be unnecessary – even if Keynes were right about saving and investment – because the economy would return automatically to full employment as a result of wage adjustments. The market for labour was seen as operating in the same way as any other market, so that an excess of supply over demand (in other words, unemployment) would automatically be rectified by a fall in prices (in this case wages). The second departure implicit in the Keynesian revolution was the assumption that such wage adjustments would not happen at all quickly: that wages were 'sticky' in a downward direction.

The IS/LM diagram

An elegant interpretation of Keynes's theory, put forward by Sir John Hicks[10] and known as the 'IS/LM diagram', has long been used as a teaching tool, and latterly as a means of explaining the differences between competing theories. It is a construction which traces out the combinations of interest rate and national income which would put supply equal to demand in two separate markets: the market for goods, and the market for financial assets.

> (Taking the goods market first, investment is assumed to be the 'active' element, with consumption being determined passively as what remained of national income after deducting the more or less fixed proportion which goes to savings. Thus national income rises as investment rises, with consumption then rising in consequence. To explain changes in national income, it is thus necessary to explain changes in investment. Investment will of course be more attractive if there is a fall in the interest rates which have to be paid for the required savings. Investment thus tends to rise as interest rates fall, and vice-versa. But this is not the end of the story: we still need an explanation of changes in interest rates. For this we have to look also at the market for financial assets.
>
> Financial assets can be divided conveniently into two categories: namely money, which is non-interest-bearing, and the rest (stocks, bonds, saving certificates, etc.) which, in one way or another, are interest-bearing. The cost of holding money rather than interest-bearing assets can be reckoned as the interest which is thereby foregone. But people will wish to hold a certain

amount of money for everyday transactions, and the higher their income, the more of it they will choose to hold. But if the amount of money in circulation is to remain constant as incomes rise, people will have to be induced to alter their choices in favour of interest-bearing assets. To bring this about, interest rates have to rise as incomes rise.

Thus the relation between interest rates and national income differs in the two markets. In the goods market, national income rises as interest rates *fall*; but in the financial markets, rising national income is associated with *rising* interest rates. Both of these relationships must be satisfied simultaneously if demand is to be in line with supply in both markets. It can be demonstrated diagrammatically that there is just one level of national income, and one level of interest rate that will satisfy both markets.)

The goods market (or IS) relationship can be represented by a downward-sloping graph showing a falling interest rate with increasing national income, and the financial market (or LM) relationship can similarly be represented as an upward-sloping line showing a rising interest rate with rising national income. The intersection of the two lines determines the level of national income at which both markets are in equilibrium as shown in figure 1.1.

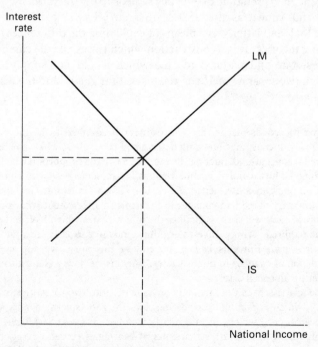

Figure 1.1   The IS/LM diagram

The importance of the IS/LM diagram for the debate on economic policy was that it provided a means of illustrating the effects of the two policy instruments: of fiscal change, and monetary change. Fiscal expansion (for example, tax reductions or public expenditure increases) can be represented by a rightward shift of the IS line. Monetary expansion can be represented by a rightward shift of the LM line. The relative effectiveness of these two policies in influencing national income is depicted on the diagram by the relative steepness of the two lines. The general conclusion of the followers of Keynes was that investment would be relatively insensitive to interest rates, so that the IS line is steep, and monetary policy is therefore relatively ineffective; a conclusion which has been greatly oversimplified into the statement that 'money doesn't matter'.

Pay and employment: the Phillips Curve

It was accepted that fiscal expansion to increase demand would raise output only at times when the economy was operating below capacity. Experience suggested that as the economy approaches its full working capacity, an increasing proportion of any demand expansion goes into price increases, rather than increases in output. This observation was formalized in 1958 by the discovery of a long-term relationship between wage increases and unemployment, which came to be known as the 'Phillips Curve'.[11] This showed that wage increases tend to rise more and more rapidly as the unemployment rate approaches zero. For policy purposes, the Phillips curve came to be regarded as the basis for deciding priorities between a wish to reduce unemployment, and the alternative of restraining inflation. The shape of the curve indicated that the 'price' – in terms of higher inflation – of a further reduction of unemployment would rise with each reduction in the unemployment rate.

V   THE POLITICAL SYSTEM

The peculiarities of the British political system had a good deal of influence upon the way in which the political attitudes and ideas of the period were translated into action. It was a system which had experienced 300 years of unbroken development since the supremacy of Parliament had first been established in the seventeenth century. The concept which had then emerged was of a system of government intended to operate in the interests of all of its citizens, granting no legal privileges to any particular group. Belief in the divine right of kings having been abandoned, the political theory which took its place in England accorded no legitimate separate role to the state beyond that of representing the

people of the country. Although revolutionary at the time of its inception –
and although the idea of a state which is superior to its people survived or
recurred elsewhere – in Britain, this theory had never since seriously been
questioned. And although the institutions of government had undergone
much adaptation since that time, the central constitutional framework, of
a titular crown, a sovereign Parliament and an independent judiciary, had
remained unchanged. In these respects, the British political system had
exhibited a far greater degree of stability than those of other Western
countries.

   The roots of that stability did not lie in the design of its institutions, and
certainly not in the process by which governments were chosen; nor in any
constitutional constraints upon what they could do when in office. With
two parties vying for power, the electoral system enabled one party to be
ousted and the other put into power – often with a decisive parliamentary
majority – as a result of a small, apparently random, change of popular
support. The winning party was then free to make sweeping reversals of
policy which, provided that it retained the support of a majority in
Parliament, could not effectively be challenged until the next election.
The system itself had the potential for violent instability of policy
formation: it was the behaviour of its participants which had avoided that
outcome. The clash of interests and of ideology between the two major
parties in the post-war period, in particular, had presented a prospect of
major changes of direction whenever there was a change of government.

The political parties

The Labour Party had its origins outside of Parliament, in the trade union
movement. It had been brought into existence in 1900 – then as the
Labour Representation Committee – as a means of promoting working-
class representation in Parliament. Since then the trade union movement
had retained an important influence over the party, providing most of its
funds and exerting a major influence upon decisions taken by its annual
conference. At an early stage the party had adopted socialist aims, and its
membership card still proclaims the intention to:

> secure for workers by hand and by brain the full fruits of their industry and
> the most equitable distribution thereof that may be possible on the basis of
> the common ownership of the means of production distribution and
> exchange and the best possible system of popular administration and control
> of each industry and service.

The phrases 'that may be possible' and 'the best possible' were, however, a reflection of the compromise with the more pragmatic party members which had to be struck in order to get that statement of aims adopted.

The Conservative Party, for its part, had no such formal aims or affiliation; but it could in a sense be regarded as the party of business, receiving each year substantial funds from private companies. Ideologically, it stood in opposition to the Labour Party's socialist aims, although it did not have the aversion to government intervention in the economy which had been the hallmark of nineteenth-century Liberalism, and which could be regarded as the viewpoint diametrically opposed to socialism.

The relatively small remnant of the Liberal Party had also abandoned its nineteenth-century philosophy, but owed no affiliation to any outside interest.

Tripartism and corporatism

For a number of reasons, the polarization of British politics which might have been expected from this combination of circumstances, did not occur. In the first place, although the Marxist rhetoric of class conflict figured in speeches by Labour leaders, wholesale nationalization was never really on the agenda. Those industries that were nationalized by the first post-war Labour administration were industries which had already been the subject of intervention by governments; and in only one case was the act of nationalization reversed by a subsequent Conservative administration.[12] The most active supporters of both parties favoured more decisive action, but the power to decide policy rested ultimately with the parliamentary leaderships; and here a convention of moderation prevailed. This created tensions, especially within the Labour Party, but calls from activists for non-parliamentary action were rare. The trade union movement, in particular, maintained its traditional respect for the supremacy of Parliament and, despite its close connection with the Labour Party, felt itself bound to work with the elected government, whatever its colour.

Conservative administrations sought to encourage this tradition and to give their policies acceptability by involving the trade unions, as well as employers' organizations, in bodies set up to advise on policy or to assist in its execution. 'Tripartite' bodies such as the National Economic Development Council and (later) the Manpower Services Commission came to assume a variety of functions within the machinery of government, and trade union leaders acquired new influence as advisers concerning the acceptability of policy to their members, and even as negotiators with government on their behalf.

Paradoxically, the growth of 'tripartism' could also be seen as part of a wider process by which the authority of Parliament was being eroded: a process which came to be known as 'corporatism'. More and more governmental decisions were taken after consultations or negotiations with interested parties, and were then presented to Parliament as *faits accomplis*. This was to some extent an inevitable consequence of increased government intervention in business and industry; consultations with those concerned being the only way in which the government could get the necessary detailed information. Government departments such as the Department of Industry adapted to this process and organized themselves into divisions, each with responsibility for the 'sponsorship' of a particular industry group. An ability to further their interests by preserving good relations with senior civil servants, became an important function of the management of the larger business organizations. Pressure groups proliferated. In those cases where the government chose to leave some power of decision in the hands of Parliament, the pressure groups sought by persuasion to influence the voting of individual Members of Parliament. The growth of corporatism gave administrators and legislators access to information on the increasingly wide range of issues which now came within the scope of government, and resulted in the involvement in the problems of government of many who had hitherto stood outside the political process.

Centralization and secrecy

But although an increasing number of people were in a position to give advice about policy, the final decisions remained highly centralized. All substantial policy issues were resolved by the Cabinet: a body of around twenty senior ministers who were appointed by (and could be dismissed by) the Prime Minister. The doctrine of collective responsibility, which had been developed in the eighteenth century to prevent the king from putting pressure on individual ministers, now served to ensure that the business of the Cabinet was conducted with the utmost secrecy. Minutes of its meetings were seen only by a limited number of ministers and their close advisers, and its decisions could not be questioned by any government minister, whether in the Cabinet or not. This meant that around a third of the Members of Parliament on the government side were debarred from open debate of government proposals. Much of the information and advice on which Cabinet decisions were based was also kept secret; the Official Secrets Act 1911 made the unauthorized disclosure of even trivial items a criminal offence. Control of information had become an important source of political power to an administration; in the increasingly complex field of government policies, the press tended gratefully to accept and print any hint of official thinking which ministers saw advantage in releasing on an unattributable basis. In this way, public reactions could be tested, or public opinion could be prepared, in advance of a formal announcement of policy.

Parliament's role

For many years, Parliament's role in initiating and designing legislation had been a minor one. The only specific role reserved to it was the approval of spending and taxation; but, as one British Chancellor was to observe concerning Parliament's scrutiny of the annual Finance Bill: 'before the Bill is published they have little chance of being heard, and after it is published there is scarcely time to heed their advice.'[13] The main function of the opposition parties in Parliament was to tease, and if possible to embarrass, the government, rather than to influence the course of policy, and it was only on the rare occasions when Members on the government side felt strongly enough about an issue to rebel against party discipline that Parliament could force the Cabinet to reconsider its proposals. For that reason, however, ministers needed to take account of the views of their own supporters in Parliament. They were helped in this by the fact that they themselves were all members of the House of Commons (or, less commonly, of the House of Lords) and that most of them had served long apprenticeships there. Ability in reading the mood of the House and performing well in its adversarial and frequently knock-about atmosphere had, indeed, for most of them been the criterion for advancement to ministerial rank.

Parliament was also able to exert some influence on an administration through the investigatory powers of its various Select Committees, but interdepartmental discussions and the transactions of the Cabinet and its committees were not open to their scrutiny, nor was anything which ministers considered that it would be against the public interest to reveal.

The administrators

Although political decision-making on major national issues was highly centralized on the Cabinet, the administration – and, to some extent, the interpretation – of policy was widely dispersed, both numerically and geographically. There were between 400,000 and 500,000 non-industrial civil servants, many of them in the regional offices of government departments. Upwards of a further 200,000 people were employed by 'non-departmental public bodies'. These included Regional Development Agencies, Sports-, Arts- and Consumer-Councils, Training Boards and

Tribunals, whose governing bodies were appointed by ministers, but who otherwise operated independently. (These figures do not include the largely independently-managed nationalized industries with their 1.5 million employees, nor the regionally-organized National Health Service with its 900,000 employees.) Most numerous of all were the 2–3 million local government officials employed by 1,400 elected local authorities who managed education, council housing and many social services.

The need for consensus

The functioning of this elaborate and complex system depended upon the existence of an informal consensus concerning the aims of government. The various elected and appointed bodies had few opportunities to influence Cabinet decisions, and the Cabinet lacked any regular means of finding whether the considerable measure of discretion available to those bodies was being exercised as it would wish. Occasionally, when things had gone far enough wrong to cause widespread public concern, a Royal Commission or some other investigatory body was set up to find facts and make recommendations; but these occasions were rare.

The unifying influence of consensus was particularly important to the smooth functioning of relations between central government and the local authorities. Local elections were for the most part conducted on party lines, and were often fought on local issues, such as comprehensive schools and council housing. But policies on these issues were defined by parties at national level, and local politicians had little influence on them. Expenditure by local authorities was partly financed by local property taxes ('rates') but this source of revenue came to be outweighed by grants from central government intended to help meet the cost of carrying out the increasing range of functions assigned by Parliament to local authorities. The total amount of these grants was, however, set by the Treasury, without consultation.

Despite the many opportunities which it afforded for confusion and conflict, the British political system functioned reasonably effectively throughout the period. The major mistakes – for example, in housing[14] – which are apparent in retrospect, were made as a result of assumptions which at the time were not controversial, and were the result of lack of expertise and experience rather than of failures of co-ordination.

VI   GOVERNMENTS AND POLICIES 1945–73

The political scene during the period 1945–73 was dominated by two parties which were evenly matched in their electoral support – with the third party never getting the support of more than 10 per cent of the electorate, nor more than a few per cent of the seats in Parliament. As table 1.11 shows, gross disparities between a party's lead in terms of

Table 1.11 The two-party system 1945–73

Election year	Winning party	Winning party's: vote lead (% of electorate)		Winning party's lead (% of seats)
1945	Labour	36.1	6.0	28.1
1950	Labour	39.9	2.3	2.7
1951	Conservative	39.5	–0.8	4.2
1955	Conservative	38.1	2.6	10.6
1959	Conservative	38.8	4.3	17.0
1964	Labour	34.0	0.6	2.1
1966	Labour	36.3	4.6	17.4
1970	Conservative	33.4	2.4	6.8

Source: Derived from figures in *British Political Facts 1900–1975*, Butler and Sloman, 1979.

electoral support and its lead in terms of parliamentary representation were common. In the seven elections between 1948 and 1973, electoral support for the Labour and Conservative parties each averaged 36 per cent of the electorate. In no case did either party get as many as 50 per cent of the votes cast, but in no case was the outcome close enough to require a coalition to be considered. Survey evidence indicates that party allegiance among voters was mainly determined by social class, but that about a third of working-class voters voted Conservative.

Changes in the electoral fortunes of the two major parties could to a large extent be seen as the electorate's response to the country's economic performance in terms of unemployment, growth and inflation. The electoral balance was in any case fine, but this observation gives an indication of the strength of popular belief in the power of governments to manage the economy. Politicians of both parties fostered this belief, especially as regards the maintenance of 'full employment'. A 1944 White Paper[15] on employment policy had set the achievement of a 'high and steady level of employment' as a prime objective of policy, and a maximum of 3 per cent unemployed, which had been proposed by Sir William Beveridge[16] as a definition of full employment, was effectively accepted by both parties as a commitment. And although the differences between the parties were emphasized in the rhetoric of campaigning and of parliamentary debate, they shared a strong consensus belief that demand management, as proposed by Keynes, was the means by which that objective could be met.

'Stop–go'

In principle, Keynesian demand management involved preparing forecasts of the state of the economy some two to three years ahead and using fiscal and monetary policy to stimulate the economy whenever the unemployment objective seemed to be in danger. In practice, however, this procedure was modified in order to meet another commitment – the maintenance of the exchange rate between the Pound and the currencies of the other members of the Bretton Woods Agreement of 1944. This made modification necessary because every stimulus to the economy brought about an increase in imports without any corresponding increase in exports, and thus led to a growing balance of payments deficit. The modified procedure required contractionary fiscal action whenever that deficit threatened to exceed the level which could be financed by capital transfers, including the use of foreign exchange reserves. Fiscal policy was thus subject to frequent reversals: a sequence which came to be known as 'stop–go'. A tendency for labour costs to rise faster in Britain than abroad added to balance of payments problems; and to counter this tendency, some form of incomes policy was from time to time adopted. Also for balance of payments reasons, restrictions were imposed in 1965 upon investment overseas in the form of purchases of securities or of UK-financed investment in physical assets, and these restrictions remained in force throughout the period.

'Butskellism'

The policies of Labour and Conservative governments toward demand management differed so little as to give rise to the term 'Butskellism' (from the names of the Conservative and Labour Chancellors, Butler and Gaitskell). There was vigorous debate among economists and political commentators concerning the competence with which demand was being managed – and there were some who claimed that government actions had actually been destabilizing[17] – but there was little questioning of its underlying philosophy.

Policy action was also taken to reduce regional disparities in unemployment rates, mainly in the form of financial inducements to employers to move into areas of relatively high unemployment, and of regulations restricting the building of factories outside those areas. This was done for social reasons, but also in the belief that increased activity levels in those areas would exert less upward pressure on labour costs than would a general increase in activity, and that it would thus enable the economy to be run at a higher level of activity without encountering balance of payments problems.

Planning and state intervention

The idea that economic planning by government could be used to promote growth remained in currency throughout the period, but failed to acquire any practical substance or consistent philosophy. Enthusiasm among Labour Party leaders that nationalization would be an effective means to this end faded rapidly in face of early experience of the difficulty of framing a consistent philosophy governing the conduct of the industries after nationalization, and of suspicions that efficiency may have been reduced by nationalization. There was a restless search under governments of both parties, for a formula by which the productivity of British industry could be brought more closely into line with its overseas competitors. Among the formulae which were tried were 'indicative planning', investment incentives, and attempts to alter the structure of industry.

In 1965 a 'National Plan'[18] was announced, which set ambitious targets for the growth of the various sectors of the economy, in the hope, apparently, that if it were believed it would determine the plans of industrialists and thus be self-fulfilling. It was not believed, and its targets were not met. Two years later, the Industrial Reorganization Corporation was set up for the purpose of encouraging mergers, in the belief that concentration of British firms into larger units would improve their efficiency – a belief which, later evidence suggests, was mistaken. In the same year, an attempt was made to transfer resources from the service sector to manufacturing industry by means of a 'Selective Employment Tax'. There were sporadic interventions of a more selective nature, ranging from industry-wide financial assistance to whole industries, such as textiles, aircraft manufacture and shipbuilding, to 'rescue operations' affecting individual firms. Very large-scale subsidization of agriculture continued throughout the period. The close contacts between the elites of industry and of government, which existed in some countries – such as France and Japan – were absent in Britain, and it seems unlikely that the governments of the period were in a position to identify, let alone rectify, the deficiencies of industry.

Competition policy

In pursuit of the same objective – although by an entirely different means – there was, in the post-war years, a substantial attempt to remove existing restraints upon competition by regulating collusive or restrictive commercial practices, and by curbing the acquisition of the power to control markets by virtue of size. With the exception of resale price maintenance, competition policy operated, not by prohibiting specified practices or behaviour as such, but by requiring their registration, and making their continuation subject to the judgement of a special court, that they were not contrary to the public interest. A broadly similar approach was taken to mergers and to the regulation of monopolies, except that in these cases there was no presumption that monopoly power is necessarily damaging in itself. These policy actions were effective in bringing about the wholesale abandonment of restrictive trade practices, but elsewhere the execution of policy tended to be permissive, and industrial concentration rose rapidly. The share of the hundred largest firms in manufacturing output rose from 22 per cent in 1940 to 41 per cent in 1972, and remained on average above the levels in other European countries.[19]

The regulation of the nationalized industries fell outside the scope of competition policy during this period but guidelines were issued in a succession of government White Papers,[20] governing pricing and investment appraisal practices in such a way as to bring their behaviour as far as possible into line with competitive industry.

Public expenditure

Direct government intervention through its own expenditure probably had more influence upon the lives of the British people than its attempts at intervention in industry. The volume of public expenditure more than

Table 1.12 The changing composition of public expenditure 1951–71 (percentages of total spending)

	1951	1961	1971
Social security	12	16	17.5
Health and personal social services	10	10.5	11.5
Education	7	10	12.5
Housing	7	5.5	5
Defence and external relations	24	18	13

Source: CSO *Social Trends*, 1982.

doubled between 1955 and 1973, and its ratio to GDP rose from less than a third to over 40 per cent. Its composition also changed substantially, as shown in table 1.12, mainly as a result of the abandonment of overseas defence commitments and the expansion of the social services. The extent of support to housing is understated by these figures because a substantial proportion of it took the form of tax relief on loans for house purchase. Relief of the social problems caused by the post-war housing shortage had received high priority from governments of both parties, particularly in the early post-war years, and the tax privileges and subsidies then introduced became politically very difficult to remove. Popular support for the health and social services was also a strong political influence upon the policies of both parties. The consequences for the level of taxes and social security contributions, which by 1972 had reached 38 per cent of national income – not a high proportion compared with other European countries – were generally considered to be acceptable, as against the alternative of restricting these services.

VII   ECONOMIC PERFORMANCE 1948–68

Relative decline

Britain's economic performance in the post-war period was, as noted at the opening of this chapter, probably the best in its history. The comparison with other industrialized countries in table 1.13 makes that performance

Table 1.13 Comparative economic performance 1955–68

	Output growth – annual rate 1955–68[a] (%)	Inflation average 1955–68[b] (%)	Unemployment rate 1960 (%)	1968 (%)
UK	2.8	3.2	1.6	2.4
USA	3.7	2.0	5.5	3.6
Japan	10.2	3.8	1.6	1.2
France	5.5	4.9		
West Germany	5.5	2.3	1.3	1.9
Italy	8.2	3.1	4.0	3.5

[a] GDP/GNP for UK, USA and Japan: industrial production for the others.
[b] Consumer prices.

Source: OECD *Industrial Statistics*

look less impressive, however. (The comparison is confined to the period up to 1968 because the special circumstances of the following years are discussed separately in the following section). Unemployment in Britain had been kept below the 3 per cent maximum set by its policy-makers by a comfortable margin: in fact it had exceeded 2 per cent in only three of the twenty years before 1968. The inflation rate had hardly exceeded 5 per cent except briefly in 1951/2, during the Korean War, and had shown no consistent upward trend. In neither of these respects did Britain show up badly compared with others.

But Britain's output growth rate put it firmly at the bottom of the league. Faster growth rates had enabled other countries to catch up with, or overtake, Britain. In table 1.14, some of the individual figures may be

Table 1.14 Comparisons of GDP per head 1953–73

| | GDP/head, percentage of UK GDP/head (in US dollars at current exchange rates) | | | |
	1953	1963	1968	1973
UK	100	100	100	100
USA	255	204	252	197
Japan	24	47	83	122
France	106	106	140	155
West Germany	75	101	123	180
Italy	43	60	80	81

Source: UN Handbooks of International Trade and Development Statistics 1970 and 76.

misleading, but the general trends are unmistakable: in twenty years, Britain had been overtaken by Germany, France and Japan. Its position in world markets had also shown a marked deterioration, especially when compared with its pre-eminent position in the nineteenth century, as table 1.15 shows.

The reasons

Many attempts were made to explain Britain's relative decline. Some industrialists attributed it to the uncertainties facing business as a result of 'stop–go' economic policies, but in fact the fluctuations which occurred in industrial production were less severe in Britain than in the other countries in the above tables.[21] For a time, it was widely believed that inadequate investment was responsible, but international statistics later showed that the amount of capital employed per unit of output in Britain

Table 1.15 Shares in world exports of manufactures 1881–1973 (percentages)

	1881–85	1950	1964	1973
UK	43.0	24.6	14.0	9.1
USA	6.0	26.6	20.1	15.1
Japan	0	3.4	8.3	13.1
West Germany	16.0	7.0	19.5	22.3
France	15.0	9.6	8.5	9.3
Italy	2.0	3.6	6.2	6.7

Source: Matthews et al., *British Economic Growth*.

was higher, not lower, than in competitor countries. One study indicated that the increase in output associated with a unit increase in capital was some 60 per cent higher in other countries than in Britain.[22] It appeared that the problem lay, not in the amount of investment, but in its quality or in the use to which it was put.

A series of studies by a team of American economists, using the statistical technique of 'growth accounting', failed to find a satisfactory explanation of the relatively low levels of productivity which they observed throughout British industry, and were at first forced to attribute them to some unmeasured residual factor. But their later report observed that there was 'strong statistical evidence to support the negative influence on industrial productivity of both poor labour–management relations and deficiencies in British management'; and that 'the industries with poor prospects are those needing large managerial cadres or managers requiring a high level of administrative skill.'[23]

Disruption of production caused by strikes had become a familiar news item in the 1960s, but international strike statistics indicated that the British experience in this respect had been no worse than the average among other industrialized countries. A comparison which took account of plant size showed that the working days per employee lost in small firms as a result of strikes were fewer in Britain than in the United States, but that as plant size rose above 2,000 employees, the losses in Britain became increasingly worse than in the USA.[24]

This and other studies pointed to quality of management as a significant factor. It had been noted that the educational standards of British management were generally low by international standards,[25] and it appeared that the characteristic British management style was ill-adapted to sophisticated and large-scale modes of production. The frequent attempts which had been made to tackle management problems by

mergers had probably made matters worse.[26] Further confirmation of the
importance of management and labour relations came from econometric
analyses of Britain's trade performance. These showed that declining
export shares and rising import penetration could not be explained solely
in terms of the relative prices of British and foreign products and of
changes in levels of prosperity. After these factors had been allowed for,
significant 'time trends' remained, indicating that British products were
becoming progressively less saleable for reasons other than their price.[27]
The precise nature of this fall in 'non-price competitiveness' could not be
identified, but it was surmised that it must have had to do with such
factors as low reliability, erratic delivery and insufficient attention to the
needs of potential buyers.

The balance of payments constraint

Falling export shares and rising import penetration led to a succession of
balance of payments crises, including no fewer than four between
November 1964 and May 1967. The 1944 Bretton Woods agreement,
which had fixed the rates of exchange between the currencies of its
signatories, provided for devaluations when they appeared to be unavoidable; and a British devaluation had taken place in 1949. But devaluation
was regarded very much as a last resort. In the 1960s, as these pressures
mounted, governments sought both to halt the fall in competitiveness by
wage restraint and to reduce the growth of imports by fiscal measures to
reduce spending. Matters came to a head in 1966 when, after a damaging
seamen's strike had caused another run on the pound, the then Labour
government increased taxes on consumption and then made cuts in
planned spending on defence, health and housing, finally imposing a
statutory wage freeze. Despite these desperate remedies, the crisis
continued until after the pound was again devalued – by 14 per cent in
November 1967.

Press commentators at the time, and since, have suggested that 1948–68
was a period of persistent fiscal expansion, and some of them have
concluded that this had been responsible for the low levels of unemployment during that period. The facts suggest otherwise. Under the constraint of recurrent balance of payments problems, fiscal policy had
probably not, on average, been expansionary. To quote one group of
economic historians:

> The most important question is whether the high average level of demand in
> the post-war period was attributable to government policy. As far as fiscal
> policy is concerned, the facts on their face suggest that the answer is

unequivocally no. Net government savings were substantial and positive throughout the post-war period. . . .[28]

It seems likely that the significant influences upon Britain's economic performance during the twenty years following the Second World War had been the rapid growth of world trade and the declining competitiveness of its manufactured products. After 1968, further problems arose which were to have a more immediate impact.

VIII ECONOMIC PERFORMANCE 1968–72

During the twenty years to 1968, the inflation rate and the unemployment rate had both fluctuated within relatively narrow limits. During this and previous periods, rising inflation had been associated with falling unemployment, and vice versa. After 1968, this pattern changed, and for the first time rising inflation was associated with *rising* unemployment. This dramatic change of pattern is brought out in table 1.16: in the four years to

Table 1.16 Inflation and unemployment 1963–72

| | Average annual increase in: | | Average level of: | |
	consumer prices	wages and salaries per unit output	employment	unemployment
	(%)	(%)		(thousands)
1963–67	3.4	2.8	25,000	440
1968	4.8	2.1	24,841	574
1969	5.5	3.7	24,857	566
1970	5.9	9.5	24,753	602
1971	8.6	9.1	24,511	775
1972	6.5	9.0	24,489	826

Source: CSO *Economic Trends*, 1985.

1972, unemployment increased by 43 per cent; the rate of consumer price inflation rose by 35 per cent; and the rate of increase of unit labour costs quadrupled.

Prices and pay

The reasons for the surge in inflation were complex. The prices of imports had been raised by the 14 per cent devaluation of the pound in 1967, but this explains only a part of the initial rise in prices. Other countries which had not devalued, also experienced a rise in inflation, also associated with increases in labour costs per unit of output. This happened in Japan and in France in 1968–9, and in Germany and in Italy in 1969–70. In Britain, labour costs were at first held down by the incomes policy of 1968–9, but afterwards they rose rapidly.

Part of the reason for this world-wide surge of inflation may have been the growth of currency reserves resulting from the deficits incurred by the United States in connection with the Vietnam War – which to some extent relieved other countries of balance of payments constraints upon fiscal expansion. It was associated with a growth in the strength and in the militancy of labour unions. A study by the Organization for Economic Co-operation and Development noted that deductions from pay to finance public spending had been taking an increasing proportion of the pay packets of people in all the main industrialized countries, and surmised that pay claims may have been raised in an attempt to recoup the loss.[29]

British trade union membership was rising fast, and since around 1960 it had become general practice to make annual pay claims in order to protect the spending power of pay from erosion due to creeping inflation. As time went on, this became more urgent, and 'leap-frogging' pay claims designed to defend or improve relative positions in the 'pay league' became common. The initiative for negotiating such claims was also passing from regular trade union officials to locally-elected 'shop stewards' and the process was becoming less co-ordinated. But the question of whether the unions had created the inflation, or merely responded to it, has never been conclusively settled.

Unemployment

The growth in unemployment reflected another change in patterns of behaviour. In previous recessions there had been a tendency for the growth in output per employee to fall, as employers held on to surplus labour in anticipation of a recovery. This time, output per man actually rose faster than the previous trend. As a result, as shown in table 1.17, employment fell; and despite a fall in the working population, unemployment rose.

Something unusual also seemed to have happened to the relationship between unemployment and vacancies, again indicating a change in labour market behaviour. It seemed possible that the improved redundancy payments introduced in 1965 had made it more acceptable to shed labour. But the change which had occurred was not so much in the numbers

Table 1.17 Output and employment changes 1961–66 and 1967–72 (percentage changes over five years)

	1961–66	1967–72
Output	+16	+13
Output per man	+12.5	+15
Employment	+ 3.5	− 2
Working population	+ 3.5	− 1
Unemployment	0	+ 1

Source: Economic Trends (CSO, 1985).

becoming unemployed, as in the duration of unemployment of those who did. It later appeared that the payment, from 1966, of an earnings-related supplement to unemployment benefit had extended the duration of unemployment slightly for those experiencing short spells of unemployment; although not by nearly enough to explain the rise in unemployment.[30]

By previous post-war standards the level of unemployment seemed scandalous, but for most of those affected it was in the nature of a temporary interlude: the average duration for a man who lost his job in the period 1967–70 was only eight weeks, and for younger men it was even shorter. But there was an upward trend in long-term unemployment, especially among older unskilled men.

Prosperity and discontent

The period from 1968 to 1972 was a time of rapidly rising prosperity – average spending power in 1972 had increased by 17 per cent since 1968. But it was also a time of rising discontent. Strike statistics, which – if mineworkers are excluded – had previously shown no appreciable upward trend, rose rapidly after the mid-1960s reaching an all-time record in 1971. In industry in particular, attitudes were changing.

IX THE BACKGROUND IN RETROSPECT

The purpose of this opening chapter has been to make what follows more comprehensible. The story of the period 1973 to 1983 presents many historical puzzles, but the answers to some, at least, of its questions must lie in what went before. What happened to the British economy in 1973, and subsequently, must have been influenced greatly by its structure, institutions, technology and working practices, as they existed in 1972. To an equally important extent, the way people behaved and acted in the course of the story that follows must have been influenced by ideas and attitudes which had been acquired over the course of the previous generation. Economic and political history makes very little sense if it fails to take account of the fact that people learn from experience.

This account of the British economy, from post-war recovery to 1973, may have given the impression of a sustained period of peace, stability and steady growth. Unemployment was low, prices stable, and there was a considerable degree of social and political consensus. That is broadly how it looks from a 1986 perspective, but it is worth remembering that the people living at the time may have had a rather different view. The interesting question is: what did the experience which has been described lead people to expect of the future?

In answer to this we may guess that people expected a continued growth of prosperity. What is beyond doubt is that they expected the maintenance of an economic growth rate which would be sufficient to keep unemployment to a low level. There was disquiet when, in 1972, the unemployment rate rose above the 3 per cent level, which had for over twenty years been regarded as the policy limit. Some even believed that if unemployment rose above one million (or about 4 per cent) it would become impossible to maintain law and order. It was generally assumed that any government would do whatever was necessary to prevent that level being reached.

Attitudes to inflation were less firmly founded. There had not in living memory been any previous peacetime experience of inflation rates as high as the 8 per cent level reached in 1971, and the new experience caused feelings of insecurity. Those who had been unable to obtain compensating pay increases were by then being forced to face the need to reduce their purchases; and pay bargainers seemed to be working on the assumption that the inflation rate would increase.

In many respects, what follows could be presented as a self-contained story, attributing its developments mainly to the immediately preceding events and policies of the period. Indeed, it is difficult in a consecutive narrative to avoid such an impression. But, dramatic though some of those events and policies were, it is unlikely that their influence could have been strong enough to account for the full extent of the change which occurred. The possibility that more deeply-rooted influences were also playing an important part, deserves recognition throughout.

NOTES

1. J. H. Goldthorpe and D. Lockwood, 'Affluence and the British class structure', *Sociological Review*, July 1963.
2. M. Young and P. Willmott, *The Symmetrical Family* (Routledge and Kegan Paul, 1973), p. 3.
3. E. Newson and J. Newson *The Family and its Future* (J. A. Churchill, 1970), p. 142.
4. A. Heath *Social Mobility*, (Fontana Paperbacks, 1981), p. 49.
5. G. C. White 'Employee participation in work redesign', *Employment Gazette*, November 1983 (Dept of Employment), p. 465.
6. P. Brannen, *Authority and Participation in Industry* (Batsford Academic 1983), p. 90.
7. F. Wilkinson, C. Craig and J. Rubery, 'Women and Payment Structures' (Department of Employment Research Paper, 1984).
8. M. B. Stewart 'Racial discrimination and occupational attainment in Britain', *The Economic Journal*, September 1983.
9. For a rigorous treatment, see: I. M. D. Little, *A Critique of Welfare Economics* (Oxford University Press, 1957).
10. J. R. Hicks 'Mr Keynes and the classics, a suggested interpretation', *Econometrica*, April 1937.
11. A. W. H. Phillips, 'The relation between unemployment and the rate of change of money wages in the UK 1861–1951', *Economica*, November 1958.
12. The steel industry was nationalized in 1951, denationalized in 1953, and renationalized in 1965.
13. Sir G. Howe, 'Reform of British tax machinery', *British Tax Review*, 1977.
14. Many of the high-rise buildings constructed in the 1960s have since been abandoned or destroyed.
15. Cmnd 6527 (HMSO).
16. W. H. Beveridge, *Full Employment in a Free Society* (Allen and Unwin, 1944).
17. J. C. R. Dow, *The Management of the British Economy 1945–60* (Cambridge University Press, 1964).
18. Cmnd 2764 (HMSO).
19. See 'A Review of Monopolies and Mergers Policy' (Cmnd 7198, May 1978, HMSO).
20. For example: 'Nationalised Industries: A Review of Economic and Financial Objectives' (Cmnd 3437, 1967, HMSO).
21. A. Whiting, 'An International Comparison of the Instability of Economic Growth', *Three Banks Review*, March 1976.
22. See 'Company Investment and Taxation' in *Economic Progress Report* (HM Treasury, May 1984).
23. R. E. Caves and associates, *Britain's Economic Performance* (The Brookings Institution, 1980).
24. S. J. Prais, *Productivity and Industrial Structure* (Cambridge University Press, 1981), p. 80.
25. M. Fores and D. Clark, 'Why Sweden manages better', *Management Today*, February 1975.
26. For a survey of evidence on the effect of mergers, see ref. 19 above, pp. 100–04.

27. See HM Treasury Macroeconomic Model Technical Manual 1982.
28. R. C. O. Matthews, C. H. Feinstein and J. H. Odling-Smee, *British Economic Growth 1856–1973* (Clarendon Press 1982), p. 310.
29. Organization for Economic Co-operation and Development, *Expenditure Trends in OECD Countries 1960–70* (OECD July 1972).
30. S. J. Nickell, 'The effect of unemployment and related benefits on the duration of unemployment' (*Economic Journal*, March 1979).

2

Confrontations and Crisis: 1973–76

I THE HEATH LEGACY

By the beginning of 1973, the Heath government had been in office for two and a half years. In that time it had already left a legacy for the future which went well beyond a continuation of the trends described in the previous chapter. The opening section of this chapter gives a brief account of five aspects of that legacy.

The legacy of U-turns

Little of what was done by the Conservative government under Edward Heath was in line with what had been intended when it was elected. At the election it had promised 'a new style of government' which would reduce public expenditure, cut income tax, reform industrial relations, strengthen competition, and give overriding priority to bringing inflation under control (without, however, the use of a statutory incomes policy). In style it was certainly different, but in substance its actions do not in retrospect look radically different from what might have been expected of its predecessors.

The first two and a half years of the Heath administration had in fact seen the abandonment – or the reversal – of nearly all of its original policies. It had been the fear of rising unemployment, not the need to reduce inflation, which had dominated its economic policy, and which had led it in 1972 to introduce the most expansionary budget in British history. So far from reducing public expenditure, it had driven it to record heights; and despite the introduction of a rigid statutory incomes policy, the inflation rate had reached an unprecedented level. After promising not to rescue 'lame ducks', it had rescued Rolls Royce and Upper Clyde Shipbuilders, and given itself powers of industrial intervention going far beyond anything contemplated by previous Labour administrations. These had been some of the reversals which had led journalists to coin the phrase 'U-turn' – a phrase which was to have a profound influence upon the thinking and the conduct of the next Conservative administration.

The legacy of confrontation

The other catch-phrase applied to the Heath administration by the journalists of the day was 'confrontation' – applied to the government's relations with the trade unions. After resisting – largely successfully – pay claims by the power workers and the postmen, the government was forced in 1972 to give in to the coal miners who had gone on strike in support of a pay claim vastly in excess of the announced 'pay norm'. This was a significant episode, not so much because of its effect on the credibility of the government's pay policy (it could always be argued that the miners were a 'special case') but because of the demonstration of what could be achieved by aggressive picketing. For the first time, British television viewers witnessed violent scenes at picket lines, as 'flying pickets' organized by the mineworkers' union sought to prevent the delivery of coal to power stations. This tactic succeeded so well that, within five weeks, power cuts had become a regular feature of life, most of industry was on a three-day week and over one and a half million people found themselves out of work. In this way, the miners won themselves a 30 per cent pay rise.

Equally significant was the confrontation which developed between the government and the trade union movement concerning the 1971 Industrial Relations Act. The background to this legislation had been the rapid growth of strike activity since the mid-1960s and the defects in collective bargaining procedures reported on in 1968 by a Royal Commission under the chairmanship of Lord Donovan.[1] This had prompted the previous government to publish a White Paper 'In Place of Strife'[2] proposing reforms which, however, were abandoned in face of strong union opposition.

But the Heath government had been more ambitious: it had promised to 'create a new framework of law' that would 'provide for agreements to be binding on both unions and employer'. As the legislation was finally drafted, however, agreements would not be binding if both sides agreed that they should not be, and this widely-used loophole made that provision largely ineffective. Another provision of the Industrial Relations Act required unions to register and submit their rules for approval. If they failed to do this, they would lose their extensive immunities against civil actions. For a time this provision, also, was ignored by unions and employers, but in July 1972 the National Industrial Relations Court sent five shop stewards to prison for failing to obey an order of the Court; in response to which the Trades Union Congress called a one-day national strike. This episode was resolved by a legal device, but it had been a reminder of the strength of union feeling against the intrusion of the courts into industrial relations disputes, of the reluctance of employers to seek legal remedies against their employees, and of the dangers of using imprisonment as a means of enforcing discipline in industrial relations.

Although there had been general support for the proposition that British industrial relations had been in need of reform, it was by then clear that the 1971 Industrial Relations Act would not improve matters. To trade unionists it was a politically-motivated attack upon their only means of protection against exploitation, and for them it remained a source of bitter resentment against the government. To many employers it was at best an ill-considered measure: the Director General of the Confederation of British Industry was later to observe that it had 'sullied every relationship at every level between unions and employers'.[3]

The European Community

From a political standpoint, the Heath government's most important legacy was, however, its successful negotiation of Britain's entry into the European Community. At the time of the 1971 election, all three parties had promised to take Britain into Europe if the terms were right, and the Labour government had, in fact, already obtained parliamentary approval to open negotiations. A White Paper in July 1971 had estimated that the cost to the balance of payments would be around £1,000 million, but had argued that, against the 'substantial' cost of membership, should be set the 'dynamic' effect that it would have on the economy.[4] When the new administration took up the negotiations, it found the going far from easy, and the terms which were finally agreed were not over-generous to Britain. But a transitional period of up to six years was agreed before the Common External Tariff, the Common Agricultural Policy, and contributions to the Community budget were to be applied fully. Opinion in Britain had in the meantime hardened, especially in the Labour Party, whose National Executive passed a resolution condemning the proposed terms of entry. But both Labour and Conservative parties were divided on the issue. Many were concerned about the loss of sovereignty implied by the fact that British legislation would become subordinate to Community law. Among the Conservatives, Mr Enoch Powell felt so strongly on this issue that he advised people to vote Labour at the next election – and did so himself. In the end, after a parliamentary process lasting five months and involving 104 divisions, the necessary Bill became law, and Britain entered the Community on 1 January 1973.

Monetary control

Two innovations which had been introduced by the Heath administration were to have effects upon the future conduct of economic policy going far beyond anything that was contemplated at the time. The first of these was a new system of monetary control, introduced under the title of 'Competition and Credit Control'.[5] Before 1971, monetary control had been exercised mainly by the use of quantitative ceilings upon bank lending to the private sector, with interest rates being used mainly to influence the exchange rate. The Bank of England had also been concerned to fund government expenditure by sales of gilt-edged securities (bonds), but it did so when favourable opportunities arose (that is, when the market expected interest rates to fall so that the value of fixed-interest stock would rise), and there was seldom any attempt to use this method to reduce the banks' ability to lend to the private sector, even when the money supply was growing very rapidly.

Under the new system the main method of control over the banking system was to be through the price mechanism, that is, by interest rate adjustments. The intention was that money supply growth should be restrained when required, by raising the rate at which the Bank of England relieves the normal shortages in the market (the Bank Rate, or, later, the Minimum Lending Rate), or by a call for 'Special Deposits'. At the same time, a change had been made in the rules governing the minimum ratios of reserves to liabilities at which banks were to operate (to require all banks to hold specified 'reserve assets' amounting to a minimum of 12.5 per cent of their 'eligible liabilities', where previously they had been required to maintain cash reserves of 8 per cent and 'liquid assets' of at least 28 per cent of deposits). These changes were to have long-term implications, but their immediate consequence was an unexpected explosive growth in bank lending.

The floating pound

The second, and more important, innovation was the move to a floating exchange rate. The Chancellor in his 1972 Budget speech had commented that 'it is neither necessary nor desirable to distort domestic economies to an unacceptable extent in order to maintain unrealistic exchange rates.' And on 23 June 1972 the Treasury announced a 'temporary' floating of the pound.

The immediate reason for this decision seems to have been a massive outflow of short-term capital prompted by troubles in the docks arising from the Industrial Relations Act and by Britain's relatively high inflation rate, but it was a move which had long been advocated by a number of eminent economists. Professor Milton Friedman, for instance, described it as 'a fundamental prerequisite for the economic integration of the free world through multilateral trade'.[6] It was seen by its advocates as a means of liberating economic policy from the balance of payments constraint which for so long had limited governments' ability to pursue objectives of their own choosing. But, in any case, the existing Bretton Woods system of 'fixed' exchange rates was to prove unsustainable, and most other industrialized countries were shortly to follow Britain's example. The history of the world economy was moving into a new phase in which many of the accepted rules would require substantial revision.

II   1973: FROM OPTIMISM TO DISASTER

Optimism

The opening months of 1973 were a time of great optimism for most observers of the British economy. Output had been growing over the previous year at the unprecedented annual rate of around 10 per cent, unemployment was rapidly falling, and the inflation rate – though high, at around 8 per cent – was lower than it had been. The buoyancy of the economy was due in part to the rapid growth in world trade, but mainly to the sharp increase in consumers' spending power resulting from the cuts in income tax and purchase tax in the 1972 budget, and to the surge in bank lending following the implementation of 'Competition and Credit Control'.

The monetary expansion may have been partly accidental, but the fiscal stimulus had been a calculated act of policy, prompted by the fear that unemployment might grow to over a million. The need for such a stimulus to the economy had been widely accepted and, with few exceptions, criticism had come from those who doubted whether it had been large enough. The influential National Institute for Economic and Social Research, for example, had advocated tax cuts twice as large as the Chancellor's £1.2 billion,[7] and a *Times* editorial had advised that he should 'respond flexibly and speedily to any evidence that too little has again been done too late'.[8] Peter Jay of *The Times* and one or two monetarists had, it is true, expressed concern about longer-term effects on inflation and the balance of payments, but this was very much a minority view.

By early 1973 the Chancellor had decided that fiscal relaxation had gone far enough, and his March budget was broadly neutral, based on the expectation of continued growth at the rate of about 5 per cent a year. In May, he decided to put the process in reverse, and announced a £500 million cut in public expenditure plans for 1974–5.

The mood of optimism continued well into the year. The Confederation of British Industry's *Industrial Trends Survey* of May 1973 was possibly the most optimistic since 1958, speaking of record increases in production, new orders, investment and employment. A report from the National Economic Development Office on 5 July said that there was no serious overheating of the economy, nor was it likely to occur in the future, although a 5 per cent growth rate would produce serious problems for many industries if it persisted for a long period. The National Institute accepted that demand had been growing faster than productive potential, but considered that sufficient slack remained in the economy to justify the Chancellor's 5 per cent growth forecast.

The boom fades

Unknown to these commentators the boom was, by that time, already over. It had reached its peak in May 1973, and the economy had moved into a state of uneasy stagnation. Over the fifteen months since the trough which had occurred in the first quarter of 1972, output had grown by 9 per cent, productivity by 6.5 per cent, and the growth of employment (which, definitionally, makes up the difference) had thus been 2.5 per cent. Employment growth had been partly offset by an increase in the number of those seeking work, so that the actual fall in unemployment had been about 1.5 per cent of total employment – a fall from 940,000 to 560,000.

The main driving force behind the boom had been an 11 per cent increase in consumer spending power ('real personal disposable income'), partly offset by an increase in saving. Consumers' expenditure, together with increases in stockbuilding by firms, had accounted for 85 per cent of the growth of demand, with only minor contributions from investment and from the trade balance. Productive potential had probably changed very little, and what spare capacity had been available was rapidly disappearing. By July, 60 per cent of firms were working at or above normal capacity, delivery dates had become the major constraint on exports, and shortages of skilled labour were limiting output growth. Vacancies notified to employment offices had risen to a record 340,000 (probably about a third of total vacancies). These were all signs that output was approaching the limit of which the economy at the time was capable.

The driving force behind the boom was in any case spent. With no further tax reductions in the 1973 budget, and with inflation catching up with pay rises, real personal disposable income ceased to rise. To make matters worse, consumers – mindful, presumably, of the way that inflation was eating into the value of their savings – continued to increase the ratio of savings to disposable income, and consumers' expenditure began to fall. And an increasing proportion of the diminishing amount of domestic expenditure was being used to pay for imports. The volume of imports had been rising, as production bottlenecks prevented domestic producers from meeting the increased level of demand; and, more importantly, import prices were soaring. This was due in part to an increase in commodity prices under the influence of a simultaneous rise in demand in virtually every industrialized country; but also, in large part, to the 15 per cent fall in the exchange rate, by the third quarter of 1973, since Sterling was floated in June 1972. Inflation had been rising faster in Britain than in most other countries, and overseas perception that it was not under control here was itself contributing to inflationary pressure. The balance of payments was making an increasingly negative contribution to economic growth, and efforts by firms to rid themselves of (by then excessive) stocks, added further to the down-turn which developed in the latter part of the year.

The monetary explosion

The money supply (on the broader M3 definition) was, in the meantime, continuing to grow at a rate of between 20 per cent and over 30 per cent a year. In July 1973 the Bank of England had brought about a sharp increase in interest rates 'for external reasons' (that is, to prevent a further fall in the exchange rate), raising the Minimum Lending Rate from 7.5 per cent to 11.5 per cent. The fact that this did not lead to the expected reduction in money supply growth provided the first hint that the interest rate was a less reliable means of control than had been thought.

The very rapid expansion of credit which had occurred had been used, to a large extent, to finance property purchases (widely thought to provide a 'hedge' against inflation), with the result that house prices were driven by the end of the year to some 40 per cent above their normal multiple of average earnings. A number of 'secondary banks' were to find themselves in serious trouble when this speculative bubble finally burst.

Prices

By the early autumn of 1973 – well before the onset of the oil crisis – it was evident that the British economy was in a highly unstable condition, with the prospect of renewed growth in unemployment and, failing some effective action to combat inflation, a further acceleration of prices. Inflation, rather than unemployment, had by then become the most pressing of the economic worries felt by the British people. Prices had, on average, risen by 13 per cent since the first quarter of 1972, and – more importantly for low-wage families – food prices had risen by 19 per cent.

Pay policy

The government had, by late 1972, abandoned its election commitment to tackle inflation by purely voluntary means, and had introduced a statutory prices and incomes policy, starting with a ninety-day freeze. In the absence of an electoral mandate, this was a move which, from the outset, faced a problem of legitimacy, or at least of acceptability. Formal legitimacy had been conferred upon it by Parliament, but this was no more than a reflection of the government's substantial majority there, and of the control which it maintained over its voting behaviour. Its acceptability by those who would be expected to submit to the restrictions which it implied, was altogether another question. In an effort to gain such acceptability, it was presented as something in the nature of a bargain, in which economic growth at a rate of 5 per cent a year was offered in exchange for wage restraint.

Predictably, in the light of the prevailing atmosphere of confrontation, such a bargain was publicly rejected by the leaders of the trade unions; but there is little doubt that consultations with union leaders took place behind the scenes in the traditional manner. Len Murray, who had been the General Secretary of the Trades Union Congress at the time, is quoted as saying: 'There was some doubt about talking to Heath at Chequers and Downing Street but the feeling of hostility was not very strong. We were trying to see how we could best settle issues with the government.'[9] The role of the Trades Union Congress – or, more accurately, of members of its General Council – as a sounding board for union opinion was thus not far different from the role in which it had been cast by previous administrations. It is not likely that any bargain was struck – nor that either side would have been thought by the other to be fully capable of delivering on one – but it is reasonable to suppose that these discussions had an influence upon policy.

In January 1973 the government announced that, on pay, the freeze was to give way, in Stage 2 of its incomes policy, to a 'norm' of a weekly increase of £1 plus 4 per cent, with a maximum annual increase of £250. This would amount to an average increase of 7–8 per cent, but with the lower-paid faring better, and the better-paid faring worse. Manual workers' wage rates were, at the time, rising by about 15 per cent per annum. On prices, the rule was to be that only 'unavoidable' costs were to be passed on – and pay increases above the norm would not be considered unavoidable. Two new bodies, a Pay Board and a Price Commission, were to be set up to administer the rules. In cases of breach of the rules, the Pay Board would issue warnings, followed if necessary by orders prohibiting the increases.

Stage 2 came into operation in April 1973 amid protests from the Labour Party and the Trades Union Congress, who rejected an invitation to nominate members to the Pay Board and the Price Commission. Apart from a token 'day of action', it encountered little real challenge from union members, and it was generally effective in meeting its aim. Stage 2 was in any case to be only an interim set of measures, to be replaced in the autumn by a more sophisticated – and rather more conciliatory – Stage 3.

When finally unveiled on 6 October, Stage 3 was seen to have two important new features. One was a system of 'threshold' increases under which every 1 per cent increase in the retail price index beyond a level 7 per cent above that of October 1973, would 'trigger' automatic pay increases of 40p a week. The other was the provision for special increases for those who worked 'unsocial hours'. As was later revealed, this had been a device agreed with Joe Gormley, President of the National Union of Mineworkers, to enable bigger increases to be given to miners, in exchange for an understanding that the miners would not then oppose the new measures.[10] These two innovations contained, in quite different ways, the seeds of disaster.

The 'thresholds' gamble

The 'thresholds' system was seen as a way of reassuring the trade unions that their members' pay would not fall seriously behind inflation. It seems to have been founded upon the belief that the inflation rate would in any case fall from its current 9–10 per cent to below 7 per cent. The success of Stage 2 may have encouraged this belief but the fact was that, by the middle of 1973, import prices were already rising at a rate of some 24 per cent a year under the combined influence of commodity price increases and a falling pound. Import prices on their own were contributing some 5 per cent to the inflation rate. It can thus be assumed that the Treasury was forecasting that import prices would cease to rise, and would soon start to fall. This indeed was the central assumption adopted by the forecasters at the National Institute for Economic and Social Research, on the basis of which they estimated that retail prices would rise by only 6.4 per cent in the year to the fourth quarter of 1974. On an alternative 'high import price' assumption, that figure would be 7.3 per cent; and on a 'high wage' assumption, it would go to 8.2 per cent.

Thus, at best, the thresholds scheme was something of a gamble. It was a gamble which would have failed even if there had been no oil crisis, because in the event, the prices of imported food were to rise by 17.5 per cent and those of basic materials excluding oil, by 35 per cent in the following year. Quite apart from its general implications for prices, the rise in import prices inevitably meant a fall in Britain's real income – and a consequent need for the economy to adjust, by moving resources out of consumption into the balance of payments. Such an adjustment would require that unit labour costs should rise less rapidly here than overseas – an outcome which the new policy put very much at risk.

The miners

The disaster over the handling of the miners' pay seems, on the other hand, to have arisen from tactical errors rather than errors of strategic judgement. The National Coal Board opened negotiations by offering at once the maximum award payable under the new policy – 7 per cent on basic pay, but averaging more like 13 per cent, when an allowance for 'unsocial hours' for some miners was taken into account. This tactic of opening the procedure with their final offer may have seemed to the Coal Board to be a business-like acknowledgement of reality, but to the union side it was so much a departure from traditional bargaining procedure that they felt bound to reject the offer. By 11 November, a chain of events had been set in motion which would require a reversal of the union's decision or further concessions to the miners by the government.

The oil producers

In the meantime, another chain of events had been set in motion, which was to lead to a quadrupling of the price of oil. It had started with a ban by the Arab oil producers on oil shipments to Holland, and had developed by 5 November into a 25 per cent cut in oil supplies to Western countries – including Britain. The initial objective of the Arab states was to put indirect pressure upon Israel to withdraw from territory captured during the Yom Kippur war – an objective which was never, in fact, achieved. They did, however, administer a major shock to the world economy; and, incidentally, greatly strengthened the bargaining position of the miners, and others concerned with the supply of energy. The miners, the power engineers, and the train drivers all launched industrial action in pursuit of pay claims. This led rapidly to cuts in the supply of electricity to households and to industry.

Crisis measures

In December, the government announced cuts in public expenditure, new restrictions upon credit, and plans for industry to move to a three-day week in the New Year. These were by way of an immediate reaction to a rapidly developing crisis, the full consequences of which were at the time quite impossible to foresee.

III WHO GOVERNS BRITAIN?

The miners' strike

Even more urgent than the problems posed by the oil crisis was the need to resolve the miners' dispute. Desperate efforts to devise a formula which would be acceptable to the miners without destroying the credibility of the government's pay policy continued throughout December and January. Union leaders indicated that other unions would not regard a generous settlement with the miners as a precedent in pressing their own pay claims; implying that if the miners were given what they wanted, the rest of the unions would comply with Stage 3. Doubts about their ability to deliver their side of such a bargain led to its rejection. A proposal by the Pay Board to use an independent investigation of pay 'relativities' as the basis for a settlement was also rejected by the government. On 5 February, after a ballot of their members which gave a four-to-one majority in favour, the National Union of Mineworkers announced that a full-scale strike was to start in five days' time. Two days later, the Prime Minister called a general election for 28 February.

The 1974 general elections

Serious handicaps faced both Labour and Conservative Parties in making their appeals to the electorate. Labour suffered from their association with the trade union movement and from the suspicion that the real purpose of the strike was to bring down the elected government – a suspicion which was confirmed in the minds of many by statements to that effect by the Communist Vice-President of the miners' union and by its General Secretary. It seems probable that, in fact, only a small militant minority of miners saw the strike in this light, and that most saw it as a means of restoring the pay differentials over other manual workers which they had traditionally enjoyed, and which, over recent years, had been eroded.

The Labour Party was also handicapped in the eyes of some, by claims by their opponents that they had become a party of extremists: claims which gained some credibility from the distinct leftward movement which had recently taken place in the composition of their National Executive Committee. The proposal by that committee to nationalize the country's twenty-five largest companies which had been endorsed by the party conference had, however, been rejected by Harold Wilson as Party Leader

– to the dismay of party activists. On the credit side for Labour was their claim to be able to make an effective attack upon inflation by means of a 'Social Contract' with the unions. Although, according to the opinion polls, most people thought that the unions were already too powerful, this seemed preferble to continued industrial disruption and power cuts.

The Conservatives, for their part, were severely handicapped by their failure to bring down inflation – and, above all, by doubts whether a victory for them would really settle anything. They made the best of their position by putting themselves forward as the champions of the moderate, law-abiding majority who did not have powerful unions to defend their interests. The election campaign reflected the resurgence of class-consciousness, to which the Industrial Relations Act had contributed, and was conducted with more bitterness than any since the war.

The election result (table 2.1) indicated a marked loss of support for

Table 2.1 The election result, February 1974

	Votes	MPs
Conservative	11,868,906	297
Labour	11,639,243	301
Liberal	6,063,470	14
Welsh Nationalist	171,364	2
Scottish Nationalist	632,032	7
Ulster Unionists, etc.	717,986	12
Others	240,665	2

both the major parties. Only 30 per cent of the electorate voted for the Conservatives – their lowest level of support for fifty years. Support for the Labour Party – at 29 per cent of the electorate – also represented a serious set-back, but it was so distributed as to give them slightly more seats in Parliament than the Conservatives. The result was inconclusive in that it gave no party an absolute majority in Parliament. After an unsuccessful attempt to form a coalition with the Liberals, Edward Heath resigned and Harold Wilson was appointed Prime Minister.

Wilson decided to act for the time being as though his government had a majority, and to seek to carry out his party's manifesto promises without making any arrangement with other parties. In this, he was able to count on the reluctance of the other parties to force another election – and to incur the opprobrium of the voters in so doing. By September he felt sufficiently well established to seek to strengthen his position in Parliament and he called an election for 10 October.

In the October election, the Labour Party did no better than hold its previous level of support, the Conservative vote fell even further to 26 per cent of the electorate, the Liberal vote also fell, and the only gainers were the Nationalist and Ulster Unionist parties (see table 2.2). The govern-

Table 2.2 The election result, October 1974

	Votes	MPs
Conservative	10,464,817	277
Labour	11,457,079	319
Liberal	5,346,754	13
Welsh Nationalist	166,321	3
Scottish Nationalist	839,617	11
Ulster Unionists, etc.	702,094	12

ment's position had indeed been strengthened, but when allowance was made for possible by-election losses, their overall majority of three, over other parties combined, left them with a distinctly precarious command over Parliament. This was to be a continuing restraint upon the government's freedom of action over the next four years.

IV 1974: UNCHARTED SEAS – 'THE PHONEY PHASE'

The conduct of economic policy by the new government was to be against a background quite different from anything that had gone before. As will be shown in the next chapter, the intellectual framework of demand management, which had served as the almost unquestioned guide to policy-formation for the previous thirty years, seemed no longer to provide reliable answers to the problems facing the economy; and alternative theories leading to quite different prescriptions were gaining acceptance.

Intellectual changes apart, the problems to be faced were different, and so were the domestic and the world environments in which they had to be tackled. Forecasting relationships, which had long been used to provide successive Chancellors with a tolerably reliable guide to the consequences of their actions, began to perform erratically, and in some cases broke down completely. Even the jargon had to change: terms such as 'reflation' and 'deflation' had become confusingly ambiguous in a world in which fiscal contraction could coexist with price inflation, and in which rising prices were frequently accompanied by rising unemployment. The commitment to defending the exchange rate having been abandoned, there was no longer a balance of payments constraint upon demand management, but exchange rate movements could affect domestic prices and international competitiveness; and could not therefore be ignored.

Taken together, these developments imparted a totally new sense of uncertainty to policy-making, marking as they did a departure from any sense of continuity with the past. The results of this loss of continuity were to be serious and far-reaching.

Coping with the oil crisis

The Arab-dominated oil cartel, The Organization of Petroleum Exporting Countries (OPEC), had in the meantime engineered a four-fold increase in oil prices to replace the quantitative restrictions which had initially been imposed.

The most obvious of the consequences for Britain was an increase in its import bill by over £2 billion a year, and a resulting massive deterioration in its balance of payments. Normally, the prescription in face of such a development would have been action to restrain domestic demand, and thus to reduce the demand for imports to the extent required to restore the balance. In this case, the move into deficit was being experienced, not by Britain alone, but by all the oil-importing countries. If each of those countries were to attempt to improve its balance of payments by reducing its imports from the others, the result would be a vast reduction in world trade; and, since each country's exports would also be reduced, the objective of eliminating deficits would not be met.

The alternative, of attempting to restore the balance by immediately reducing imports from the oil-producing countries alone, would have been ludicrously impracticable. In Britain, for example, oil imports supplied almost half of energy needs, and they would have to be reduced by two-thirds to eliminate the deficit. In the longer term, the price increase would encourage both economies in the use of energy, and the development of new energy supplies. The exploration of the North Sea for this purpose, following earlier discoveries, was, for example, given great stimulus. Finds which had previously seemed to be of marginal value, suddenly offered a promise of great profitability. But for the time being, oil imports on a little-reduced scale would continue to be a necessity, and a way of living with the deficits would have to be found.

For countries like Britain, the problem of living with the oil deficit was by no means insuperable. With a few exceptions, the oil-exporting countries were incapable of spending the enormously increased incomes that they were now receiving. In most cases their populations were too small to make this possible, especially in light of a tradition among their governments of protecting their peoples from the moral dangers thought to be posed by material prosperity. While this limited – although it did not eliminate – the possibility of increasing British exports to the oil-producers, it also implied the availability of the funds needed to finance the British deficit. A trade deficit does not, of course, raise any immediate problem if overseas suppliers are prepared, on a sufficient scale, to accept promises and claims upon wealth, in exchange for their exports. Britain, with its highly developed banking system and its capital markets, was in a very favourable position to square this particular circle. It could offer to the oil exporters, a safe and accessible home for the money which they were unable to spend, by exchanging claims upon wealth for the oil supplies which it needed. A number of other developed countries were in a similarly favoured position, but the underdeveloped countries in particular lacked this means of financing their oil imports. Without outside help, many of them would have faced severe impoverishment. Such help was, however, to be made available by the private-sector banks in Britain and the United States, who rapidly assumed the profitable role of intermediaries, accepting deposits from the oil-exporters and lending them on to the governments of those oil-importing countries who were unable to attract those funds more directly.

While, by their adaptability, the Western countries' financial institutions thus served to avert what might otherwise have been a world-wide economic disaster, they also brought about changes in the economic system which were to create their own problems, and which were to add further to the uncertainties surrounding the consequences of policy formation. Nothing by way of previous experience was available to serve as a guide to the behaviour of a system in which exchange rates were no longer fixed – other countries having followed Britain's example in this respect – and in which the demand for a particular currency could change rapidly in response to movements of funds which could now occur on a vast scale at the whim of a few investors. These developments were to bring the concept of 'international confidence' into a prominent place in policy analysis. Financial arrangements of this sort could not, in any case, provide a permanent solution to the problems created by the oil price increase; all they could do was to offer a breathing space during which longer-term solutions could be sought.

A more fundamental problem was posed by the fact that a substantial transfer of resources out of the British economy had taken place, which was bound to bring about a reduction in the resources available for domestic consumption and investment. At the same time, the rise in oil prices was – even if partly absorbed by a reduction in profit margins – bound to feed through into an increase in prices in the shops. Any attempt to maintain living standards by getting compensating pay increases would at first put downward pressure upon profits and investment, but ultimately would be self-defeating when finally it brought about a reduction in the opportunities for the profitable employment of labour. Any such attempt would, in the meantime give a further stimulus to inflation.

The social contract

For an incoming government which had no strong political commitments, an attractive way of tackling these problems might have been the immediate imposition of a statutory pay freeze. Whether such a move would have been successful must be a matter for speculation. In the event, the new government felt itself committed to a manifesto which effectively excluded such a possibility. The nearest approach to pay restraint which it had been able to negotiate with the unions had been an undertaking that negotiated pay increases should be confined to compensating, either for price increases which had occurred since the last pay settlement, or for anticipated future price increases before the next settlement. And to make matters a great deal worse, the 'thresholds' arrangement of the previous administration's pay policy was left in operation. By October of 1974, most workers received eleven automatic pay increases totalling £4.40 a week.

The new government's first action was, of course to arrange a settlement with the miners. Pay increases ranging from 22 per cent to 32 per cent were awarded. There was then an immediate return to work, and an end to the three-day week for the rest of industry. In addition an agreement was reached between the government, the National Coal Board and the unions (the 1974 'Plan for Coal') under which the coal industry was to be expanded and modernized. This provided for increased investment to provide 40 million tons of new capacity by 1985, together with the abandonment of old capacity at a rate of 3–4 million tons a year.

Another early action was the repeal of the 1971 Industrial Relations Act, and its replacement by the Trades Unions and Industrial Relations Act (1974). Almost total immunity was restored to trade unions against civil actions for tort, although individual workers remained subject to actions for breach of contract.

The government's remaining commitment as its part of the Social Contract was to bring about 'an irreversible transfer of wealth and power to working people and their families'.[11] A start was made in this direction in Denis Healey's first budget as Chancellor, in March 1974. Income tax was increased, particularly on unearned incomes and on the highest earned incomes. Corporation tax was increased and brought forward, and gift and wealth taxes were promised. Council house building was to be increased; new regulations giving rent control and security of tenure to tenants of privately-owned premises were introduced; and substantial increases in pensions and in food and rent subsidies were announced. The intention was also announced of phasing out the subsidies to nationalized industries, which the previous government had instituted to enable them to avoid increasing their prices; but this was not immediately implemented. The government regarded these changes as providing an increase in 'the social wage'; which, it hoped, people would take into account in seeking pay increases.

The crisis in company finance

It was not until later in the year that the extent to which a transfer of wealth had already occurred became evident. A substantial part of the profits on which Corporation Tax was payable was discovered to be attributable to an accounting illusion associated with 'stock appreciation' (the apparent growth in the value of stocks between the time of purchase and the time of sale, which was in fact due to inflation). When these illusory gains were deducted, it was seen that profits had fallen. The share of profits in domestic incomes – which had long been on a downward trend – had fallen from over 11 per cent to under 8 per cent in the course of a single year. Companies were finding it increasingly difficult to finance investment out of profits. They had increased their borrowing – largely from the banks – to the point where their financial deficits had reached record levels, and many feared that such levels could not be sustained.

The depressed financial position of British companies was reflected in the value placed upon them by stock market investors, which was estimated to amount on average to less than a third of the replacement cost of their physical capital.[12] Nowhere did there seem any prospect of an investment that would yield a positive return after allowing for inflation.

The Chancellor's response was to introduce a November budget (his third in ten months), which had the main purpose of giving financial relief to companies by reducing Corporation Tax payments in respect of stock appreciation, and by easing the provisions of the Price Code.

The pay explosion

Before the end of 1974, the failure on the part of trade union leaders to

uphold their side of the Social Contract had already become painfully
apparent. Over the first six months of its operation, wage rates had
increased twice as fast as prices, and they were now 26 per cent higher
than a year ago. This prompted the Chancellor to say in his budget speech
that, if the unions were not willing to abide by the guidelines of the Social
Contract, he would be forced to tighten demand, which would inevitably
result in higher unemployment.

The public spending problem

The total effect of the Chancellor's first three budgets had been intended
to be moderately expansionary, but startling gaps between intentions and
outcomes were emerging. By November, the excess of expenditures over
revenues (the 'Public-Sector Borrowing Requirement') for 1974–5,
which in the March budget had been put at £2.7 billion, was estimated to
have risen to £6.3 billion. Of this increase of £3.6 billion, only £1.4 billion
could be accounted for by budget changes. Expert witnesses warned a
Parliamentary Committee that public expenditure was running out of
control.[13]

Industrial policy

1974 also saw the setting up of the National Enterprise Board as a state
holding company, the institution of voluntary 'Planning Agreements'
between firms and government, and a number of apparently random
episodes of government support to industry; none of which appear in
retrospect to have had much relevance to the problems facing the
economy.

'The phoney phase'

Little, if anything, seems in fact to have been done in any sphere of
government in the course of 1974 to tackle the massive problem of
adjustment which faced the British economy. In the words of the then
Chief Secretary to the Treasury, this had been 'the phoney phase'.[14]

V   1975: SETTING A COURSE

Recession

Economic trends had, in 1974, been difficult to distinguish from the
effects of the miners' strike and from the period of recovery which
followed the return to work. By the second quarter of 1975, it was evident

that Britain had experienced the first sustained fall in activity since the Second World War.

Although consumers' spending power had increased, with after-tax earnings still rising faster than prices, consumer spending failed to keep pace with inflation because the proportion of disposable income going into savings had continued to increase. After rebuilding their stocks after the three-day week, firms had responded to the financial pressures on them by cutting back sharply on their stocks. Since de-stocking by one firm means a loss of sales by its suppliers, they in turn find that they have higher stocks than they need, and the de-stocking process snowballs; leading to what in the United States is termed an 'inventory recession'. In 1974, this had been accompanied by a substantial reduction in capital investment. By the first quarter of 1975, output was 2 per cent below its peak value of the second quarter of 1973 – and still falling.

Previous post-war recessions had been due to a fall in output relative to its normally rising trend. This time, output had fallen in absolute terms also.

By April 1975, unemployment was again approaching the 900,000 level (which, in 1971, had caused the Heath government to embark on its policy of expansion), and was rising at a rate of about 30,000 a month. Employment had not fallen from its 1973 levels; it had merely ceased to rise fast enough to keep pace with the numbers wanting work; which were increasing because of population growth, and because of the continuing increase in the number of married women going to work. With firms keeping their work-forces on, despite falling output, productivity was falling, and unit costs were rising faster than ever.

Retail prices were by now rising by more than 20 per cent a year – a faster peace-time increase than at any time in the previous 300 years. Uncertainty about the future course of inflation was having a damaging effect upon the confidence of consumers and industrialists alike.

On the stock market, however, confidence was recovering after a disastrous year which had seen the demise of a number of property companies and some financial institutions, following the collapse of the 1973 property boom, a secondary banking crisis, and the rescue from collapse of British Leyland and Burmah Oil. But by February, some investors had decided that fears had been exaggerated and that there were bargains to be had. After falling from 430 (in the autumn of 1973) to below 150 (by the end of 1974), share prices, as measured by the *Financial Times* Ordinary Index, recovered to nearly 300 (in the early months of 1975). The panic was over, but the experience was to have a lasting effect upon operators in the financial markets.[15]

The 1975 budget – a break with the past

When the time came for Denis Healey to introduce his fourth budget in April 1975, he could look back on a year of failure in respect of all the accepted objectives of economic policy: (1) economic growth, (2) full employment, (3) stable prices and (4) a satisfactory balance of payments. The financial deficit of the public sector and the deficit on the balance of payments had both reached levels far higher than had been previously recorded.

The situation was unprecedented. So, in post-war history, was his reaction to it. In what was seen to be a clear break with the traditions of Keynesian demand management, he introduced measures which would reduce demand at a time when unemployment was rising. In his words at the time: 'the budget judgement is conventionally seen as an estimation of the amount of demand which the government should put into the economy . . . for many reasons I do not propose to adopt this approach today.' He announced increases in income tax and value added tax, the net effect of which, he acknowledged, would be to reduce output growth and cause unemployment to rise to perhaps a million by the end of the year. And he announced plans to cut back public expenditure in 1976–7.

Part of the reason for these moves lay in the expectation on the part of the Treasury forecasters that world trade would increase and that an export-led recovery would be under way by the end of the year – a forecast which turned out to be correct. The Chancellor would also have had in mind his November warning to the unions that tax increases would be the penalty for excessive pay claims. Some commentators suggested that he had also been influenced by the 'New Cambridge' theory (explained in the next chapter) which was then temporarily in vogue – and by 'monetarist' economics.

Money supply growth was certainly receiving attention – several paragraphs in the budget report were devoted to it – but it is unlikely at this stage to have been a constraint on policy. After peaking at over 25 per cent a year at the end of 1973, the growth rate of broadly-defined money (M3) had fallen to about 10 per cent, as firms reduced their need to borrow from the banks by cutting back on their stocks. With money supply growth now substantially slower than the inflation rate, the authorities were apparently already applying a tight monetary policy. In fact, they were probably less concerned with the domestic money supply than with the need to hold British interest rates far enough above American rates to attract the funds needed to finance the huge balance of payments deficit without risking a further fall in the exchange rate, and the additional upward pressure on prices which that would entail.

The public spending battle

The budget caused comparatively little public protest but the public expenditure proposals caused problems of a political nature and of a technical nature. Under British conventions, public expenditure is dealt with separately from tax changes, and by different procedures. The Chancellor of the Exchequer is not bound to discuss his tax proposals with his Cabinet colleagues, and normally he does little more than inform them of his decisions shortly before they are announced. Public expenditure plans, on the other hand, are discussed, first in outline, and later in detail; and are put to Parliament only after agreement has been reached between the Chancellor and the ministers concerned. These discussions are normally a source of friction between Treasury ministers and ministers in the spending departments. In 1975 and 1976, however, disagreements were so strong as to provoke threats of resignation on both sides at the time,[16] and recriminations within the Labour Party for many years after.

The Chancellor's concern was a practical one: that expenditure was likely to rise to a level at which it could not be financed without requiring unacceptable levels of taxation or of borrowing. His Cabinet colleagues were equally reluctant to see further tax increases, but could not see why increased spending could not be met by more borrowing from the public, especially at a time when the public were evidently inclined to save more of their income. Most of them saw both the main categories of public expenditure as politically desirable: increased expenditure on goods and services served to increase the government's control over the economy, while increased 'transfer payments' (such as state pensions and social security benefits) served to bring about a socially desirable redistribution of wealth.

Increased borrowing was in any case generally accepted to be the appropriate means of tackling unemployment. As noted in the next chapter, the Keynesian theory on which this approach to unemployment was based was at the time coming increasingly under question on theoretical grounds, and this may have influenced Treasury thinking. But for most of those concerned, the problem was simply that of reconciling what was desirable with what was practicable.

There was also concern in some quarters that public expenditure had been rising over the years, both in absolute terms and as a proportion of national income. On one definition it reached about 60 per cent of GDP by 1975-6, but a variety of alternative definitions could be used to yield much lower estimates. Using the definition favoured by the international Organization for Economic Co-operation and Development, the figure for Britain in 1974-6 was 44.5 per cent, compared with about 54 per cent for

Scandinavia and the Netherlands, 44 per cent for West Germany, and 35 per cent for the United States. But whichever definition is used, the proportion had risen substantially between 1970 and 1975.[17]

This concern was accentuated by the discovery (already mentioned) that a substantial part of the increase could not be accounted for in terms of publicly-announced expenditure decisions, leading to fears that the whole public expenditure system was out of control.[18] It turned out that these apparently unplanned increases could – to a large extent, at least – be explained by the inherent tendency of the costs of the government's activities to rise more rapidly than the cost of the average private-sector activity.[19] One possible reason for this 'relative price effect' is that fewer opportunities for increasing productivity tend to occur in public-sector activities such as medicine and teaching. Another is that, since the output of much public-sector activity is not – and cannot readily be – measured, no means of measuring its productivity is available; and that this leads too readily to an assumption that no improvements are possible.

Uncertainty as to whether it would prove possible to finance the highest-ever budget deficit (the public-sector borrowing requirement was approaching 10 per cent of GDP) as well as the highest-ever balance of payments deficit, was the deciding factor. Public expenditure plans were cut back, and changes in the methods of public expenditure control introduced. Instead of targeting public expenditure in 'volume terms', and subsequently making allowances for cost increases, a wide range of spending plans were to be expressed in terms of the expected outcome, including any relative price effects.

This system of 'cash limits' required the adoption of forecasts (or 'planning assumptions') covering the price and wage increases to be expected over the planning period. The implication was that if the planning assumptions were overshot, offsetting economies would somehow have to be made in the conduct of the programmes affected. Changes were also made in the methods used to control spending by local authorities and by the nationalized industries, both of which are included under the heading of public expenditure.

The European Community

After the budget, political attention turned again to the question of Britain's membership of the European Community. At the Dublin 'summit' meeting of Community leaders in March, Harold Wilson had obtained some concessions over the terms of Britain's membership. He had announced on his return that the objectives of the renegotiation had been 'substantially although not completely achieved'. A majority of the

Cabinet considered that the new terms were good enough to justify continued membership, but a special conference of the Labour Party in April voted two-to-one in favour of withdrawal, and a substantial minority of the Cabinet were known to agree with them. Left-wing opposition to membership was influenced by the fact that the Community rules would prevent the adoption of what came to be known as 'the Alternative Economic Strategy', under which the balance of payments constraint upon economic expansion would be evaded by the imposition of controls upon imports. The disagreement within the Labour Party over Europe can thus be seen as the first sign of a more fundamental disagreement which was emerging, concerning the entire conduct of economic policy.

Two departures from British constitutional practice were adopted in order to resolve this dispute. The traditional practice of 'collective responsibility' – under which ministers are required either to give public support to Cabinet decisions, or to resign – was suspended, and a nation-wide referendum was arranged. The result was a two-to-one majority in favour of continued membership of the Community. This was seen as a setback to the influence of the left wing of the Labour Party on the conduct of policy.

Pay policy

This distraction out of the way, attention turned again to the increasingly urgent problem of curbing what many feared might develop into a runaway inflation. In July, the Chancellor announced the government's intention to bring the inflation rate down to below 10 per cent in the course of 1976, and that it would take measures to ensure that pay increases in the next round did not exceed 10 per cent. The measures which were subsequently announced amounted to the adoption, almost in their entirety, of proposals put forward by the Trades Union Congress. The maximum pay increase was set at £6 a week, and no pay increase would be allowed for those earning over £8,500 a year. (The average male manual worker was then earning about £3,000 a year.) These rules were to be enforced by 'sanctions' against employers who did not comply with them. Private-sector employers would be punished under the Price Code by being prevented from passing on in price increases, any part of a pay increase which was over the stipulated limit. Local authorities would be penalized by a reduction in the grants which they received from central government. Reserve powers were also to be taken under which other penalties could be imposed at the government's discretion.

The industrial strategy

In November, the government's new 'industrial strategy' was unveiled. This was an attempt to replace its hitherto piecemeal and *ad hoc* interventions in industry with systematic policies based upon detailed studies of industry's needs. The existing National Economic Development Council, made up of representatives of government, trade unions and employers organizations, was to be the main instrument of the new policy, and under its auspices a number of 'Sector Working Parties' were to be set up.

VI 1976: ECONOMIC RECOVERY AND FINANCIAL CRISIS

In the early months of 1976, the government's policies seemed to be succeeding. There had been no known breaches of the pay policy, and average earnings had risen by 7.5 per cent in the first six months of its operation, compared with over 12 per cent in the previous six months. Over the same period to February, prices (excluding seasonal food) had risen by 6.7 per cent, which was under half the increase in the previous six months. World trade had picked up as expected, and the economy was experiencing an export-led recovery. Output was rising at a rate of about 2.5 per cent a year, which was expected to lead before long to an end to the fall in employment, which by then was some 400,000 below its 1974 peak. Unemployment was over 1.2 million and still rising – but by around 10,000 a month, compared with 30,000 a month a year previously. The exchange rate had remained stable since November, and interest rates fell about 2 per cent in the first quarter.

The Bank of England and the pound

Prices were, however, rising more rapidly in Britain than in most other industrialized countries, and a gentle fall in the exchange rate was thought to be desirable in order to maintain the competitiveness of British goods in international markets. But nobody wanted or bargained for the slide in the pound which then took place. Despite official attempts to halt the slide, it was to fall by nearly 23 per cent in just over six months, forcing up the cost of imports and threatening the government's anti-inflation strategy.

The Bank of England attributed the initial collapse, on 4 March, to a misinterpretation of an official sale of sterling, which had been undertaken to prevent a temporary rise in the exchange rate.[20] Foreign exchange dealers, according to this explanation, jumped to the mistaken conclusion that this was an attempt to engineer a devaluation, and started an avalanche of selling. The Bank's response was to use its foreign exchange reserves to buy sterling in the hope that part at least of the selling pressure would be temporary. This worked for a time, but in April there was renewed selling which the Bank attributed to three main factors: (1) labour problems in the motor industry; (2) statements opposing further tightening of pay policy, made by some trade union leaders; (3) the resignation of the Prime Minister.

(Harold Wilson, it appears, had decided some time previously to resign when he reached the age of sixty. He had delayed his resignation because of a parliamentary defeat on a vote over the February Public Expenditure White Paper, resulting from the abstention of the 'Tribune Group' of left-wing Labour Members. The survival of the government then depended upon its ability to win the vote on a 'motion of confidence' – a matter which Wilson felt that he should handle rather than leave to his successor. Faced with the alternative of an election, the Tribune Group then supported the government, and the vote was carried. Wilson thereupon resigned, and James Callaghan was elected his successor by Labour Members of Parliament.)

What followed has subsequently been attributed by many Labour supporters to a conspiracy by the financial community to force the government into more restrictive – or less socialist – policies. But it could also be regarded as confirmation of the Treasury's earlier fears about the difficulty of financing the government's deficit. In order to do so without borrowing from the banks and so increasing the money supply, the government needed to raise money by selling fixed-interest bonds (mainly 'gilt-edged securities') to the public. But it is well known that the value of a bond falls when market interest rates rise. The expectation that the government might have to raise interest rates in order to persuade foreigners to hold sterling thus made people reluctant to buy bonds. Unable to finance its deficit in this way, the government then had to turn to bank borrowing and the resulting increase in the money supply caused alarm among potential holders of sterling. And so the process could continue to feed upon itself.

Pay policy – Stage 2

At the time of the April budget, the exchange rate crisis was in its early stages and the Chancellor's main preoccupation was the launching of a Stage 2 pay policy. He announced tax cuts totalling £1,300 million of which £900 million would, however, be conditional upon the agreement of the Trades Union Congress to a new pay norm of 'around 3 per cent'.

This was the first occasion on which an explicit connection of this sort

had been made between taxation and pay, and it led to complaints that the
trade unions were now being allowed to determine tax policy. From the
standpoint of demand management, however, it offered the logic that if
demand were restrained by limiting pay rises, more room would remain to
expand it in other ways, and vice versa.

In May, the unions agreed to a formula under which pay increases
would be limited to £2.50 for those earning up to £50 a week, to 5 per cent
for those earning between £50 and £80, and to a maximum of £4 for all
higher levels. This was formally approved by a very large majority at a
specially-convened meeting of the full Trades Union Congress in June. It
was estimated that earnings under Stage 2 would rise on average by 4.5 per
cent at a time when prices were rising by around 14 per cent a year.

Union leaders had thus agreed to a deal under which the real spending
power of their members' earnings was to fall. Even allowing for the tax
cuts – which the Chancellor then implemented – and for the fact that
earnings were 'drifting' upwards rather faster than pay rates, the tendency
of earlier years for incomes to rise more rapidly than prices was to be
reversed. There is little doubt that the fall in real earnings was intended by
the leadership to be a temporary phase which would form the basis of
improved competitiveness and renewed growth. But it is doubtful whether
this was appreciated by their memberships.

By the middle of 1976, it had become clear that the Chancellor's
objective of bringing the inflation rate down to 10 per cent in the course of
the year, could not be achieved. Although the growth of labour costs fell
from around 15 per cent in 1975 to around 7 per cent in 1976, other costs
continued to increase; with the costs of imports, in particular, being raised
as a result of the fall in the exchange rate. Although by July the inflation
rate, at 13 per cent, was half what it had been a year previously, it was well
above the rates of most other industrial countries.

The rate of growth in the money supply which, in his April budget, the
Chancellor had forecast would be about 12 per cent in 1976–7, was also
causing concern. The increase in July alone was 2 per cent and it seemed
likely that the outcome would be well above forecast.

Sterling crisis

The exchange rate continued to fall despite the successful negotiation of
Stage 2, and despite the Bank of England's attempts to hold it up by
buying sterling. Although in June the Bank had arranged with other
central banks 'lines of credit' which would enable it to augment its foreign
exchange reserves by borrowing up to 5.3 billion dollars from them, this
did not have the desired effect of boosting confidence. It was becoming

clear that concern about the government's deficit, and about money supply growth, were now the main factors which were making people reluctant to hold sterling. Treasury ministers and officials came to the conclusion that, in light of this, the deficit was unsustainable and that action to reduce it had become a matter of urgency.

It was, however, very difficult to devise a policy which would have sufficient impact to restore overseas confidence, and which was also acceptable to other members of the Cabinet. Sir Douglas Wass, then the chief Treasury official, was to say, later on:

> . . . without doubt 1976 was the year I would least like to live again . . . the year when I did lose sleep and lose weight. . . . There was an immense struggle between those of us – including, I think, Denis Healey – who believed that we would have to modify our position either to restore stability in the markets or to get the financial assistance we needed to maintain stability, and, on the other hand, politicians who very much wanted to avoid anything resembling a U-turn on the lines that they had had to make the year before when they introduced an incomes policy. . . . The battle was not resolved until the end of the year.[21]

On 22 July the Chancellor announced reductions in expenditure plans and an increase in employers' National Insurance contributions, which together were designed to reduce the Public Sector Borrowing Requirement for 1977–8 from £10.5 billion to £9 billion. He also announced his intention of limiting the growth of the M3 money supply to 12 per cent for that financial year.

The impact of that announcement was, however, offset by worsening statistics for output and external trade. After rising more than 1.5 per cent in the first quarter of 1976, these showed output to have risen by less than 0.5 per cent in the second quarter. The volume of imports also rose rapidly in the second quarter: much faster than the volume of exports. The third quarter figures, when they appeared, were even more disturbing: the volume of both output and exports were shown to have fallen, and that of imports to have risen. Even worse, the annual rate of growth of the money supply had risen to over 20 per cent as sales of government bonds stagnated, despite a series of interest rate increases from 9 per cent in March to 13 per cent in September.

The situation was deteriorating rapidly. In the words of another Treasury official: 'The pound appeared to be in free fall and there was no knowing at what point it would touch bottom.'[22]

The International Monetary Fund

Matters came to a head in the last week of September 1976, when the pound dropped sharply. (The situation had become so serious that the Chancellor turned back at Heathrow airport from the journey to Manila which he had planned to make for the annual meeting of the International Monetary Fund). The Bank of England's foreign exchange reserves were approaching depletion, and borrowings of over a billion dollars were due for repayment in December. In desperation, the government finally applied to the International Monetary Fund for a further loan of $3.9 billion.

The Fund's representatives arrived in London on 3 November, and it soon became apparent that they would require further substantial reductions in the budget deficit as a prior condition for a further loan. Over and above the cuts which had already been announced, they proposed reductions of £3 billion in 1977–8 and £4 billion in 1978–9 in programmes totalling around £50 billion.

What followed was, in the words of a staff report to the US Senate Committee on Foreign Relations:

> a simultaneous two-tiered set of negotiations; one of them between the British Government and the IMF negotiating team . . . the other, and perhaps more difficult, took place within the British Cabinet itself as the Government struggled to agree upon a negotiating position.

In the words of Sir Leo Pliatzky, then a senior Treasury official:

> As days and weeks went by, a third tier developed, in this case between the Prime Minister on the one hand and President Ford and Chancellor Schmidt on the other . . . not merely to persuade them to exercise a softening influence on the Fund's hard line, but also to pave the way for support arrangements . . . to supplement the IMF loan. . . . There can be little doubt that these representations resulted in a softening of the initial hard line of the US Treasury . . . and to a greater flexibility in the Fund's negotiating position.[23]

Sir Leo notes that when the Chancellor put to the Cabinet proposals which he believed that the Fund would accept, they were resisted by supporters of the 'Alternative Strategy' (import controls, etc.) but that after examination of this alternative, it was decided that 'it did not offer an alternative less painful than the IMF terms.' Nonetheless, it seems to have been a fear of the consequences for confidence of a failure to agree with the Chancellor and the Prime Minister that finally persuaded the rest of the Cabinet to accept their proposals.[24]

The terms finally agreed were announced on 15 December, and were embodied in a 'Letter of Intent' to the Fund. They involved a reduction in public spending plans by only £1 billion in 1977–8 and £1.5 billion in 1978–9. To reduce the borrowing requirement further, £500 million of the government's shareholding in British Petroleum was to be sold, and an additional unspecified 'fiscal adjustment' was to be made in 1978–9. Limits were also set for the public-sector borrowing requirement of £11.2 billion in 1976–7, £8.7 billion in 1977–8 and £8.6 billion in 1978–9. Monetary objectives were set in terms of 'domestic credit expansion' (which amounts, broadly, to the growth in M3 plus the balance of payments deficit), for which limits were set at £9 billion for 1976–7, and, subject to review, £7.7 billion for 1977–8, with a further reduction to £6 billion envisaged for 1978–9.

The Fund's loan, together with other arrangements made with commercial banks, were immediately successful in restoring confidence. The exchange rate started to rise, sales of government bonds increased and interest rates began to fall.

The final irony

A final irony was the discovery, months later, that public spending and borrowing for 1976–7 had been overestimated. There had been a shortfall in spending of £2.25 billion – much more than the planned reductions – and a public-sector borrowing requirement of less than £8.5 billion, compared with the budget estimate of £11.9 billion.

Thus the conditions agreed with the Fund could have been met without any reductions in planned public expenditure. Nevertheless, this episode came to be thought of as marking a significant new departure in the conduct of British economic policy.

NOTES

1. *Report of the Royal Commission on Trade Unions and Employers Associations* (HMSO, 1968).
2. *In Place of Strife* (Cmnd 3888, HMSO, 1969).
3. C. Adamson, statement made on 26 February 1974.
4. *The United Kingdom and the European Communities* (Cmnd 4717, HMSO, July 1971).
5. See *Competition and Credit Control – a collection of articles from the Bank of England Quarterly Bulletin* Vol. II 1971 (Bank of England 1972).
6. M. Friedman, *The Case for Flexible Exchange Rates* (Essays in Positive Economics, Phoenix Books, 1953) p. 203.

7.   National Institute for Economic and Social Research, *Economic Review*, May 1972.
8.   *The Times*, leader, 22 March 1972.
9.   L. Murray, interview in the *Observer*, 2 September 1984.
10. S. Fay and H. Young 'The fall of Heath', *The Sunday Times*, 22 February, 29 February, and 7 March 1976.
11. As promised in its 1974 election manifesto.
12. J. S. Flemming, L. D. D. Price, and S. A. Byers, 'The cost of capital, finance and investment', *Bank of England Quarterly Bulletin*, June 1976, p. 193.
13. W. Godley, Evidence to the Public Expenditure Sub-Committee of the Select Committee on Expenditure, 3 November 1975.
14. J. Barnett, *Inside the Treasury* (André Deutsch, 1982) – the title of chapter 4.
15. See B. Riley, 'The worst year of my life', *Financial Times*, 29 December 1984.
16. See Barnett, *Inside the Treasury*, chapter 7.
17. Quoted in: L. Pliatzky, *Getting and Spending* (Basil Blackwell, 1982), p. 166.
18. See Godley, Evidence to the Public Expenditure Sub-Committee.
19. R. W. R. Price, *Public Expenditure: Planning and Control* (National Institute Economic Review, November 1979).
20. See the *Bank of England Quarterly Bulletin*, June 1976, p. 171.
21. Interview with Mary Goldring on BBC Radio 2, November 1983.
22. Pliatzky, *Getting and Spending*, p. 151.
23. Ibid., p. 154.
24. See also Barnett, *Inside the Treasury*, chapter 10.

3

Back to the Classics?: the Change in Attitudes and Thinking in the mid-1970s

I RE-THINKING THE FUNDAMENTALS

There are several reasons for interrupting the story at the end of 1976 to take stock of the way that ideas about the economy had changed.

By then it had become evident that – quite apart from the exchange rate crisis – the economy was not working in the way that the authorities had expected. In fact, the economy in 1976 was in a worse state in every respect than the most pessimistic 1972 forecaster had thought possible. The intervening recession had been deeper, and the recovery weaker, than any in the previous twenty-five years, and the average growth rate had been less than three-quarters of that of any comparable post-war period. Unemployment had risen by more than a half, and was at a level far higher than had previously been thought tolerable. The inflation rate had more than doubled to 16.5 per cent, having at one time topped 25 per cent. The downward trend in company profitability had become steeper, and firms had cut back on investment and training. Personal spending had risen very little, despite a rise in real incomes, because a sense of insecurity had impelled people to save more. As table 3.1 shows, similar trends could be seen in other industrialized countries, although Britain had fared worse than most.

The main reason for pausing to take stock at this point is that since 1972 a major change in attitudes had taken place, in particular to the management of the economy and to authority in general. Disappointed expectations were partly responsible, but the policy reversals and inconsistencies over the years were a more important factor. It was bad enough that governments of both parties had failed to deliver what they had promised, but even more disturbing to observe that they now seemed to lack a coherent strategy for the future. The informal consensus among the governing elites which had been the unifying feature of post-war corporatism seemed to have crumbled, and the willingness of ordinary people to accept their authority was correspondingly reduced. And

Back to the Classics

Table 3.1   Inflation and unemployment in OECD countries, 1976

| | Consumer prices – average annual increase | | | Unemployment | |
	(%) 1961–70	(%) 1971–5	(%) 1976	1976 index 1972 = 100	unemployment rate 1976[a] (%)
UK	4.1	13.0	16.5	155	5.5
USA	2.8	6.7	5.8	151	7.7
Japan	5.8	11.5	9.3	148	2.0
France	4.0	8.8	9.6	246	4.7
Germany	2.7	6.1	4.5	430	3.6
Italy	3.9	11.3	16.8	105	3.6

[a] US definition.

Source: Prices, OECD; unemployment, *Dept of Employment Gazette*, January 1978.

inflation was a disruptive influence in its own right. The prospect of runaway inflation, such as had happened in Germany between the wars, was at no time more than a remote nightmare: but price increases had been large enough to force people to make big adjustments to their life-styles over the course of a few years, unless their incomes also rose. The erratic character of price increases made people unsure about how they stood financially, and even the impeccable Retail Price Index was viewed with suspicion. British institutions were slow to adapt, there was no wage indexation, and the accounting profession was in disarray about how to cope. Groups of workers who felt themselves in danger of falling behind were increasingly disposed to rely upon their own industrial muscle to defend themselves – often in defiance of their national leadership. The industrial relations mood was getting worse, and commentators at home and abroad were asking whether Britain was becoming ungovernable.

The new mood which was emerging lent urgency to the debate going on in academic and political circles concerning the conduct of economic policy. It was recognized that the oil price increase of 1974 had been the main immediate reason for the setback which had occurred, but it was also clear that this and earlier events had exposed unsuspected weaknesses in hitherto widely-accepted theories of macroeconomics. At the practical level, it had already been found that economic management could no longer be based solely upon the Keynesian-style 'fine-tuning' of the sort which had been practised consistently throughout the twenty-five years up to 1973. At the analytical level, what was now needed was first a diagnosis of the weaknesses in existing theory, and out of that, a prescription for the future conduct of policy.

In the heat of this intellectual debate, long-neglected ideas received fresh attention, and some new ideas – or new developments of existing theories – were generated. Economic theorists found themselves in a sellers' market with politicians eager to incorporate their prescriptions into policy or even into ideology. The remainder of this chapter is an attempt, first to outline the theoretical developments which emerged, and then to assess their political impact. The starting point is the reassessment which emerged of the Keynesian theory, which has been outlined in chapter 1.

II THE LIMITATIONS OF KEYNESIAN THEORY

It had long been recognized that the usefulness of Keynes's original theory was limited by some of the simplifying assumptions which it had incorporated, and his followers had from time to time sought to produce modified versions using less restrictive assumptions.

Inflation

One of the more serious limitations of the original theory arose from its treatment of inflation. It assumed that so long as the economy is operating at below a full employment level of output, an increase in demand could not lead to an increase in prices; and inflation would occur only if demand exceeded the productive capacity of the economy. By the late 1950s, this assumption had been replaced – as already noted in chapter 1 – by the 'Phillips Curve' relationship, in which inflation rises more and more rapidly as full employment is approached, and vice versa. By the late 1960s, however, that relationship had broken down. Contrary to its prediction, the inflation rate had risen at a time when unemployment was also rising. Keynesian theory no longer offered a tenable explanation of inflation.

The Keynesian theory not only failed to explain inflation, it also failed to take it into account. In the assumed absence of inflation, any increase in demand leads – so long as the economy is operating at below full employment – to an equal increase in output. But if the possibility of inflation is allowed for, only a part of any injection of demand goes into increases in the volume of output: the rest goes into price increases. In the early 1970s, high proportions of all increases in money GDP were in fact absorbed in price increases. The effectiveness of the Keynesian prescription as a means of curing unemployment was thus put in question.

Another way of looking at it is to say that Keynesian theory has little or nothing to say about the 'supply side' of the economy. If there is unused productive capacity, output is assumed to rise instantaneously in response to an increase in demand. No account is taken of the possibility that some parts of the economy may be working at full capacity while others are under-loaded.

Expectations

A second limitation of Keynesian theory arises from its essentially static nature. It envisages movements to a position at which demand is in line with supply in the goods market and in the market for financial assets, but it says nothing about the sequence and speed of those movements, nor about the influence of previous events upon peoples' behaviour. In the original Keynesian model, and in the Phillips Curve extension to it, people always respond in the same way to what happens at the time, regardless of what had gone before or what they expect to happen next. Later elaborations attempted to take account of the fact that peoples' actions are influenced by their expectations, but in doing so, they threatened to undermine the Keynesian prescription itself.

The closed economy assumption

A third limitation arose from the assumption that the economy is 'closed': that is to say that international trade can safely be ignored. This was, of course, a deliberate simplification, and Keynes's followers subsequently developed the theory to take account of international trade. Some difficulties, however, were encountered. In a fixed exchange rate regime, the balance of payments does – as we have seen – place severe limitations upon the implementation of Keynesian prescriptions. At first sight it seemed that these limitations could be removed by devaluation, or by a move to a flexible exchange rate. But it later emerged that a single devaluation would not permanently remove a balance of payments deficit unless fiscal restraint were also employed to shift resources away from satisfying domestic demand, and into production for export. Otherwise, a progressive devaluation would be needed.[1] Devaluation would, in any case, raise the prices of imported goods. If people succeeded in getting wage increases to compensate, the overseas price of British exports would rise again, eventually cancelling out the advantage initially gained by devaluation.

The multiplier

Some further limitations were revealed by detailed analyses of economic statistics. The system of national accounts, which was the starting-point of Keynesian analysis, provided a framework for the collection of economic statistics, which was adopted after the Second World War by virtually all of the non-communist world. Keynes's system of equations also provided the framework for the construction of mathematical models of the economy, which eventually were to be used for forecasting, and for testing the effects of alternative policies.

By the 1960s, sufficiently long runs of statistics had become available to put numbers, based upon actual experience, to the coefficients in those equations. Considerable advances had been made in the techniques of correlation and multiple regression analysis, which enable the effects of particular influences or 'variables' to be separated, even when many different variables are affecting the outcome. With the help of powerful electronic computers, which by then had become widely available, these 'econometric' techniques were extensively used to make numerical estimates of how people respond to various economic influences. Many such estimates were incorporated into computerized economic models. A small model of this type was set up by the Treasury in 1969, and by the late 1970s, it had expanded to an elaborate system of over 500 equations. Similar models were set up by the London Business School, the National Institute for Economic and Social Research, and the Department of Applied Economics at Cambridge; all working independently, but with government funding.[2]

An important finding which emerged from this work was that Keynes's assumption that people save a constant proportion of any income increase (and vice versa) was not borne out by the facts. It was found that an increase in the inflation rate leads people to increase their savings – an apparently irrational pattern of behaviour, attributable to a desire to maintain the purchasing power of their accumulated savings. And when peoples' incomes fall – for example, during a spell of unemployment – they tend to draw on their savings in an attempt to maintain their living standards. Because of his simplifying assumptions, Keynes had thought that the initial effect of a fall in demand would lead through a 'multiplier' effect to a greatly magnified fall in national income; and that the initial effect of an injection of demand by government would similarly be magnified. On the basis of estimates of saving behaviour, it was thought that the magnification factor (or multiplier) would be above five. But when account is taken of this different pattern of saving behaviour, of 'leakages' of expenditure into imports, and of income tax and social security payments and benefits, the value of the multiplier is in practice much lower.[3]

One implication of this finding is that the modern economy is less vulnerable to disturbances than Keynes had supposed: that in fact it contains powerful 'built-in stabilizers'. Another implication is that demand management is not as powerful an instrument as had been thought. Some estimates of the value of the multiplier effect of an increase in public expenditure put it at less than one, implying that public spending somehow 'crowds-out' some of the private expenditure which would otherwise have occurred.

Interaction between monetary and fiscal policy

One simplifying assumption popularly attributed to Keynes, which in fact he did not make, was that 'money doesn't matter'. The supply of money plays an essential part in the IS/LM diagram as was explained in chapter 1. But this had an implication for policy which, subsequently, was sometimes overlooked. If the government chooses to finance an increase in public expenditure by borrowing from the banks, it thereby increases the total demand for credit, and for money generally. If the money supply is assumed to remain constant, this would imply an increase in interest rates, which would indeed crowd out some private spending. If this form of crowding out is to be avoided, increased public spending must be accompanied by an increase in the supply of money.

Thus a shift in the IS curve brought about by increased public expenditure is likely to be accompanied by a shift in the LM curve brought about by the increase in the money supply. Then the IS and LM curves would not move independently, as might be supposed from a casual view of the diagram shown in figure 1.1 (p. 16). Since post-war governments have frequently financed public spending increases in this way, it is misleading to think of fiscal and monetary policy as separate instruments which are used independently.

The labour market

Finally, in this brief review of the assumptions underlying Keynesian economic theory, there is the paradox which is inherent in the assumption that wages do not move downward – or do so very slowly – in face of a labour surplus. It cannot be said that this assumption is contradicted by the evidence, but it is an assumption which would seem to demand an explanation. What is it about the labour market that makes it different in this respect from other markets? Why, if wage increases at a time of high unemployment increase the risk of unemployment by their recipients, do people nevertheless press for them? If answers could be found to these questions, they might, after all, suggest policy action to reduce unemployment by influencing labour market behaviour.

III NEW CAMBRIDGE AND THE NEW KEYNESIANS

New Cambridge

Among the Keynesian economists who attempted to provide answers to the questions raised by the deficiencies of conventional Keynesian theory, the most immediately influential was the Cambridge Economic Policy Group. Their answers to the questions relating to wages and prices were straightforward. The general level of wages was, in their view, determined entirely by the processes of institutional bargaining, which were virtually unaffected by market forces. Employees adopt a negotiating target which corresponds to a steady growth of real (inflation-corrected) earnings of about two per cent a year. Employers, for their part, set prices by applying a constant percentage mark-up to costs; a procedure which is also virtually unaffected by market forces.

Inflation was thus regarded as an institutional phenomenon which proceeds independently of economic influences, except that an increase in economic growth and in real earnings would reduce the pressure for pay increases, and thus lead to a moderation of inflation. In the New Cambridge view, this was in fact the only way in which inflation could be reduced: incomes policies would have no chance of success, except in the very short term, unless they conformed to the real wage target.

The approach to demand management, which in the mid-1970s was known as 'New Cambridge', was based upon an iconoclastic view of the role of fiscal policy. This depended upon the observation that the financial balance (or net savings) of the private sector had remained reasonably constant over the years. Since, in any complete accounting system, all debits are matched by credits, and all deficits are matched by surpluses, this meant that any changes in the deficit of the public sector must have been matched by opposite changes in the surplus of the overseas sector, which is the only remaining sector in the accounting system. In other words, changes in Britain's balance of payments had been determined almost entirely by changes in the public sector deficit.

From this line of argument, they derived two policy prescriptions. First, the conventional practice of using the budget deficit to manage domestic demand, and using the exchange rate to correct a balance of payments deficit, was the opposite of what was needed. Instead, the government should use the budget deficit to regulate the balance of payments, and the exchange rate to regulate demand. Second, there should be no further attempt to 'fine-tune' the economy because the evidence indicated that the economy was in itself inherently stable, and that the main de-stabilizing influence had been government action (together with occasional overseas 'shocks').[4]

The influence of this New Cambridge theory was short-lived, however, because the stability of private sector financial balances which had been its foundation, ceased, within a year or so of its formulation.[5]

The Cambridge Economic Policy Group was also the main protagonist of what came to be known as the 'Alternative Strategy'. The justification for this strategy was the expectation that Britain's deteriorating trade performance would place a continuing constraint upon domestic growth, effectively ruling out any prospect of a reduction in unemployment. Devaluation, as a way out of this impasse, was also ruled out because it acts too slowly upon demand, and because the size of the devaluation needed to make a substantial inroad into unemployment would be so large as to bring about a sharp rise in inflation.

The proposed solution was a system of import controls designed to prevent imports from rising above pre-existing levels. Domestic demand could then be expanded steadily on normal Keynesian lines but without the constraint which had hitherto been imposed by the balance of payments. Domestic producers, assured of the full benefits of the growth in domestic demand, would add a further stimulus by investing in new capacity, and this would ensure that exports would not suffer as a result of capacity constraints. Action of this sort would break the rules of the European Community and, possibly, the General Agreement on Tariffs and Trade. But as imports would not actually be reduced, there would be no reason, it was argued, for overseas retaliation.[6]

The new Keynesians

Other Keynesian economists had been re-examining the assumptions of Keynesian theory concerning the behaviour of markets other than the labour market. By implication, these assumptions envisaged an imaginary auctioneer who eliminated any impending shortages or surpluses by making the price adjustments necessary to correct them, so that supply and demand were kept in line on a day-to-day basis. It had always been recognized that these were stylized assumptions which, although they might be approximated to in markets for financial assets and in well-organized markets for homogenous commodities, were far from realistic when applied to markets with strongly differentiated goods and services. Keynesian economists had not asserted that all markets actually behave in this way, but rather that the economy as a whole behaves as though they do.

In reality, it is known that there are cases where price adjustments cannot bring supply into line with demand. When straw hats went out of fashion, no feasible price reduction could have kept Luton's straw hat industry from declining. The adjustment in that case had to take place in supply, with automobile production eventually replacing the jobs which had been lost. And it had become evident – as has been noted in chapter 1 – that Britain's post-war loss of export share of manufactured goods had been due largely to non-price factors such as design and reliability. Supply adjustments tend, however, to be slow, sometimes leaving resources idle for several years in the course of transition to other uses. And even where price adjustments are an effective means of bringing demand into line with supply, the possibility of building or running down stocks means that they need not be made instantaneously. A supplier may, instead, choose to postpone making price reductions until it becomes evident whether a change in demand represents a firm trend or merely a fluctuation.

Thus the task of the auctioneer – even if he existed – would not be a simple one. He would need information about the behaviour of future competitors and customers, which might be expensive or perhaps impossible to obtain.

On closer examination, it turned out that in some markets, price adjustments take place slowly, if at all, and that supply adjustments may only take place very slowly. This recognition leads to an understanding of the economy which differs in several respects from that which emerged from the stylized assumptions of earlier Keynesian theory. In the first place, many of the adjustments toward an equilibrium in which supply is everywhere equal to demand may, at a particular point in time, be incomplete; and even as some adjustments approach completion, new ones may just be starting. Thus the economy may remain in a permanent state of disequilibrium, with shortages and surpluses always to be found somewhere or other. Second, the assumption that downward adjustments of prices take place very slowly, if at all, does not distinguish the labour market at all sharply from other markets. Unemployment can also arise from the absence, or slowness, of price responses in the market for goods. Third, as disequilibrium models of the economy were developed, it became evident that Keynesian demand deficiency was not necessarily always the factor responsible for unemployment. Circumstances could be envisaged in which, although in the goods market demand was equal to or even in excess of supply, wages could be too high in relation to other prices to prevent excess supply from developing in the labour market. It seemed that in some periods of its history, the economy might experience 'Keynesian' or demand-deficiency umemployment; while at other periods it might experience 'classical' unemployment.[7]

While these developments improved the explanatory power of Keynesian economics, their implications for policy were limited, and somewhat negative. The 'New Keynesians', unlike their predecessors, recognized the possibility of classical unemployment during which an expansion of demand would have no effect except of raising the rate of inflation. But beyond this, they offered no prescription.

The New Keynesians' explanation of inflation tended, like New Cambridge, to be institutional and sociological. One such explanation was that:

> The current inflation consists of a social dispute about the distribution of the national income; persistent attempts by many social groups to increase their consumption faster than is consistent with the aims of other groups or with macroeconomic stability; persistent consequential bidding up of the price level in a wage–price or wage–wage spiral.[8]

If this were indeed the true explanation, then the prospect would be of accelerating inflation for as long as the dispute persists, accompanied by a continuing transfer of earning power to those with the most industrial bargaining power. The usual Keynesian prescription in the face of such a threat was the introduction of an incomes policy. Previous experience had suggested that incomes policies tend to collapse after a few years, and that this is followed by a catching-up period during which all that had been gained is lost. But the New Keynesians saw little hope of containing inflation except in a continuing search for an effective and durable form of incomes policy.

IV   THE MONETARIST REVOLUTION

The 'helicopter money' story

In its simplest form, monetarism offers an easily understood explanation of inflation, and a straightforward prescription for its cure. It seems intuitively obvious that if pound notes were dropped by helicopter to the extent necessary to double the amount of money in circulation, then prices would double. It is a small step from this 'thought experiment' to the conclusion that inflation is caused by increases in the money supply. And it is an obvious further step to prescribe control of the money supply as the cure for inflation.

But monetary economists did not take so simple a view of the matter. The 'helicopter money' story might work in a primitive society in which a single financial asset provided the only means of payment, but it could not be assumed that it would work in a society with a banking system and with a variety of different financial assets. Whether it would work in such circumstances was what they had set out to investigate.

The monetary equation. The story can be examined in a little more depth using an equation, the two sides of which represent two alternative ways of measuring total national income in money terms:

$$MV = PT$$

The right-hand side consists of some measure of total physical output (denoted by T), multiplied by some measure of price per unit of that output (denoted by P). The left-hand side consists of the total amount of money in circulation (denoted by M), multiplied by a notional 'velocity of circulation' of that money (denoted by V). What this equation says is:

if the velocity of circulation, V, can be assumed constant;

and if the volume of output, T, can be assumed to be unaffected;

then any increase or decrease in the quantity of money, M, will lead to a proportional increase or decrease in the price level, P.

As it stands, this statement is empty of content, being no more than the consequence of the definitions which make it up. It acquires content only if the 'if' statements can be shown to be true. But there is no way of investigating their truth or untruth by contemplation alone: it can only be done by testing them against known facts. This was the task which the monetary economists tackled, and it turned out to be a far from simple one.

The behaviour of the velocity of circulation

The first question – whether the velocity of circulation can be assumed to be constant – could not be tested directly because velocity of circulation is an abstract concept, not a directly measurable quantity. It could be tested indirectly, however, by examining the relationship between nominal national income (PT) and money supply (M).

Casual inspection of published statistics indicated that if such a relationship exists, it could not be a simple one: nominal income clearly does not rise and fall with the money supply on a month-by-month basis. But this was not the end of the matter. It is not, after all, reasonable to insist that the response of nominal income to the money supply should be instantaneous. Econometric techniques were available for testing for

relationships which incorporate time-lags, and many studies were done
using these techniques. These revealed that a strong association existed
between the money supply and nominal income, with changes in the
money supply preceding the associated income changes. Results produced
by Professor Milton Friedman using United States statistics, indicated
that the lags were long and variable.[9] Other results, using both American
and British data, though indicating generally shorter time-lags, confirmed
the leading position of the money supply change. It was also found that the
velocity of circulation emerging from these relationships had not been
constant; but this did not matter in practice because trends in it had been
slow and steady.[10]

These findings were not on their own conclusive. The possibility
remained that – as some Keynesians maintained – it had been changes in
nominal income that had caused changes in the money supply, and not the
other way round. If this were the explanation, then the statistical
association which had been discovered, offered no support to the
monetarist thesis. The fact that money supply changes preceded the
associated changes in nominal income did not rule out this possibility; it
was pointed out that visits to travel agents tend to precede trips abroad,
but cannot be supposed to cause them. Work done by the Bank of
England did suggest that there was a two-way relationship with causation
running both ways.[11]

In view of this, and of the shortcomings inherent in the econometric
techniques which had been used, many economists felt that more was
needed before the evidence for the monetarist thesis could be regarded as
convincing. One thing which would help would be an account of the
'transmission mechanism' by which changes in the money supply are
converted into changes in national income.

The transmission mechanism

In the 'helicopter money' story, the transmission mechanism seems to be
obvious: those who pick up the money spend it on goods. But since the
supply of goods is not affected, the result of attempts to buy more of them
merely pushes up their price, thus their nominal or money value is
increased. This is entirely plausible so long as they can spend the money
only on goods. But if they can also exchange money for other financial
assets, the story may be different. According to Keynesian theory, they
would spend it all on interest-bearing financial assets. If they did, then
there would be no tendency to bid up prices in the goods market.

Monetary economists pointed out, however, that the distinction
between goods and interest-bearing financial assets is, for this purpose, an

arbitrary one. Durable assets such as houses, cars and record players, yield their owners a return which is none the less real for being unmeasurable. That return – which may be in timesaving, health, or merely psychological well-being – can be thought of as being the equivalent, for each asset, of its 'own rate' of interest. Households can thus be thought of as managing a portfolio of assets which includes money, other financial assets and goods; each asset yielding a different return, and differing also in respect of 'liquidity', or ease with which it can be exchanged for cash. In response to a change in the money supply, households can thus be expected to adjust their entire portfolios to restore the desired balance between interest rates and liquidity. If the money supply increases, part of that adjustment will therefore go to bidding up prices in the goods market.

In principle, this account of the transmission mechanism clearly provides a more general account of the effects of money supply changes than does Keynesian theory. But in practice, what matters is how much of the adjustment actually gets absorbed in the market for financial assets, and how much is carried over into the goods market.

If people treat interest-bearing financial assets, such as building society deposits, as close substitutes for money, then the bulk of the adjustment might well take place in the form of purely financial transactions, leaving little of it to affect prices in the goods market. In this case, the Keynesian assumption would be the closer to the truth. At the other extreme, it may be that the adjustments might have only a temporary effect on the financial market, so that in the longer term, virtually the entire effect is felt in the goods market: thus confirming the monetarist thesis. So, once again, the Keynesian/monetarist controversy hinged upon an issue which could be settled only by testing the rival theories against observed behaviour.

Many such tests were done, using British and American data over different time periods and using different measures of money supply and of interest rates. The results indicated that there was a statistically significant relationship between changes in the money supply and changes in interest rates on other financial assets, but that the relationship was not particularly strong nor stable. The looseness of the association was generally taken to indicate that other financial assets are not treated as particularly close substitutes for money, and that a substantial amount of substitution is thus likely to occur in the goods market.

Taken together with the much stronger statistical association between the money supply and nominal national income, these results gave encouragement to the belief in the importance of controlling the money supply. But, while the evidence gave no support to any extreme version of the Keynesian position, neither did it support the extreme monetarist contention that behaviour in the financial markets could safely be ignored. The possibility that controlling the money supply might produce unanticipated reactions in the financial markets, thus remained a source of worry.

Effects on unemployment

Granted that a reduction in the growth of the money supply can bring about a reduction in the growth of nominal national income (PT), the next question arose from the second 'if' (p. 77) – if the volume of output is unaffected.

In fact, that question had to be reformulated because most monetarists conceded that there would be an initial fall in output growth, and an accompanying rise in unemployment. The important questions concerned the magnitude of that initial increase in unemployment, and the course of events which would follow it. Two main mechanisms were envisaged as determining the subsequent course of inflation. The exchange rate would rise, reducing the price of imports; and pay increases would moderate under the influence of the rise in unemployment. But expectations would play an important part also. It was the 'expectations-augmented Phillips Curve' which was used to trace out the path of prices and of unemployment which would follow a reduction in the growth of the money supply.

In the particular form used for this purpose, the expectations-augmented Phillips Curve is a relationship in which the inflation rate is determined jointly by the unemployment rate and the expected inflation rate. For any given value of the expected inflation rate, this relationship is the same as that of the original Phillips Curve (except that, in this version, it is the inflation rate, not the wage rate, which falls as unemployment rises). But the higher the expected rate of inflation, the more pressure there is for pay increases to catch up. And, since high pay increases contribute to inflation, the higher the expected rate of inflation, the higher its actual rate will be. Thus, if the expected inflation rate rises, there is a corresponding increase in the actual inflation rate which corresponds to each level of the unemployment rate. The expectation augmented Phillips Curve is therefore not a single curve, but a stack of curves the higher of which relate to the higher inflationary expectations.[12]

As a point of reference, the unemployment rate at which the actual inflation rate is the same as the expected inflation rate is termed the 'Non-Accelerating Inflation Rate of Unemployment' (NAIRU), or simply the 'natural rate' of unemployment. By assumption, the natural rate of unemployment is the same at all levels of non-accelerating inflation.

The 'natural rate' of unemployment

The expectations-augmented Phillips Curve construction was used to trace out the consequences of departures of unemployment from its natural rate. For ease of exposition the story was usually told in a series of episodes. For example:

(1) Unemployment rises above its natural rate. In the short-term, the expected inflation rate does not change and the actual inflation rate falls, as predicted by the ordinary Phillips Curve.
(2) In the longer term, the expected inflation rate also falls, so that the actual inflation rates corresponding to each level of the unemployment rate, also fall.
(3) If unemployment is maintained at above its natural rate, then steps (1) and (2) are repeated until the inflation rate falls to zero. If, however, the unemployment rate is brought back to its natural rate, then the process ceases. In any case, unemployment reverts to its natural rate in the long term when the expected inflation rate comes into line with the actual inflation rate.

By substituting 'rises' for 'falls', 'below' for 'above', etc., this can be turned into a story of continually accelerating inflation.

An important feature of this story is that, although in the short-term (before inflationary expectations change) unemployment has to rise in order to get a reduction in inflation, in the longer term (when expected inflation comes into line with actual inflation) unemployment goes back to its 'natural' rate. Inflation is thus ultimately reduced without any long-term increase in unemployment. How rapidly unemployment falls back to its natural rate depends, in this scenario, upon how rapidly expectations are revised. Step 2 assumes that the expected rate of inflation falls only after the actual rate has fallen (a pattern of opinion-formation known as 'adaptive expectations'). This is not the only possibility. As some monetarists pointed out, it is reasonable to assume that people are capable of anticipation. If the monetarist thesis were generally accepted, then the mere announcement of an intention to reduce monetary growth would cause people to expect inflation to fall. If this happened, then inflation might be reduced without even a temporary increase in unemployment. (Driven to its logical conclusion, this type of argument can lead to some startling conclusions, as will be explained later in this chapter.)

The expectations-augmented Phillips Curve story had no necessary connection with the money supply; it could be told in the same way whatever the cause of the initial rise in unemployment. It provided a plausible account, both of the development of accelerating inflation, and of the process by which inflation might be cured. It was, however, a highly simplified story which omitted the influences of factors other than unemployment and pay; and because of the problems of measuring expectations, it was difficult to test against experience. Nevertheless it became an important part of the monetarist thesis.

This was not the whole story, however; another part of the transmission mechanism worked through the effect of the money supply on the exchange rate. Since this mechanism had a considerable bearing upon events before and after 1976, it merits separate examination in its own right.

V MONEY AND THE EXCHANGE RATE

In the brief account of Keynesian economic theory in chapter 1, and in the section on its limitations which appears earlier in this chapter, it was noted that in its original form, that theory embodied the assumption of a 'closed economy', and therefore took no account of international trade. In fact, post-war Keynesian economists had developed a sophisticated synthesis between Keynes's original theory and earlier theoretical work on the balance of payments. This had provided the intellectual framework for the practice of demand management in an open economy, throughout the 1950s and the 1960s. In practice it amounted, as we have seen, to an acknowlegement of the constraint which the balance of payments imposed upon the exercise of demand management. But in the late 1960s and early 1970s, this 'conventional' view of the balance of payments faced a strong challenge from a new monetary approach to the balance of payments.

Conventional theory

The essence of the conventional theory had been that the exchange rate is determined by the balance between the supply and the demand for exports and for imports. Domestic economic expansion increases the demand for imports without necessarily affecting exports. In a regime of nominally fixed exchange rates, this limits the scale of expansion unless it is accompanied by a devaluation. It could be demonstrated, moreover, that devaluation provides no long-term escape from this constraint except under narrowly-defined conditions and assumptions.

The monetary approach

The monetary approach to the balance of payments (pioneered in Britain by Professor Harry G. Johnson)[13] treated the exchange rate as the relative price of the moneys in circulation in the two countries in question, and related it to the supply of and the demand for money in each of those two countries. An increase in the domestic money supply, relative to that of an overseas currency, would therefore cause the rate of exchange of the domestic currency against that currency to fall.

Payments received in exchange for exports, constitute an increase in the domestic money supply, and payments made for imports cause it to decrease. A balance of payments surplus thus means a net inflow of money, and its effect is to increase domestic activity and domestic prices. The consequence of the increase of domestic activity is an increase in imports, and the consequence of the increase of domestic prices is a fall in exports. Both effects act to remove the surplus, and put an end to the inflow without any change in the exchange rate. In the absence of other effects, a balance of payments deficit is similarly self-correcting. But if the domestically-created money supply is increased, the self-correcting mechanism is defeated and the domestic currency tends to depreciate.

The balance of payments thus both influences, and is influenced by, the domestic money supply. In particular, the changes to the domestic money supply which accompany a change in the balance of payments, affect domestic activity and prices. The conventional assumption that the demand for imports is determined solely by domestic demand and relative prices is thus an over-simplification.

The policy implication is that if the authorities maintain the domestically-created money supply constant, then the balance of payments will be self-correcting. A balance of payments deficit, for example, leads to a monetary outflow which leads to a domestic contraction or price-reduction, either of which would tend to restore the balance without any change in the exchange rate. Devaluation would in any case be ineffective unless accompanied by a reduction of domestic credit expansion.

The monetary approach to the balance of payments had a particular appeal for the economists in the International Monetary Fund. The Fund could be approached by member governments who faced balance of payments problems for loans to strengthen their foreign exchange reserves. Customarily (as in 1967 and 1976, in the case of Britain) the Fund attached conditions to such loans which were designed to make applicants adopt policies which would tackle the causes of their problems, and thus avoid the need for further loans. Its economists saw a limit on domestic credit expansion as a simple and effective way to require the adoption of such policies. The spread of monetary thinking in the 1970s owed much to the influence of the Fund's economists.[14]

An explanation of British inflation

Proponents of the monetary approach to the balance of payments did not claim that monetary developments were the sole influence on exchange rates but they pointed to the importance of money in their short-run determination. It seemed likely to be important because, while price changes may take some years to bring about a balance in the goods markets, international monetary flows could take place very rapidly. Their thinking had not, at this stage, developed to the point of offering a comprehensive theory of exchange rate determination, taking account of interest rates and inflationary expectations. Moreover, it offered only a qualitative explanation which had not been rigorously tested against statistical observations. Nevertheless, it provided a framework within which the story of the inflationary mechanism in the British economy could be re-told in a more convincing way than had hitherto been possible.

Economists at the London Business School re-told the story in three episodes.[15]

(1) The first episode covered the period from the Korean war to the 1967 devaluation. This was a period of fixed exchange rates and a time when the world price level showed only a modest average increase. Britain traded substantially in the market for manufactured goods, in which competition increased steadily through the years. The trend in Britain's prices of manufactures was substantially set by the world price level. (The fact that Britain's prices rose somewhat faster, is attributed to a process of adjustment following an excessive devaluation in 1949). The artificially low exchange rate, which followed that devaluation, was responsible for the low unemployment rates of the period, and led to a mistaken belief that these were consistent with the balance of payments equilibrium. Finally, the 1967 devaluation was due to a mistaken belief that it had been an incorrect exchange rate, and not an over-ambitious unemployment target, which had caused the balance of payments to deteriorate.

(2) The second episode ran from 1967 to 1972. This had many of the same characteristics as the pre-1967 period, except that there was a sharp acceleration of the world price level, and also an upward movement of British import prices, following the devaluation.

(3) The third episode ran from 1972 to 1976; a period during which the world inflation rate continued to rise, and the sterling exchange rate was allowed to fluctuate. Without a fixed exchange rate, the link between British and world prices had been severed. The world value of sterling fell by over 20 per cent as a result of the rapid expansion of the British money supply, and domestic prices were pushed up as a result. The fact that inflation increased more

rapidly in Britain than elsewhere, was due to its faster monetary expansion.

It is to be noted that this story accounts only for the difference between British and world inflation. It does not account for the rise in world inflation. A plausible explanation of this, which is consistent with the story, would lay the blame upon the United States deficit financing of the Vietnam War, which might be held responsible for an increase in the world money supply.

Implications for monetarism

An interesting implication of the monetary approach to the balance of payments arises from its stipulation that if the exchange rate is fixed, the authorities cannot control the money supply independently of what is happening elsewhere in the world. (What happens is that the authorities respond passively to variations in the demand for money, and any shortages or surpluses which develop are eliminated by means of balance of payments surpluses or deficits.) Under such a regime, therefore, any statistical association between the money supply and prices must be due to the effect of prices on the money supply, and not the other way round. Those associations which were discovered in the statistics of open economies during periods of fixed exchange rates cannot, therefore, be taken as supporting the monetarist thesis. This would appear to discredit all of the British studies, but not the United States studies, since international trade plays too small a part in the United States economy to justify regarding it as an open economy. Nevertheless, its explanation of events when exchange rates are not fixed, depends on an acceptance of the monetarist thesis – if the Keynesian version of the direction of causation holds (from income change to money supply change) then the story collapses.

If the basic monetary thesis is accepted, however, this approach provides another element in the transmission mechanism between the money supply and prices. In this element also, expectations can be important; if currency dealers accept the monetary thesis then they, too, might respond to an announcement of monetary restraint by buying pounds, thus raising the sterling exchange rate and bringing about a reduction in the British inflation rate.

VI THE NEW CLASSICAL ECONOMICS

The disagreements between monetarists and Keynesians were seen by some (including Professor Milton Friedman) as disagreements over facts, rather than over theoretical analysis. This, indeed, is how they have been treated so far in this summary. But some others claimed that Keynes's theory was not merely factually unrealistic, it was logically flawed. This second line of attack on Keynes's theory thus went deeper than the 'monetarist revolution', and it was in the long run to have wider implications for economic thinking and for policy.

The objection which the 'new classical' economists raised against Keynes's theory was that it embodied a 'money illusion', namely the assumption that people resist downward movements of money wages rather than of real wages. They interpreted Keynes's prescription as a proposal to take advantage of that supposed illusion, and to tackle unemployment by allowing inflation to erode real wages. Such a proposal stood no chance of more than temporary success. If it is granted that people are capable of learning from experience, then it is illogical to suppose that such an illusion would persist. It runs counter to the dictum that 'you can't fool all of the people all of the time'.

Whatever the truth of this accusation, there does seem to be something unsatisfactory about a theory which depends upon an assumption of irrational or unexplainable behaviour.

The Rational Expectations Hypothesis

While the assumption that people fail to learn from experience and make persistent forecasting errors is clearly unsatisfactory, the opposite assumption also raises some difficulties. The 'Rational Expectations Hypothesis' postulates that, in forming their expectations, people make use of all relevant information; and that, although they may make random errors, their forecasts are not systematically biased. Concerning doubts about its credibility, proponents of that hypothesis replied that it was not necessary to suppose that individuals actually form their expectations that way, but only that the economy as a whole behaves 'as if' they do. While not claiming that it was literally true, they did claim that it offered a better hypothesis concerning the working of the economy than the available alternatives.[16]

The hypothesis seemed to raise some awkward problems.[17] Apart from the practical problem of how people were considered to be able to obtain access to all of the relevant information, there is the conceptual problem of how they are to be supposed to interpret it. To suppose that people could correctly interpret information for forecasting purposes, was to suppose that they were all in possession of the 'correct' model of how the economy works. This is to presuppose a consensus among the population at large which is not to be seen among professional economists; and also to presuppose that the Rational Expectations Hypothesis is itself embodied in that consensus.

Notwithstanding these convoluted implications, the rational expectations hypothesis seemed to be a powerful and fascinating intellectual construction, whose implications were worth further exploration. Sweeping conclusions follow the implication that, among the developments that people can correctly foresee, are the future actions of governments. Given this foreknowledge, it was argued, individual agents would adjust their plans concerning the 'real' world in such a way as to thwart any attempt by governments to influence the outcome. Thus governments could influence inflation, but their actions could not affect 'real' physical outcomes, such as the level of output – except, possibly, if their actions were random and unpredictable. Keynesian demand management, in particular, is ruled out.

The role of government

This corollary of rational expectations offered some interesting insights, but also some further difficulties. It had to be accepted that the contrary assumption, that people take no account of expected government behaviour, is rather absurd; as also is the assumption that their expectations of such behaviour must be systematically biased. The notion of a wise and benevolent governing elite, manipulating a passive population like pawns on a chessboard (as Keynesian theory seemed to envisage) also seemed to be logically unacceptable. But, on the other hand, a complete reversal of roles so that the Government becomes the passive agent seems equally unthinkable. The 'new classical' economics does in fact assign to governments the role of maintaining price stability. It acknowledges that, unless such a role is performed, a monetary economy is 'unanchored' and inherently unstable. But it was maintained that this role would have to be performed by adherence to a fixed rule, such as a predetermined path for the money supply. Discretionary 'fine-tuning' produces undesirable effects because it tends to introduce a random or unpredictable factor which threatens stability. Beyond the maintenance of price stability and of law and order, the proponents of the New Classical economics appeared to assign no effective role to government.

Government action to stabilise the economy, it was argued, would in any case be unnecessary because, given price stability, the economy is inherently self-stabilizing. The theoretical basis for this contention was derived from the concept of 'general equilibrium' originated by the nineteenth-century economist Leon Walras. This envisages the economy as a series of inter-linked markets, with supply in one market determining demand in others in a manner which could be represented by a vast set of simultaneous equations. An imaginary auctioneer permits trading only at prices which keep demand constantly in line with supply in all markets, so that there can be no shortages or surpluses anywhere in the system. Under rational expectations all concerned are in fact sufficiently well-informed to achieve this without the auctioneer.

This 'Walrasian' system was, in effect, a mathematical formulation of Adam Smith's concept of the 'hidden hand', which guides the economy without the need for central direction. Over a wide range of economic activity, it could be shown to be a more effective way of carrying out the wishes of the people than any other form of collective decision-making.

The labour market

Categories of activity to which the stylized Walrasian system cannot, or does not, apply can readily be identified; and the debate among the proponents of the New Classical economics concerned the circumstances under which the Walrasian concept could usefully be assumed to apply. The debate was conducted in the spirit of what Professor Milton Friedman described as 'positive economics', under which theories were to be adjudged not by the realism of their assumptions (since assumptions can never be fully realistic) but by their usefulness for the purpose of analysis.[18]

One of the challenges which faced the new classical economists was the need to construct an account of the working of the labour market which did not embody irrationalities of the sort which they attributed to Keynesian theory, but which would be analytically useful in the sense of providing an explanation for unemployment. It was pointed out that some unemployment could be accounted for by the fact that some people spend time searching for suitable work.[19] This is rational behaviour which, presumably, is advantageous to those who engage in it. But it was recognized that this could account for only a small part of the unemployment experienced in the 1930s and the 1970s.

Another line of thinking developed the implications of long-term contracts. Outside of the labour market some contracts, such as tenancies at a fixed rental, could be thought of as agreements to shift the risk of price changes, for example, from tenant to freeholder, in exchange for a risk premium. This is a rational form of behaviour, much the same as the purchase of insurance, but it could delay the otherwise instantaneous price adjustments which were assumed to occur under the Walrasian system.

Long-term contracts of this sort are not common in the labour market but in the mid-1970s a number of economists were investigating the possibility that it behaves 'as if' such contracts exist. They hypothesized an unspoken agreement or 'implicit contract', under which employees receive the same pay rates in good times and in bad times, so that they are paid less than they are worth to their employers in good times, and are correspondingly over-paid in bad times.[20] This could plausibly be represented as rational behaviour, except that under rational expectations, employees must be presumed also to accept the consequences of such an arrangement, among which is an increased prospect of becoming unemployed in bad times. The rationality of such an arrangement is then less obvious, but its plausibility is enhanced when account is taken of unemployment insurance. The concept of 'moral hazard' was also borrowed from insurance theory, to bring out the possibility that unemployment benefit might lead some of the unemployed to prefer that status, or at any rate to prolong the process of job search.

Related studies developed the idea of a segmented labour market, with a favoured category of employees whom employers are reluctant to dismiss, because of the investment represented by their skills or loyalty; and a remaining category, on which the main burden of unemployment tends to fall.[21] Others put forward the hypothesis that the objectives of trade unions might differ from those of individual workers, giving less weight to the risks of unemployment, and attempted to relate unemployment to the growth of trade union power.[22]

Stabilization policies versus supply-side policies

When considerations of this sort were taken into account, it became evident that the 'natural rate of unemployment' was not immutable, but depended upon such structural factors as the conventions and institutions of the labour market, the level of unemployment insurance, geographical mobility, etc. And while the new classical economists denied that governments could bring about a lasting shift of unemployment below its natural rate: they also argued that they should be able to bring about a downward shift of the natural rate itself, by means of structural changes. But the distinction between stabilization policies and policies to produce structural change was not always clear-cut. A reduction in taxes on energy, for example, might alternatively be seen as part of a stabilization package, or as action to bring about the substitution of energy for labour in production processes. Most government actions fell to some degree in both categories, weakening the practical force of the contention that governments could not influence the real economy. Nevertheless, emphasis had shifted from an almost exclusive preoccupation with demand management, to an

increased concern with the effect of economic policy on the supply side of
the economy.

Room for doubt

The intellectual debate of the early 1970s was conducted both at a
theoretical level and on the basis of the results of econometric testing of
rival hypotheses. At neither level could the outcome be regarded in 1976
as having been conclusively settled. When econometric methodologies
were closely scrutinized, it was found that there were many pitfalls and
that there were few practical studies which could fully live up to the
standard required to place their findings beyond reasonable doubt. The
proper conduct of economic policy was a matter on which, as seldom
before, honest and reasonable men were entitled to differ.

VII   PRACTICAL AND POLITICAL IMPLICATIONS

Economic policy is not entirely a matter of economics; nor is the
economics which it involves, all a matter of high theory. It is an activity
concerning which the cliche about 'the art of the possible' is at its least
trivial. This is brought out most clearly by considering the importance of
credibility and confidence. It had become very clear by 1976 that, no
matter what the intellectual justification for a policy, it is liable to fail if
people doubt the government's ability and determination to sustain it. An
incomes policy breaks down if people expect inflation to continue
unchecked. A deficit cannot be financed if lenders fear that they will be
repaid in depreciated currency. The government may itself be convinced
that such fears are misplaced, but it dare not ignore them. Conversely, a
policy which creates confidence has political attractions which may
transcend its intrinsic merits.

Presentational considerations

In political terms, the adoption of a money supply target had important
presentational advantages. In a sense, it was constitutionally irrational,
because the money supply has no implications for the people whom the
government had been elected to represent, except through its effects upon
prices, output and employment. The rational procedure would seem to be
to pursue an objective, formulated as an intended path of prices, output
and employment. But this would have raised insuperable presentational
problems. The government had no reliable means of forming an estimate
of the consequences of its policies for prices, output and employment,

except within a very wide range of uncertainty. To reveal the extent of that uncertainty would hardly be likely to inspire confidence, and there might be public dissension if it appeared possible that a policy to reduce inflation might involve very high levels of unemployment. The pursuit of a more readily controllable intermediate objective such as a money supply target, on the other hand, offered a prospect of demonstrating the government's ability to achieve what it had set out to do.

This was to be an experimental operation, and there were persuasive arguments against telling the patient too much about the risks involved. The immediate objective was the restoration of lost confidence, and the stage seemed to have been reached at which this could only be done by announcing the adoption of a new operating technique.

Monetary policy operates, as has been explained, by influencing the growth of nominal national income. In principle, this could be done by a variety of combinations of monetary, fiscal and exchange rate policies. But the other alternatives lacked the presentational simplicity and the other presentational advantages of a money supply target. The immediate reason for the adoption of such a target in 1976 had been pressure from the International Monetary Fund, but there are thus good political reasons for supposing that something of the sort might have been done in any case, whatever party had been in power.

Technical problems

At a practical level, the adoption of a money supply target had to be preceded by a number of decisions of a technical nature. In principle these concerned the definition of money to be used, the choice of the path for the money supply so defined, and the technique of control to be used to follow that path. In practice, the decision-making process also required some sort of estimate of the consequences of those decisions for the economy at large. In Britain, those decisions were taken with the minimum of public debate by a central executive made up of the Treasury and the Bank of England. The decisions which they took in 1976 were strongly influenced by their experience of working to undisclosed monetary targets since 1973. Since those decisions were to have a significant influence upon subsequent events, it will be worth dwelling briefly on how they were arrived at.

The choice of M3

In keeping with monetary theory, it would appear that the appropriate definition of money would be one which excludes interest-bearing assets. In statistical terminology this is M1 (currency plus current account deposits). But for several reasons, the more broadly-defined M3 (currency plus current and deposit account deposits by UK residents with UK banks) was preferred.[23]

One reason was presentational. Unlike M1, M3 was a readily-distinguishable component of the International Monetary Fund's 'domestic credit expansion' (the other component being external flows from abroad). And, again unlike M1, it could be neatly split into three accounting 'counterparts'; namely, the public sector's borrowing from the banks, the private sector's borrowing from the banks, and external flows. The public sector's borrowing from the banks could in turn be split into the public sector borrowing requirement (public expenditure less revenues) less whatever the public sector borrows directly from the public by sales of bonds (for example, 'gilts') and savings certificates, etc. The use of M3 thus enabled the authorities to explain their actions in terms of the accounting relationship between public expenditure, taxation and the money supply. (The economic relationship is more complex because it has to take account of behavioural responses.)

A second reason for choosing M3, in preference to M1, was a practical one. It was thought that any attempt to control M1 would lead people to transfer funds from current accounts (which are included in M1) to interest-bearing deposit accounts (which are not).

The choice of M3 as the subject of control had also been influenced by the requirement that there should be a stable relationship between the measure of money chosen; nominal income on the one hand, and interest rates on the other. The existence of such a relationship was, as we have seen, a fundamental tenet of monetarism. On the basis of statistics for the period 1964-71, it had appeared that a stable relationship of this sort did exist, both for M1 and for M3. After 1972, it had become evident that the M3 relationship had broken down,[24] but this was thought in 1976 to be a temporary consequence of changes in the banking system, brought about by the previous government's 'Competition and Credit Control' regulations. M3 was retained as the target measure in the hope that a stable relationship would re-establish itself when things had settled down.

The target path and the technique of control

There had been two schools to choose from, as regards the numerical targets to be adopted. The 'instant monetarists' advocated a sharp reduction in monetary growth to a level to correspond to the required inflation rate. The 'gradualists', on the other hand, considered the consequences of such action to be too unpredictable to risk, and advocated a steadily reducing rate of monetary growth. The choice of the British authorities, in common with those of many other countries, was 'gradualism'.

It was intended that, in the long term, the growth of M3 would be influenced by operating on its public-sector borrowing requirement, bond sales and external flows counterparts; but for month-by-month control the intended procedure was to influence bank lending by varying interest rates. For this purpose, techniques were required to forecast bank lending and to determine the interest rate adjustments needed to correct any divergences from its required track. Bank lending had, however, proved to be volatile and difficult to forecast; and the picture seemed to have been confused by changes in the behaviour of the banks in the early 1970s.

Partly to overcome these difficulties, the supplementary special deposits scheme (popularly known as 'the corset') had been introduced in 1973. This had the effect of imposing financial penalties upon banks whose lending exceeded stipulated limits. The corset was not in operation in 1976, but remained in the authorities' armoury, as an expedient to be employed if the money supply threatened to get out of control.

It was hoped in 1976 that the technical problems of controlling the money supply would yield to the expertise which would come with further experience. It was also intended that the underlying problem should be eased by downward pressure on planned public spending.

The control of public spending

It was not fully appreciated at the time that the British system of government was ill-adapted to that task. Some of the costs of arbitrary expansions of public expenditure had become apparent. A vast surplus of electrical generating capacity had, for example, become inevitable as a result of the previous government's public spending programmes, and of its policy of artificially holding down electricity prices. Arbitrary reductions in public spending plans were liable to be equally damaging. The available channels of communication were not equal to the task of ensuring that the cuts fell upon the least economic parts of a programme; and the system of ministerial 'horse-trading' which allocated the cuts was, in any case, not capable of assimilating such information. Thus, cuts tended to fall arbitrarily; some of them upon wasteful projects, but others upon expenditure which could be postponed only at high cost. The lack of effective communication between central government and the local authorities – whose expenditure was, of course, part of public-sector spending – was a particularly telling weakness in this context.

VIII   THE CONSERVATIVE PARTY AND THE NEW RIGHT

The centralization of political power which characterized the British
system of government had, particularly in times of crisis, allowed Cabinet
ministers little time to discuss policy with their supporters, even if they
had the inclination to do so. The policy changes of the 1970s had
consequently created a sense of bewilderment and alienation among
members of both the major political parties. In the Conservative Party,
this and the authoritarian management style of Mr Heath, had caused
some discontent among Members of Parliament outside the Cabinet; and
after the electoral defeat of February 1974, this had turned into recrimi-
nation. There was general agreement that the Cabinet's conduct of
economic policy had been faulty; but uncertainty as to whether its policies
had been mistaken in principle, or merely ill-judged in execution. The
alternatives were in any case not clear. Monetarism was getting a good deal
of attention from economic commentators in the press, but in early 1974,
it remained very much a minority view in political circles. Mr Enoch
Powell – by then a figure on the fringes of the party – was its only
prominent advocate.

Sir Keith Joseph's influence

In the course of 1974 the position changed with the sudden conversion of
Sir Keith Joseph (formerly Secretary of State for Health and Social
Security, and then a member of the Opposition Shadow Cabinet). Sir
Keith formed the view that, in attempting to compete for the political
middle ground, the Conservative Party had allowed itself to be moved step
by step in the direction of state socialism. He proposed a radical
re-orientation of policy away from Keynesian demand management and
other forms of state intervention, towards a much greater reliance upon
the free operation of market forces. First priority should go to the control
of inflation, but this could not be achieved by incomes policies. Sir Keith's
philosophy now included a strongly-held belief in a strict form of
monetarism, which denied the possibility of wage-induced inflation in the
absence of monetary expansion. He acknowledged that monetary control
of inflation might involve some increase in unemployment, but maintained
that the official statistics had greatly overstated the true levels of involun-
tary unemployment; which, he estimated, had fluctuated between 100,000
and 300,000 or so since the war.

Assisted by the Conservative Party's Centre for Policy Studies, of which
he was founder and chairman, Sir Keith Joseph made vigorous attempts to
convert his Cabinet colleagues to his view. He was met with assent to the

proposition that mistakes had been made, but resistance to the radical policy reversal which he proposed. He found a staunch ally in Mrs Thatcher (formerly Education Secretary, and then an Opposition spokesman on Treasury affairs) and was supported by Sir Geoffery Howe and Mr David Howell, but Mr Heath, Mr Prior and others were unconvinced by his case.

The debate within the Cabinet became public when, in September 1974, Sir Keith Joseph gave a public speech which was generally interpreted as an attack on the policies of his own party when in office.

> . . . on each occasion the government – by which I mean almost every post-war government – has chosen to boost demand by deficit financing, in spite of a virtual certainty that the additional balance of payments deficits generated would oblige them to call a halt fairly soon and thereby lose as many jobs as they were creating, while keeping the additional inflation. . . .
> . . . We cannot talk about fighting inflation as the overriding priority and then in the same or another speech say that we can take no monetary action which might threaten some jobs. We cannot have it both ways.[25]

One newspaper commented that Sir Keith had 'handed a blunderbuss loaded with duck shot to Mr Wilson and invited him to blow the Conservative Party's head off'.[26]

Mrs Thatcher's role

Following its further electoral defeat in October 1974, the decision was taken to hold an election by Conservative Members of Parliament for the leadership of the Party. Sir Keith did not offer himself as a candidate, and most of Mr Heath's other colleagues were at first reluctant to stand against him. Mrs Thatcher did so, and was elected. It does not appear, however, that her monetarist views were an important element in her favour. In the words of one commentator:

> Mrs Thatcher became leader of the Conservative Party in February 1975 because she was not Edward Heath, not because of a widespread commitment to her views. She was the only serious candidate willing to challenge Mr Heath at a time when a majority of Tory MPs wanted a change.[27]

Sir Keith Joseph was thus free to pursue his campaign for a new economic policy with the enthusiastic support of the leader of his party.

'The Right Approach'

The outcome was a policy statement, published in 1977, entitled 'The

Right Approach to the Economy', and signed by James Prior as well as Sir Geoffery Howe, Mr David Howell and Sir Keith Joseph. This was generally more cautious in tone than Sir Keith's speeches on the subject. It did not contain an all-out attack on Keynesian demand management. It did, however, reject incomes policies in favour of a return to free collective bargaining. And it did contain a strong commitment to a gradualist monetary policy:

> . . . our prime and overriding objective is to unwind the inflationary coils which have gripped our economy and threaten to throttle the free enterprise system.

> . . . we shall aim to continue the gradual reduction in the rate of growth of the money supply, in line with firm monetary targets.

> . . . That is not to say that one only has to follow the right money supply path and everything in the economy will become right . . . but it is certainly the case that if the management of money is handled wrongly, everthing goes wrong.

Beyond that, the document proposed lower personal taxation, an 'enterprise package' to stimulate business growth and action to 'reduce the preponderance of state ownership'. There was to be an arms-length relation with the trade unions, but the National Economic Development Council was to be used to ensure that pay bargaining would be well-informed; and there would be a new code of practice for bargaining.

Between 1974 and 1977, there had thus been a radical shift in the policies of the Conservative Party, even if they had not moved quite as far as Sir Keith or Mrs Thatcher would have wished.

IX   THE LABOUR PARTY AND THE NEW LEFT

The divisions which had been developing within the Labour Party had been less public, but went even deeper than those in the Conservative Party. Unlike the Conservative Party, the Labour Party had a constitution which, in principle, gave its rank-and-file members the right to determine policy. However, in practice, it was different. In the words of one of its leaders:

> Since it could not afford, like its opponents, to maintain a large army of paid party workers, the Labour Party required militants – politically conscious socialists – to do the work of organising the constituencies. But since these

militants tended to be 'extremists', a constitution was needed which maintained their enthusiasm by apparently creating a full party democracy, while excluding them from effective power. Hence the concession in principle of sovereign power to the delegates at the Annual Conference, and the removal in practice of most of this sovereignty through the trade union block vote on the one hand and the complete independence of the Parliamentary Labour Party on the other.[28]

The National Executive Committee of the Labour Party, which is a body elected by the party's Annual Conference, had for some years been moving to the left of the leadership of the Parliamentary Party. In October 1973, the annual conference had approved a policy document entitled 'Labour's Programme 1973' which had been prepared earlier in the year by that committee. The document proposed the nationalization of twenty-five major companies and the powers – under the heading of 'Planning Agreements' – to issue directives to privately-owned companies concerning prices, profits and investment, with powers to dismiss recalcitrant directors. Harold Wilson had made no secret of his rejection of these proposals and he insisted that the party's 1974 election manifesto should make no reference to the document's nationalization proposals. After the election, he instituted planning agreements which were not compulsory as proposed, but entirely voluntary (and, as it turned out, entirely ineffective).

The Campaign for Labour Party Democracy

Indignation with this flouting by the party's leadership of the wishes of its conference, led to the formation of the 'Campaign for Labour Party Democracy'. The aim of this body was to ensure that policy decisions taken by the party's annual conference should in future be binding upon the Parliamentary Labour Party. To this end, its supporters proposed a succession of changes to the party's constitution. But the underlying dispute was ideological rather than constitutional.

Ideological undercurrents

The British Labour movement had always been an amalgam of, or a compromise between, two strands of thinking. They had in common a determination to put an end to the exploitation of working people by the employers, which had been so vividly described by Dickens and by Marx. But they differed fundamentally about the means to achieve that objective. The Marxist strand of thinking saw it as coming about as a result of the historically inevitable overthrow of the economic system by the working class; whereas the earlier English socialists had thought to bring it about by getting full voting rights for all working people, and then using the parliamentary system to redress the economic balance.

It had been the latter 'social democratic' strand of thinking which in practice had dominated the policies of the Labour Party. But there had always been a reluctance, particularly among active party members, to make an explicit rejection of the Marxist alternative. The party's 'Statement of Aims' had, since 1918, included the aim of securing the common ownership of the means of production, distribution and exchange (the famous 'Clause IV', quoted in full in chapter 1) and an attempt by the then party leadership in 1959 to get that clause deleted had been defeated by the party conference.

In the 1960s, the dominant social democratic wing of the party could successfully argue that it was well on the way to achieving the party's true aims. National Insurance, the Welfare State, employment protection legislation, and immunities against legal action for the trade unions, had done much to redress the balance. And, contrary to Marxist predictions, the material condition of working people had greatly improved. More needed to be done to remove the remaining inequalities, but further growth in the size of the national cake would further the interests of working people more than could any feasible redistribution of wealth or ownership. The best course was thus to seek further improvements while preserving the 'mixed economy' in broadly its existing form, without any sweeping programme of further nationalization.[29]

By the mid-1970s, this argument had become somewhat less persuasive. The prospects of further rapid growth in the size of the national cake seemed to have receded, and the importance of how it was distributed had correspondingly increased. Unemployment was hurting more and more working people and inflation was creating feelings of insecurity. On top of this, there was a suspicion of a conspiracy among companies – particularly multinational companies – and international financiers to thwart any further moves toward socialist objectives.

The 'Outside Left' and the 'Inside Left'

The changes in the economic situation, and the perception that outside influences were depriving a Labour administration of its freedom to pursue socialist aims, tended to tilt the balance somewhat in favour of the Marxist alternative. Conventional Marxist thinking did not, however, suggest an alternative course of action for a Labour government: it did not concern itself with the action required of a socialist government because it assumed that after the historically inevitable revolution, the state would simply fade away.

Trotskyite socialists were more specific, however; they saw the objective as universal control by workers' councils, from which non-manual workers would be excluded. In principle, they saw no merit in attempting to further this end through a parliamentary system, whose collapse it was their purpose to hasten. The proper route to that objective was in their view through 'direct action' in the factories and in the streets. Groups who held broadly to this view came to be known in Britain as the 'Outside Left' to distinguish them from the more moderate groups of Labour Members of Parliament known as the 'Inside Left', who were attempting to move the party's policies toward a more rapid achievement of socialist objectives.

In the 1970s, the Inside Left saw further nationalization and compulsory planning agreements as a means of restoring the internal control over the economy which the government had lost, and the 'Alternative Strategy' of extensive import restrictions as a means of removing the constraints imposed by overseas influences. They did not advocate the wholesale transfer of power to workers' councils, but they did envisage an extension of 'industrial democracy' as a means of increasing the influence of workers over the decisions taken by privately-owned and publicly-owned companies, together with stronger national control over the activities of multinational companies.

The Inside Left consisted in 1976 of a loose grouping of Labour Members of Parliament known as the 'Tribune Group' (after a weekly paper of that name). It was exclusively a parliamentary group, and it made no attempt to organize any following in the constituencies. The Outside Left consisted of a variety of small organizations operating inside and outside the Labour Party. Among those operating within the Labour Party were the Trotskyite 'Militant Tendency' (also named after a weekly paper) and the 'Socialist Campaign for Labour Victory'. Though small in numbers, these were highly-organized and disciplined groups which exerted a significant influence upon activists in the constituencies; but not, at this stage, in the trade unions.

The Campaign for Labour Party Democracy was not a Trotskyite organization. It did not, in fact, argue for any particular ideology but sought only to increase the influence of party activists upon party policy. It received support from many who did not share the aims of the Inside Left, but to the extent that it succeeded, it was likely to increase their influence.

The party leadership

The Labour Party leadership was at that time preoccupied with practical rather than ideological problems. It, too, had undergone some changes in its thinking. In a speech to the party conference in 1976, James Callaghan uttered a rejection of Keynesian demand management at least as forthright and articulate as any made by Sir Keith Joseph:

> We used to think that you could spend your way out of a recession and increase employment by cutting taxes and boosting government spending. I tell you in all candour that that option no longer exists, and that insofar as it ever did exist, it only worked by injecting a bigger dose of inflation into the economy, followed by higher unemployment as the next step. Higher inflation followed by higher unemployment. We have just escaped from the highest rate of inflation this country has ever known; we have not escaped from the consequences: high unemployment. That is the history of the last twenty years.

In view of what was to follow, many people regard that speech as having overstated the change which had taken place in the government's thinking. Nonetheless, it is clear that a very substantial change had taken place.

NOTES

1. See for example: W. M. Corden, 'Balance of payments theory old and new', in *Inflation, Exchange Rates and the World Economy* (Clarendon Press, 1977).
2. See: Holden, Peel, and Thompson, *Modelling the UK Economy* (Martin Robertson, 1982).
3. G. R. Lewis and P. A. Ormerod, 'Policy simulations and model characteristics', (in P. M. Jackson and S. T. Cook, *Current Issues in Fiscal Policy* (Martin Robertson, 1979).
4. See the evidence to the Public Expenditure Committee by Messrs. Cripps, Godley, and Featherstone. (Ninth Report from the Expenditure Committee, 1974, HC328, HMSO).
5. For an account of the breakdown of 'New Cambridge' see: J. A. Bispham, 'The New Cambridge and monetarist criticisms of conventional policy-making', *National Institute Economic Review*, November 1975.
6. The case for import controls is set out in the *Cambridge Economic Policy Review* (Gower Press, April 1979).
7. Disequilibrium macroeconomics is expounded in: R. J. Barro and H. Grossman, *Money, Employment and Inflation* (Cambridge University Press, 1976).
8. M. Posner, letter to *The Times*, 4 September 1973.
9. M. Friedman and D. Meiselman, 'The relative stability of monetary velocity

and the investment multiplier in the United States 1897–1958', in *Stabilisation Policies, CMC Research Papers*, (Prentice-Hall, 1964), p. 165.

10. For a summary of empirical findings, see: C. A. E. Goodhart, *Monetary Theory and Practice* (MacMillan, 1984), p. 44.
11. Ibid., p. 87.
12. For a diagrammatic exposition, see K. A. Chrystal, *Controversies in British Macroeconomics* (Phillip Allen, 1979), p. 129.
13. H. G. Johnson, *International Trade and Economic Growth* (George Allen & Unwin, 1958), chapter 6.
14. For an early example of the IMF's thinking see: J. J. Polak, 'Monetary Analysis of Income Formation and Payments Problems' (*IMF Staff Papers*, November 1957).
15. R. J. Ball, T. Burns and J. S. E. Laury, 'The role of exchange rate changes in balance of payments adjustment – the United Kingdom case,' *The Economic Journal*, March 1977; R. J. Ball and T. Burns, 'The Inflationary Mechanism in the UK Economy', *The American Economic Review*, September 1976.
16. For an elementary exposition see: G. K. Shaw, *Rational Expectations* (Wheatsheaf Books, Harvester Press, 1984); for an account of some of the difficulties see: D. G. Mayes, 'The controversy over rational expectations', *National Institute Economic Review*, May 1981.
17. For an academic attack see: W. H. Buiter, 'The economics of Dr Pangloss. A critial survey of the new classical economics', *The Economic Journal*, March 1980.
18. M. Friedman, *Essays in Positive Economics* (Phoenix Books, 1966), chapter 1.
19. P. Fallon, 'Job creation, search duration and induced migration' (Centre for Labour Economics Discussion Paper, No. 163, 1983).
20. C. Azariadis, 'Implicit contracts and unemployment', *Review of Economic Studies*, 1975, p. 1183).
21. See N. Bosanquet and P. B. Doeringer, 'Is there a dual labour market in Great Britain?', *Economic Journal*, June 1973.
22. A. Oswald, 'The microeconomic theory of the trade union', *Economic Journal*, September 1982.
23. J. S. Fforde, 'Setting monetary objectives', *Bank of England Quarterly Bulletin*, June 1983.
24. C. A. E. Goodhart, *Monetary Theory and Practice. The UK Experience* (MacMillan, 1984), p. 261.
25. Speech given by Sir Keith Joseph at the Preston Town Hall, 4 September 1974.
26. *The Times* leader, 5 September 1974.
27. P. Riddell, 'The Thatcher Government' (Martin Robertson, 1983), p. 21.
28. R. H. S. Crossman, 'Introduction' in Bagehot, *The English Constitution*, (Fontana, 1963), p. 41.
29. This philosophy was propounded in: C. A. R. Crosland, *The Future of Socialism* (Jonathan Cape, 1956).

4

Doubts and Discontents: January 1977–March 1980

I THE WORLD BACKGROUND

Exchange rates

The events of the period 1973–6 demonstrated the growing extent to which a national economy could be affected by developments overseas. Even under the new regime of flexible exchange rates, it was difficult for one major industrialized country to persist in policies which differed much from the others. It has been estimated that if one such country were to experience a growth in demand three percentage points faster than the others, it would move into a current account deficit of around one per cent of its GDP.[1] Other things being equal, a deficit of that size would normally create problems severe enough to necessitate a major change of policy. Exchange rate changes had proved to be a slow-acting way of dealing with deficits; often taking two to three years to have full effect, besides having inflationary side-effects. International capital movements, on the other hand, could have a rapid effect upon exchange rates, although not necessarily in the desired direction, and were frequently on a very much larger scale than trade flows. Thus the freedom for each country to pursue its chosen policy, which it had been hoped would result from the move to flexible exchange rates, did not materialize.

The fact that exchange rates were no longer fixed did not, however, mean that they were now freely determined by market forces. In fact, intervention continued to occur on a massive scale, as the central banks in many countries used their currency reserves to influence their exchange rates. In the 1970s, and especially from 1973, countries with weak currencies financed their intervention by 'sovereign borrowing' from the private sector, predominantly from the large commercial banks. One of the first countries to exploit this source of funds was Britain; which from 1973 onward, encouraged local authorities to do their borrowing in dollars, and to pass the proceeds to the Bank of England in exchange for sterling. By the mid-1970s, sovereign lending by commercial banks came to occupy a central position in providing external finance, particularly to the developing countries, as the banks 'recycled' the surpluses of the oil-producing countries.

Exchange rate policies among the industrialized countries differed considerably, however. The United States adopted a policy of 'benign neglect', intervening only to smooth out day-to-day fluctuations. In Europe, a group of countries, including West Germany and the Benelux countries, had set up a currency union in 1972 (generally known as 'The Snake') under which fluctuations in exchange rates between participating currencies were restricted to a maximum of 2.5 per cent. Most other countries attempted to manage their exchange rates independently.

Managing the oil deficits

The 1974 oil price increase had initially moved the structure of international payment balances sharply in favour of the oil-producing countries, but their surpluses diminished thereafter, as indicated in table 4.1, as they increased their imports from the industrialized countries.

Table 4.1 World current account balances 1973–6 (US $ billion)

	1973	1974	1975	1976
Major oil exporters	6	67	35	41
Industrialized countries	12	–10	19	1
Other non-oil producing countries	–10	–44	–53	–40
(residual error)	(8)	(14)	(0)	(–1)

Source: IMF *Annual Report*, 1977.

Early in 1974, the major industrialized countries had agreed to 'accept' their oil-induced deficits, and to avoid policies that would serve only to shift the payments problems among themselves to the detriment of world trade and economic activity.[2] But the interpretation placed upon that agreement varied, in the event, among the countries concerned. Three countries, the United States, Japan and West Germany, immediately adopted deflationary policies, which enabled them to offset their oil-induced deficits by surpluses elsewhere. Other oil-importing countries postponed the adjustment, and their total current account deficits rose.

Britain and Italy followed policies almost opposite to those of the United States, Japan and Germany; and France followed an intermediate course.

By 1976, the position of these countries was causing international concern; and the Director of the International Monetary Fund observed that the danger was no longer of deepening recession, but of worsening inflation. The time had come, he said, to place 'more stress on the adjustment of external positions, and less emphasis on the mere financing of deficits'.[3] From then on, Britain and Italy were forced to adopt more restrictive policies; and Germany and the United States felt free to move in the direction of fiscal relaxation.

Table 4.2 Output, inflation and unemployment in OECD countries 1973–7

	Industrial production (index 1973=100)		Inflation rate[a] (%)	Unemployment rate[b] (% of labour force)		
	1975	1977	1977	1973	1975	1977
Britain	93	95	14.3	2.8	5.1	7.6
USA	91	106	6.5	4.7	8.3	6.9
Japan	87	100	8.1	1.3	2.0	2.1
France	94	105	9.8	2.6	4.1	5.2
Germany	93	103	3.9	0.9	3.6	3.5
Italy	94	105	18.4	2.8	5.1	7.6

[a] Consumer prices.
[b] broadly comparable definitions.

Source: NIESR *Economic Review*, May 1978.

As table 4.2 shows, the outcome as regards output, prices, and unemployment indicated that those countries which had initially adopted restrictive policies had fared best.

Trade

The volume of world trade did not suffer anything approaching the catastrophic collapse which occurred in the 1930s. The General Agreement on Tariffs and Trade was generally observed, so that damaging tariffs against trade were avoided; but there was a move toward non-tariff restrictions, especially against trade in textiles and steel. After growing at an average rate of 9 per cent a year between 1964 and 1974, world trade contracted by 6 per cent in 1975, but then picked up rapidly to average 4 per cent over the period 1973–7.

Substantial exchange rate changes occurred in 1976, with depreciations for the pound, the Italian lira and the French franc, and appreciations for the US dollar, the deutschmark and the yen. The instability which had developed in the currency markets was primarily the result of sometimes massive capital movements, under the influence of interest rate differentials and inflationary expectations, rather than of changing trade flows.

II 1977 THE BRITISH SCENE

By the beginning of 1977, British output had recovered from its recessionary trough and was above its previous peak level. But it remained well below the level which would have been reached had the pre-1974 trend continued without interruption. A rough estimate prepared in 1978 assigned the shortfall to different factors, as shown in table 4.3. Rising

Table 4.3 Percentage contributions to the shortfall of GDP in 1975–7 below the 1963–73 trend

Increase in private-sector saving	−4.0
Reduction in private-sector investment	−1.5
Total	−5.5
Increased imports	−12.0
Increased exports	+8.5
	−3.5
Increased fiscal deficit	+2.5
Total	−6.5
(Actual shortfall)	(7.0)

Source: Bank of England Quarterly Bulletin, March 1978, p. 39.

import penetration emerges as the largest factor, with higher import prices accounting for 4.5 per cent of the 12 per cent negative contribution. But this was offset to a considerable extent by increased exports, despite a shortfall of world trade. The total trade effect was contractionary compared with the previous trend, but less so than the combined effects of reduced investment and increased saving; and their contractionary influence was only partly offset by relatively expansionary fiscal policies.

The limited nature of the economic recovery was to have an important influence upon events in 1977, and beyond. A number of other trends had gradually been established, which were also to have a significant impact on the economy.

North Sea oil

In economic terms, the most important of these trends was Britain's
emerging status as an oil-producer. This had been made possible by the
1958 Geneva Convention, which assigned rights of under-sea natural
resources to countries with bordering coastlines. Britain, as a signatory to
that convention, in 1964 issued its first set of offshore exploration licences,
and this was followed in 1965 by the discovery of large deposits of natural
gas under the North Sea. In 1970, a left-wing government came to power
in Libya, and immediately cut oil production and raised the price of oil.
This marked a shift in bargaining power in favour of the oil-producing
countries, and gave the oil companies an incentive to develop the North
Sea as a possible new source of oil, despite the fact that finds there seemed
likely to be only marginally profitable at 1970 prices. A large oil deposit
was discovered in the Forties field north-east of Aberdeen, in October
1970, and another in the Brent field east of the Shetlands, in June 1971. By
the end of 1973, further discoveries had been made which were large
enough to give Britain the prospect of eventual self-sufficiency in oil.

These oil discoveries were to have little effect upon employment in
Britain, but were to have substantial and growing effects upon the balance
of payments and upon tax revenues. Until 1977 their effect upon the
balance of payments had been negative because of the imports required to
develop the oil fields; but their contribution to the current account was to
rise from £3 billion in 1977, to around £12 billion (current prices) a year by
1981. The tax system which had been introduced, allowed the companies
who were developing the fields to recover their capital costs at an early
stage, after which a substantial proportion of their revenues would go to
the government. The government's oil revenues were consequently very
small in 1977, but were to build up to around £6 billion a year by 1981. Oil
and gas production together were to add 1.2 per cent to GDP in 1977,
rising to 3.6 per cent in 1981.

As Britain moved toward self-sufficiency in oil, it could expect to move
also toward invulnerability to further increases in the world price of oil.
This prospect was to add greatly to the attractiveness of sterling to foreign
investors and was to have an effect upon the exchange rate which, in the
short term, could be even more important than the effect of oil on the
current account of the balance of payments.

Scottish and Welsh nationalism

Another development which was to assume some importance, this time in
the political sphere, was the upsurge of nationalism in Scotland and
Wales. Together with Northern Ireland, Scotland and Wales were

experiencing higher unemployment and a generally lower level of prosperity than England, as shown in table 4.4.

Table 4.4 Regional economic differences 1977–78

	Unemployment rate[a] 1977	GDP per head 1977	Average household income 1977–8	Public spending per head 1977–8
England	98	102	101	95
Scotland	128	97	101	121
Wales	126	89	98	115
Northern Ireland	172	75	80	142

[a] Index numbers, UK = 100.

Sources: HMSO *Regional Trends*, 1985; *Treasury Economic Progress Report*, January 1979.

In an attempt to reduce regional disparities of output and unemployment, special treatment had for years been afforded to designated 'Assisted Areas' in England and Wales, Scotland and Northern Ireland. Regional Development Grants were given to encourage investment, a regional employment premium to support employment, and selective assistance of various sorts under the Industry Act 1972. Because of their higher proportions of assisted areas, Scotland, Wales and Northern Ireland had received net financial benefits from these measures, and it is likely that they benefited financially in other ways. The report of a Royal Commission gave the following assessment:

> There is no official information on the subject, but we believe that a geographical breakdown of revenue and expenditure would show large surpluses of revenue over expenditure in the South-East and West Midlands regions of England, and deficits in Northern Ireland, Wales, Scotland and probably all the other English regions. Some of the deficits would be substantial – areas with low tax revenues tend to require the highest public expenditure.[4]

But the disparities nevertheless persisted, partly because of the relatively high proportions in Scotland, Wales and Northern Ireland of declining industries such as coal, steel and shipbuilding.

The extent of the political integration into the United Kingdom of Scotland, Wales and Northern Ireland varied. Wales, which had first been annexed in 1282, still had its own language but was politically fully integrated, with no separate say in its affairs. Scotland, which had been joined with England and Wales by the Act of Union of 1707, had retained its own legal and educational systems, but no independent control of other aspects of government. Northern Ireland, on the other hand, had its own legislature, giving it independent control of many aspects of its domestic affairs, from the time of the partition of Ireland in 1921, until 1972. The ruling Protestant majority had not, however, been able to administer the province in a manner which produced a stable reconciliation with the Catholic minority, and after numerous outbreaks of violence, the legislature was disbanded in 1972. Since that time, Northern Ireland has been governed in the same way as the rest of the United Kingdom, directly from Westminster.

In Scotland, there had long been a minority in favour of independence from England, and in Wales the nationalist 'Plaid Cymru' had long campaigned for self-government and for a better status for the Welsh language. By late 1969, Celtic nationalism had combined with a wider feeling of dissatisfaction at the remoteness of central government. (The Scottish Nationalist Party were later to argue that independence for Scotland would give it an exclusive claim upon the revenues from North Sea oil and that this would give Scotland financial independence.) The government of the day responded by setting up a Royal Commission to study the problem. The Commission's report, published in 1973, rejected a federal solution but recommended 'devolution' – a delegation of certain powers to provincial assemblies, with final control resting in the hands of Parliament. In 1977, the government placed before Parliament a Bill to give Scotland and Wales each a separate assembly. The fortunes of this Bill were to be important to the Scottish and Welsh Nationalist Members of Parliament and the support of these Members was to be important to the government.

Unemployment and the inner cities

By the opening months of 1977, unemployment in Britain had reached 1.4 million, a rate of 6 per cent of the working population – almost three times as high as in 1973. To make matters worse, that national average was greatly exceeded in some localities, and the incidence of unemployment was greater among certain groups of people. In Liverpool, for example, the unemployment rate approached twice the national average, and in some central districts of the city it was probably much higher than that. Urban areas in places such as Birmingham, Bolton, Leeds and parts of inner London were also suffering from a disease which came to be known as 'urban decay'. Over the years, the cities' better-off inhabitants had moved out into the suburbs, leaving behind a less mobile and generally lower-skilled population, and also reducing the number of service-sector jobs open to those who remained.

In combination with a general decline in manufacturing employment, ill-considered housing and town planning policies together with a rating (property tax) system which discouraged new development, had left areas of the inner city in a depressed and decaying condition. The jobs that remained open to inner-city residents tended to be low-paid jobs in transport, hospitals and housing maintenance. These jobs had increasingly been taken up by immigrants from Britain's former colonies in the Caribbean and the Indian sub-continent.

There was a tendency, among white wage earners in particular, to blame black and Asian immigrants for the poor and run-down condition of their surroundings, and for much else besides. Despite the very small size of the immigrant population in Britain compared with many other countries, this became a keen issue. The 'new Commonwealth' immigrants had at first taken up jobs that white people did not want, mainly in areas of low unemployment. But as unemployment rose in Britain as a whole, it rose fastest in these inner-city areas, and fastest of all among the black populations that were concentrated there.[5] In the inner cities there was, to quote a government White Paper, 'mounting social bitterness and an increasing sense of isolation'.

Youth unemployment

There had also been a tendency during the 1970s for unemployment to fall disproportionately on young people. This was partly because employers preferred to reduce recruitment rather than to dismiss existing employees; but it was partly due to a steep increase which had occurred in the early 1970s in the pay rates of young people, relative to those of adults.[6] By 1975, 46 per cent of eighteen and nineteen year-olds were receiving adult rates of pay, compared with 14 per cent in 1970. The reasons for this shift in relative pay are not known, but the reduction of the legal age of majority from twenty-one to eighteen in 1969 may have been a factor. The raising of the age limit for compulsory education from fifteen to sixteen in 1972, and the increase in numbers staying on for post-compulsory education, had temporarily alleviated the surplus of young people seeking work, but youth unemployment rates continued to rise. In early 1977, when the overall unemployment rate was 6 per cent, the youth unemployment rate was 13.5 per cent for sixteen and seventeen year-olds, and 10.5 per cent for seventeen and eighteen year-olds. The average duration of unemployment was, however, shorter for young people than for adults. The median duration was eleven weeks in January 1977 for males under eighteen, compared with twenty weeks for all males. Among unemployed males of all ages, the proportion who had been unemployed for more than a year was about 25 per cent, but was highest among older and less-skilled men.

Special employment measures

A number of schemes to alleviate unemployment had been instituted,[7] of which the largest was the Temporary Employment Subsidy, under which firms were paid £10 a week in respect of each redundancy which they undertook to defer. Under the Job Creation Programme, the government financed labour-intensive projects sponsored by local authorities and others; and under the Job Release Scheme, employees were offered an inducement to retire early, provided that they were replaced by people formerly unemployed. About 250,000 people were on such schemes in April 1977, as a result of which unemployment was reduced, perhaps by about 100,000. There was also a small urban aid programme to alleviate the inner-city problem.

III   JANUARY 1977 TO MARCH 1978: THE UNCERTAIN RECOVERY

Prices and jobs

With the financial crisis over, attention turned again in the early months of 1977 to the continuing problems of inflation and unemployment. The inflation rate was still running at over 15 per cent, and the prospects of a reduction to single figures seemed to be tantalizingly remote. But the underlying position was, in fact, much more favourable than that figure would appear to indicate. Settlements in the 1976–7 pay rounds were generally within the government's Stage 2 guidelines; the growth of basic wage rates over the past year had fallen to 9 per cent from 25 per cent the previous year; and real (inflation-corrected) wage rates had actually fallen by over 5 per cent. Earnings (including overtime, bonus payments, etc.) rose faster in money terms than wage rates, but their growth was still well below the inflation rate.

The bulk of the price increase over the year had been due, not to increased labour costs, but to transitory factors, whose effects upon the rate of inflation might be expected to fade out over the coming year. Over five of the fifteen percentage points increase in prices over the past year were attributable to import price increases resulting from the fall in the exchange rate in 1976; and a further four or five percentage points could be traced to increases in expenditure taxes, and to a rebuilding of profit margins which had been severely squeezed during the recession. Barring a sharp resurgence of earnings growth, the inflation rate could be expected to fall as these temporary effects wore off.

The success of the Labour government's voluntary incomes policy had been due partly to the threat of financial sanctions against employers who breached it; but it had owed a great deal to the support of the Trades Union Congress, who had even gone so far as to threaten the expulsion of member unions who pressed for increases above the government's guidelines. But the fall in real earnings which their members had suffered, together with the continuing threat of higher unemployment, were causing a strong underswell of discontent within a number of unions; and the policy changes of 1976 had caused concern, even among the leadership of the Trades Union Congress. After its initial failure, the 'Social Contract' between the government and the trade unions had become a powerful influence upon the course of events. Much was now to depend on whether that influence could be sustained.

The continuing rise of unemployment could also be attributed to temporary factors. Output had grown at an average rate of 3.5 per cent to 4 per cent a year over the past eighteen months; a rate which, under normal circumstances, would be more than sufficient to prevent unemployment from rising. But employers who had held on to labour despite falling demand during much of the recession were in a position to expand output during the upturn without taking on more people. Total employment had, in fact, fallen by 140,000 since the middle of 1975, and productivity had consequently risen at the historically high rate of over 4 per cent a year.

That pattern of initially high productivity growth had been seen in previous upturns. Experience suggested that productivity growth would fall back to a more normal rate before long, and that employment growth would then be resumed. The working population was, however, growing at a rate of around 0.5 per cent a year; so that employment growth in excess of this would be needed to bring about a fall in unemployment.

Fears of stagnation

In the early months of 1977, there was a widespread fear that the momentum of recovery had been lost, and that there was a prospect of only slow growth of output, or even of stagnation. On Keynesian assumptions, the fall which had occurred in real incomes could be expected to lead to a proportional reduction in the volume of consumption. This in itself would be sufficient to reduce the rate of growth of domestic demand by about one percentage point, when taken together with an expected continuation of the fall in investment and a reduced growth of exports. Considerations of this sort led the forecasters of the National Institute for Economic and Social Research to say that 'GDP is forecast to rise very little in 1977' and 'we expect employment to fall a little in 1977, and rather more sharply in 1978',[8] and to conclude that unemployment would rise to 1.5 million by the end of 1977, and continue to rise through 1978.

The fact that these fears were unfounded did not become apparent during 1977, because they appeared to be more than confirmed by the official statistics published during that year, and in early 1978. On April 1978 figures, GDP had fallen by 1.7 per cent between the fourth quarters of 1976 and 1977. A year later, the statistics had been revised to show a rise of 2.7 per cent over the same period; and by a year after that, the figures had been again revised to show a rise of 1.7 per cent. Consumer spending volume did fall in the first six months of 1977, but by less than one-third of the fall in real incomes, and this was offset by continued strong growth in exports and – after a dip in the first quarter – by a recovery of investment. After faltering briefly, output resumed its trend of recovery. This was not known at the time, however, and forecasters were puzzled to see a slight increase in employment and a flattening-off of the growth in unemployment in the second half of 1977.

The Lib–Lab pact

In early 1977, the belief that its policies were likely to lead to a persistent growth in unemployment had undermined the government's authority. As a result mainly of defections and abstentions amongs its supporters, the government's ability to command a majority in Parliament was eroded to the point where, in mid-March, it faced the prospect of defeat on a vote of confidence – an event which, (except on a minor issue) leads automatically, under the British constitution, to a general election.

That outcome was averted by a pact with the Parliamentary Liberal Party under which, subject to certain conditions, the Liberals would afford the government the support which it needed for survival. The conditions included the setting-up of a joint consultative committee on policy and other issues, regular meetings between the Chancellor and the Liberal economics spokesman, and the achievement of progress toward devolution. The 'Lib–Lab pact', as it came to be known, was initially to run only to the end of the current parliamentary session, but it was renewed in July 1977. Although it contained no specific policy commitments, the effect of the pact was to give the Liberals a veto over policy proposals of which they did not approve.

Monetary policy

Even after concluding its pact with the Liberals, the government was to have unprecedented difficulties in getting parliamentary approval for its budget proposals. For many people, however, the centre of the economic policy stage was now occupied, not by budgetary questions, but by monetary policy. To maintain confidence in its policies, the government's overriding priority was to ensure compliance with the targets set out in its 1976 'Letter of Intent' to the International Monetary Fund, and this effectively set the limits within which budgetary policy could be framed, or so it would appear. In fact, this was not the case. Ironically, in view of the political stresses which that letter had occasioned, it became apparent, within a few months of its dispatch, that it had ceased to apply any effective constraint upon the government's freedom of action. The situation as it appeared in April is set out in table 4.5.

Table 4.5 Targets and Out-turns 1976–7

	Target (£ billion)	Out-turn
Public-sector borrowing 1976–7	11.2	8.7
Domestic credit expansion	9.0	5.1

The formal targets for 1976–7 had been met with a wide margin, and it seemed likely that the somewhat tighter targets for 1977–8 would also be met.

The monetary targets which were in fact to impose a constraint upon fiscal policy, were not the domestic credit expansion targets agreed with the Fund. Targets for money supply growth had already been set; but not, as has sometimes been implied, by the International Monetary Fund. The Letter of Intent to the Fund had offered no undertaking about money supply growth except to say that 'I am satisfied that the resultant course of sterling M3 will be consistent with a reduction in inflation.' A target growth rate of 12 per cent for M3 had been set by the Chancellor in July 1976, before his approach to the Fund; and had been modified in December to a range of 9–13 per cent for the more narrowly-defined sterling M3. In the first half of 1977, with confidence restored, the government was having no difficulty in meeting its reduced borrowing requirement, without expanding the money supply, by selling bonds to the public. By April, the growth of sterling M3 over the year was below the bottom limit of the 9–13 per cent range; although its path had been erratic, and it was showing a rapid growth rate.

The 1977 budget and the 10 per cent pay policy

In light of this generally reassuring monetary situation and the apparent deterioration of employment prospects, the Chancellor decided that there was scope for a carefully controlled fiscal stimulus. In his March 1977 budget he proposed an increase in the personal allowances against income tax, and a reduction of the basic rate of income tax from 35 per cent to 33 per cent, together with partly offsetting increases in the duties on petrol and cigarettes. The net effect was to be a reduction in taxation of £1.5 billion; but only £0.5 billion of that was to take immediate effect. The remainder would be conditional upon the negotiation of a new pay policy to follow Stage 2 at the end of July.

The Trades Union Congress was by then opposed to the setting of any new limit upon pay increases, and negotiations with them proved fruitless. The Cabinet decided eventually to impose a 10 per cent limit upon the growth of earnings, without their agreement. The limit was to be enforced, as before, by penalties against employers who breached it. It was recognized that this was a high-risk strategy, but it was thought to be better than the alternative of doing nothing.

The 'Rooker–Wise' amendment

The passage through the necessary parliamentary procedures of the Finance Bill, which gives legislative effect to the budget, is normally a routine process. On this occasion, it was a bitter struggle, in which disaffected Labour Members of Parliament frequently supported Opposition amendments. Among the amendments which were carried against the government was the 'Rooker–Wise amendment', devised by Nigel Lawson (then a Conservative spokesman on Treasury matters) but proposed by the two Labour Members with whose name it is associated. Its effect was to require that income tax allowances should be increased in future years by not less than the increase in the retail price index over the previous year. This was to put an end to the phenomenon of 'fiscal drag', which had led to automatic increases in the burden of taxation, as inflation had eaten into the value of tax allowances.

The tax reductions finally implemented in July 1977 reduced the basic tax rate by 1 per cent, rather than the 2 per cent originally proposed; but tax allowances were also increased in October, in anticipation of the increases which would be required the following April under the Rooker–Wise amendment. The intended net effect was a larger fiscal stimulus than had been envisaged in March.

As often happens there was, in the event, a large divergence of outcomes from intentions. At the time of the March budget it was forecast that its full effect would be to increase the public sector borrowing requirements from £7.4 billion to £8.5 billion. The final outcome was £5.5 billion – a reduction of around 30 per cent in real terms compared with 1976–7. This unintended fiscal contraction was due largely to underspending against planned public expenditure. The new system of cash limits had required those responsible for the detailed planning of public expenditure to anticipate, and allow for, possible price increases. It appears that the uncertainties which this introduced had made for an attitude of caution among planners, of which the Treasury forecasters had been unaware.

Exchange rate policy

The efforts by the Bank of England to carry out the government's monetary policy were also encountering difficulties. With the financial markets now paying meticulous attention to month-by-month variations in the money supply figures, success in this aspect of economic management had become of great importance to the maintenance of confidence. But the figures were moving in an erratic and unpredictable manner, and were themselves subject to frequent revision. The forecasting relationships governing bank lending had broken down, and the management of bond sales to offset expected deviations from the target path of sterling M3, had become largely a matter of subjective judgement. To make matters worse, a conflict was beginning to emerge between monetary and exchange rate policy.

Among the conditions for the loan from the International Monetary Fund, the government had undertaken to manage the exchange rate in such a way as to maintain international price competitiveness. This was at first interpreted as a policy of maintaining a stable rate of exchange with the dollar. In July 1977, as the dollar weakened, this was changed to stabilize the effective (weighted average) rate against all other currencies. With growing exports of oil and of other goods, and with the inflows of overseas capital needed to finance further spending concerned with North Sea oil, massive amounts of money were coming into the country from abroad and there was strong upward pressure on the exchange rate.

The Bank of England attempted to resist this pressure by selling sterling and by reducing interest rates. The Bank's Minimum Lending Rate was reduced in stages from 15 per cent in October 1976 to 6 per cent in

September 1977. But the effect of the maintenance of the exchange rate at what was widely regarded as an unduly low level was to encourage the inflow of foreign funds, which when exchanged for sterling added substantially to domestic money supply growth. By October 1977 it was realized that either the exchange rate objective or the money supply objective would have to be abandoned. It was decided to give priority to the money supply and to allow the exchange rate to rise.

IV   THE 1978 BUDGET

The economic policy adopted by the Labour government after 1976 has been described as 'monetary-constrained Keynesianism'. But this categorization belongs to the world of academic theory, and it conveys little of the real process of putting new ideas into practice. A glimpse of that reality can be obtained by looking at the circumstances surrounding the 1978 budget.

The pressure for tax cuts

The statistics before the Chancellor of the Exchequer as he contemplated his budget options were, on the whole, reassuring. They carried some worrying portents, but they showed the economy in early 1978 to be in a better state in most respects than it had been a year previously. The inflation rate had fallen from over 16 per cent to under 10 per cent. And, what mattered more to ordinary people, the increase in pre-tax income needed to keep abreast of inflation, had fallen even further, from over 18 per cent to less than 5 per cent. Employment had risen by almost 100,000 and, after flattening out in the second half of 1977, unemployment had begun to fall. The unemployment prospect was far from satisfactory, but some of the constraints upon the Chancellor's freedom to tackle it had been lifted. The constraints imposed by commitments to the International Monetary Fund, in particular, had been eased.

The latest Letter of Intent (15 December 1977) to the Fund had stated the government's determination to 'continue its firm control of public spending and the counter-inflationary thrust of its monetary policies', noting that these would require 'both control over the money supply and moderation in domestic credit expansion'. The Chancellor had made no new commitments, however; only statements of his expectations. On Domestic Credit Expansion, he had noted that the 1977-8 outturn was expected to be well within the required £7.7 billion limit, and he merely added that in 1978-9 'I expect DCE to come back nearer to the levels envisaged earlier and possibly to make up some of the earlier shortfall.' All that he had said about fiscal policy was that 'I expect the public sector borrowing requirement for 1978–9 not to exceed the (existing) figure of £8.6 billion.' That existing figure for 1977–8 had, in fact, been undershot by about £3 billion, and since the Treasury were then forecasting a borrowing requirement of only £7 billion for 1978–9, this left some scope for tax cuts.

There was strong political pressure for tax cuts. Without them, the prospects of a continued reduction of unemployment seemed poor. The forecasters (influenced by official statistics which then understated the strength of the recovery) had concluded that the current decline in unemployment was transitory and likely to be reversed. In the opinion of the National Institute for Economic and Social Research, even a £2 billion cut in direct taxation would only 'significantly moderate the rise in unemployment (though it would not reverse it) during 1978'.

This, moreover, might well be the last budget before the next election. The government's standing in the opinion polls had fallen sharply since the last election and it was much in need of measures to restore its popularity. Above all, there was the need to preserve the Social Contract, and it was thought that tax cuts offered the best prospect of reconciling the trade unions to continuing pay restraint.

The battle for financial confidence

Political pressures were not the only influence upon the Chancellor. To maintain the confidence of the financial community he would have to announce a new target range for sterling M3, to replace the 9 per cent to 13 per cent range which he had set for 1977–8. Financial commentators expected a lower range, but they would also be looking for consistency between monetary and fiscal policy. They had become accustomed to giving minute attention to the accounting presentation which provided a reconciliation between money supply growth and the borrowing requirement, and its other 'counterparts'. The financial community were not merely passive observers of these figures. Any hint in them that the government might need to raise interest rates, in order to avoid overshooting the money supply limits, could prompt a reluctance on their part to buy government bonds; this reluctance would, itself, make overshooting more likely.

By way of illustration, table 4.6 shows broad trends exhibited by the counterparts of the money supply over the period since April 1976. In view of the volatile and approximate nature of these figures they are shown as six-month totals rounded to the nearest half billion. At the time,

Table 4.6 Money supply counterparts April 1976–March 1978

	April–September 1976	October–March 1977	April–September 1977	October 1977–March 1978
	(£ billion seasonally adjusted)			
Public-sector borrowing	5	3.5	3	3
Less: Debt sales to non-bank private sector	2	5	4	3
	3	–1.5	–1	0
Plus: Bank lending to private sector	2.5	1	2	2.5
Domestic credit expansion	5.5	–0.5	1	2.5
Inflows from abroad	–2.5	0.5	1	1.5
Change in Sterling M3	3	0	2	4

Source: Economic Trends, November 1978.

however, markets were sensitive to monthly changes of a much smaller order.

As the second row of figures shows, sales of government bonds were, after October 1976, sufficient – or more than sufficient – to cover the public sector borrowing requirement. But after April 1977, an increase in bank lending, together with in-flows from abroad, raised the growth of sterling M3 to a total of £6 billion in the year to March 1978. This took its percentage growth to 15, as against the target range of 9–13 per cent. By this time, the change of exchange rate policy in October 1977, which had been designed to reduce inflows from abroad, had not yet had its intended effect. Apart from this temporary overseas influence, monetary objectives had been met, and it had even been possible to reduce the Bank of Englnad's minimum lending rate from 15 per cent in October 1976 to 6.5 per cent in march 1978. Against this background, the Chancellor had to decide whether to take full advantage of the opportunities for tax cuts implied by a borrowing requirement of £8.5 billion; bearing in mind the need to announce new and tighter monetary obectives.

The Chancellor announced his decision in his budget speech on 11 April 1978. There were to be tax cuts leading to an estimated borrowing requirement of £8.5 billion. The minimum lending rate was to be raised to 7.5 per cent. And the target range for the growth of sterling M3 was to be reduced to 8–12 per cent per year.

Over the months that followed, the Chancellor and his colleagues found themselves fighting bitter rearguard actions on two fronts: for parliamentary acceptance of his budget proposals; and for the restoration of financial confidence which collapsed almost immediately after the budget. The reasons for this collapse are not entirely clear, but reports at the time suggest that gloomy interpretations were being put on volatile and erratic statistics. The current account of the balance of payments went temporarily into deficit in the first quarter of 1978, by an amount which was greatly overstated at the time. And the April money supply figures showed a rise in sterling M3, which the Bank of England described as 'erratically and quite unexpectedly high', and which took the increase over the previous year to over 16 per cent. By annualizing the growth rate over three months, some commentators put the annual rate of growth at an alarming 22 per cent. Worried by these figures, the financial institutions cut back on their purchases of government bonds, thereby increasing the upward pressure on the money supply.

The battle for the confidence of the financial markets was finally won in June, by which time the minimum lending rate had been raised to 10 per cent, and the government had reintroduced controls on bank lending, using the Supplementary Deposits Scheme known as 'the corset'. Bond sales immediately picked up, and the growth rate of sterling M3 dropped rapidly to well below the bottom of the new 8–12 per cent range.

Meanwhile, in Parliament, the government had been defeated on two amendments to its Finance Bill which had the effect of raising the public sector borrowing requirement by an estimated £440 million. The government attempted to restore the position by an increase in an employment related charge upon employers (the 'National Insurance Surcharge') which had been announced as an emergency measure in June 1976. The opposition responded by a protest, framed as a motion to reduce the Chancellor's salary; and it became clear that defeat on this motion would mean a general election. The Liberals who, despite the Lib–Lab pact, had voted against the government on the two amendments, then gave the government the support it needed for survival. As the price for their support, they exacted a token reduction of £140 million in the proposed charge on employers.

What was it all about?

The conduct of these battles had exhibited some curious features. One was the stance of the Conservative opposition in seeking to increase public borrowing despite recent policy statements to the contrary. Another was the device adopted by the government in increasing what was, in effect, a tax upon employment. Above all, there was the preoccupation over changes of a few hundred million pounds in the estimated public sector borrowing requirement; which could, in fact, be estimated only within margins of error running into billions of pounds.

There was, indeed, no basis in economic theory for the particular significance which was at this time being attached to the size of the public-sector borrowing requirement. Monetary economists such as Professor Milton Friedman pointed out that the accounting relationship with the money supply was not evidence of a causal connection: that it would be possible to maintain the same monetary growth at a variety of different levels of public borrowing.[9] It was also pointed out that the public-sector borrowing requirement would automatically tend to rise during a recession, because tax receipts fall, and benefit payments rise. This did not necessarily mean that the money supply would rise: quite possibly there might be an offsetting fall in private sector borrowing.

(Also, the Treasury had already developed ways of making presentational adjustments to public sector borrowing which would have little or no effect on the economy. The then Chief Secretary of the Treasury recalls that 'finding ways of cutting the PSBR without having any real effect, especially on employment, occupied our most fertile minds' – an activity which he refers to as 'fiddling the figures'.)[10]

V THE EUROPEAN MONETARY SYSTEM

An episode which threw further light on the way in which ecnomic policy was developing, culminated oddly in a non-event. In 1978, Britain decided not to become a full member of the European Monetary System. That decision was of some importance for its influence upon events to follow, but from an historical standpoint the reasons for it are of equal or greater interest.

The system of fixed, but adjustable, exchange rates, set up at Bretton Woods in 1944, had come to an end in 1971. Since April 1972 there had been another arrangement, known as 'the snake', for keeping European currencies together during a period of generally floating exchange rates. By 1978, only West Germany, the Benelux countries, Norway and Denmark remained within the snake, others including Britain, France, Italy, and Ireland having left it at various times since 1972. In July 1978, at a 'summit' meeting of European Community heads of government, the West German Chancellor and the French President proposed the replacement of the snake by a stronger and, it was hoped, wider system of fixed but adjustable rates.

Member governments under this arrangement would be required to take corrective action if their exchange rates diverged by more than a stipulated percentage against other currencies individually or against a weighted average of all European currencies. Members wishing to intervene by buying their own currencies would be able to borrow from a credit pool, amounting to about 20 per cent of the official reserves of all member states.

In Britain, his proposal led to an intense debate. Many industrialists saw commercial advantages in the prospect which it seemed to offer of some reduction in the uncertainties concerning the future course of exchange rates. But economists and bankers were almost unanimous in their opposition to membership. On the face of it, the agreement on this question between Keynesians and monetarists seems surprising. They were united in the assumption that, if Britain did not join, its exchange rate would fall. But they were concerned in different ways about the policy adjustments to prevent this, which membership would require.

Among the Keynesians, the Cambridge Economic Policy Group used their forecasting model to compare prospects under a fixed exchange rate and under a regime in which the exchange rate was allowed to fall sufficiently to maintain the price competitiveness of British manufactures. The model runs showed falls in output growth and of employment which increased when assumed earnings growth was increased: but which were much smaller under a floating than under a fixed exchange rate. They took their results to indicate that membership would result in substantial losses of output growth and of employment. (In light of the subsequent debate on the subject, it is interesting to note this as an early example of work showing an explicit connection between pay increases and unemployment.) The National Institute came to the same conclusion, noting that the devaluation which would take place in the absence of membership would have little effect upon inflation but that preventing it would have serious adverse effects upon output and employment because of the resulting loss of competitiveness.[11]

Among the monetarists, Alan Budd and Terry Burns of the London Business School reached the same conclusion by a different route. They reasoned that because productivity growth would be slower in Britain than elsewhere in Europe, its inflation rate would have to be lower in order to maintain a stable exchange rate. They estimated that monetary growth in Britain would have to be at a rate some five percentage points lower than the European average; which would need a savagely deflationary reduction of the public sector borrowing requirement, from the planned £8.5 billion to about £4 billion. Other monetarists argued that membership should at least be delayed until the necessary reduction in money supply growth had been achieved. One of them referred to the possibility of a rise in the exchange rate, but since he considered that it could then be countered by the abolition of exchange controls, he evidently thought that it could be no more than a temporary move.

It is not unreasonable to suppose that the advice which the Chancellor of the Exchequer received from Treasury economists was to the same effect. But on this occasion there were reasons for concealment going beyond traditional secretiveness. The Chancellor had declared a policy aim of maintaining a stable exchange rate. He could not, therefore, use the prospect of a depreciation as an objection to membership. And there was, as always, the danger that the public acknowledgement of such a prospect would be immediately and violently self-fulfilling.

The reasons advanced by the government for not seeking full membership were significant, even if they were not the whole truth. The consultative Green Paper, published in November 1978, set out the Keynesian arguments as above, but effectively dismissed them in its conclusions, noting that 'the Government has made it clear that it does not regard exchange rate depreciation as a solution to the economic problems facing the UK.' And in an argument which appeared to favour membership, it noted that:

> A higher average exchange rate may make British goods dearer to foreigners but it will also reduce costs to British business. It should lead to lower rates of wage increases without any loss to living standards. . . . Once a virtuous circle of exchange rate stability, lower costs and greater stimulus to efficiency, has been established, the effects of any initial loss of competitiveness may be removed.

– but then all but discarded the argument with the observation that: 'It would be pure guesswork to predict how much higher the rate of exchange would be in an EMS regime, or whether it would be higher at all.'[12]

The device that the government finally adopted was to erect a set of requirements for the new system which would be unacceptable to other governments.[13] In December, it announced that its conditions had not been met, and that it would not undertake to intervene to maintain the pound within the 2.25 per cent limit of divergence adopted by other countries except Italy, nor within the 6 per cent limit adopted for Italy.

Postscript: the pound rises

As a postscript to this revealing episode, it has to be noted that the European Monetary System started operating in March 1979, and that the pound had moved outside the 2.25 per cent divergence limits by mid-

April, and outside the 6 per cent limit by May or June. The pound had not, however, fallen as predicted – it had risen. The economic advice concerning British membership had thus been worthless because it had been founded upon a false premise. As a result, attention had been diverted from the question whether membership would contribute to financial stability.

VI THE END OF CONSENSUS

While the debate about the conduct of economic policy continued, relations betwen the government and the trade unions were deteriorating, and a course was being set which was to lead to the disaster which the newspapers were to call 'the winter of discontent'.

Pay policy under attack

On the government's side, there was concern that the gains which had been made in the fight against inflation might be lost – with a consequent loss of international competitiveness. Part of the fall in the rate of inflation could be attributed to the success of Stage 2 of its pay policy, but the continuing fall since the middle of 1977 had owed more to reduction in the prices of imports due to falling world commodity prices, and to the rise in the exchange rate. On figures reported by the Department of Employment, there had not been many overt breaches of the 10 per cent Stage 3 guideline; but average earnings had nevertheless risen by 15 per cent in the 1977–8 pay round.

Some of the discrepancy could be explained as being the effect of bonuses, overtime payments and self-financing productivity deals. But there was a strong suspicion that a good deal of ingenuity had gone into schemes which violated the spirit of the policy, while observing the letter of the law. Pay was rising a great deal faster than prices; and even after allowing for productivity increases, unit labour costs were rising by over 9 per cent a year. The downward trend in import prices could not be expected to continue, and when they turned up again, a resurgence of inflation would be inevitable, unless there were a renewal of pay restraint.

It seems paradoxical that the Stage 2 policy had been successful, even though it had meant a fall in real earnings; but that it had since become difficult to restrain pay increases at a time when real earnings were, in any case, rising rapidly. The easing which had taken place in the financial pressure on employers, may have been partly responsible. Growing dissatisfaction with the way in which pay policy was being operated seems to have been an important factor. The principle of pay policy continued to command popular support, but its practice attracted complaints of which the following comment by the National Institute is an example.

> We regret that the guidelines . . . are both crude and ambiguous, that the machinery of adjudication has had to be hastily contrived and that it operates behind closed doors according to principles unknown to the general public. . . . It is noticeable that the thrust of criticism of incomes policies is directed to their inflexibility and to the consequent build up of more and more anomalies and distortions.[14]

The machinery of pay policy was discredited. The opposition to it by rank-and-file trade unionists was such that trade union leaders refused to enter any formal negotiations regarding its continuation. They advised the government informally that a norm of 8–9 per cent, in line with the inflation rate, might be acceptable, but that anything less than this would lead to serious industrial strife.

In reaching their decision about the figure to be adopted for the next pay round, the Cabinet were influenced by the expectation that a general election would be held before it could be put to the test. On the experience of the previous round, the figure chosen would in any case be overshot by a big margin. The figure of 5 per cent, which had been mentioned by the Prime Minister in a speech earlier in the year, seemed under the circumstances to be an attractive one; and, against union advice, that was the figure which was announced.[15]

That much-regretted decision can be seen in retrospect as symptomatic of the lack of communication between the Cabinet and its supporters. Members of the Cabinet seem to have reasoned that the unions would not risk a confrontation with their party leaders in election year. Some union leaders, for their part, argued that with the economy now in a consumer boom, high claims had a good chance of success; and that they would not be effectively resisted by the government in an election year.

The end of pay sanctions

At its annual conference in September, the Trades Union Congress passed a motion that: 'Congress declares its opposition to government policies of intervention and restraint in pay bargaining including government sanctions.' And at the Labour Party Conference in October 1978, a resolution was passed with a two to one majority, rejecting 'any form of pay restraint by whatever method'.

The sanctions which could be used against employers who yielded to claims exceeding their guideline now seemed to be the government's last card. But when the 5 per cent limit was challenged, it was a card which the government found itself unable to play. In November, after a short strike, the Ford Motor Company conceded pay increases averaging about 15 per cent. The government decided to apply 'sanctions' against Ford by refusing them contracts. However, before this policy could be applied, the Conservatives forced a vote on the sanctions policy in the House of Commons. Due to Labour abstentions, they succeeded in having the policy rejected.

The 'Winter of Discontent'

Many trade unionists saw this as the end of pay policy, and hastened to put in large pay claims. The road haulage workers and the petrol tanker drivers went on strike and shortages of food and fuel began to appear. The most serious trouble was to come from the public sector. Average public-sector pay had risen faster than private-sector pay between 1973 and 1976, but some groups had been left behind. Strict application of Stage 2 and Stage 3 pay policies had since kept pay increases much lower in the public sector than in the private sector and, as a result, some serious anomalies had developed. The fact that unskilled public sector jobs were some of the lowest paid in the country, added to the sense of grievance. The National Union of Public Employees put in a claim for a 30 per cent increase, and others followed suit. When these claims were rejected, there were widespread strikes, and other forms of protest.

The industrial disputes which thus developed in the winter of 1978–9 caused a significant loss of output. They also had immediate and dramatic effects upon the public. Patients were refused admission to hospitals; vermin-infested refuse piled up on the streets; bodies were left unburied in the graveyards; and water supplies became contaminated. These different events happened at different times, and in different places, and most were of short duration. However, they received a great deal of publicity in the national press and on television.

The public resentment generated by these disputes was directed as much at the conduct of the strikers as at the damage which they caused. The use of mass pickets to discourage strike-breaking had on several previous occasions led to threatening and violent scenes on television, and these tactics were again in use. Picketing of employers not involved in disputes (so-called 'secondary picketing') was seen as particularly unfair. Trade union leaders, under pressure from ministers, tried to discourage the more unpopular of these forms of behaviour; but it was apparent that they had little influence over their members.

Within the Labour movement, the breakdown of relations between the government and the unions seemed, for a time, to be complete. One

Cabinet Minister observed that 'the trade unions are now the most unpopular institution for 100 years', and one trade union leader was quoted as saying 'if the government falls that's OK, the trade union movement is indestructible'.[16]

But, after a period of what appeared to be horrified paralysis, the government moved to retrieve the situation. On 16 January 1979, the Prime Minister announced important changes to its pay policy. To deal with the problem of the lower paid, he announced that increases up to £3.50 a week would be allowable, even where they amounted to more than 5 per cent. To deal with the problem of public sector pay, he proposed that 'the guiding principle should be the achievement of comparable pay for comparable work and effort'. And to replace the lost weapon of sanctions, he proposed changes to the powers of the Price Commission which would make it more difficult for firms to pass on high pay increases into higher prices.

The 'Concordat'

Negotiations were started with trade union leaders in January 1979, and on 14 February, a joint Government/Trades Union Congress statement was issued which announced a fresh approach to pay increases. Instead of a pay limit, an inflation target would be used as a future guide to pay settlements. The aim would be to get inflation down below 5 per cent within three years. It was noted that 'there is no precise arithmetical relationship between, for example, getting price rises down to 5 per cent, the economy growing at 3 per cent, and a particular level of pay settlements'. There would be an annual 'National Assessment' by government and both sides of industry from which, it was implied, would emerge pay guidelines for the year. 'The Concordat', as the statement came to known, also contained guidelines for the conduct of disputes, including picketing, and for closed shops.

Comparability

Settlements were eventually reached with the public-sector unions. A Standing Commission on Pay Comparability was set up, and back-dated rises were agreed, to which would later be added whatever the Commission ruled as appropriate. Awards of the Commission were to be binding on both sides.

On paper, the government had succeeded in repairing much of the damage which had been done to its economic strategy. But that achievement was received with scepticism, not least because of the loss of confidence in trade union leaders' authority over their members. The

'Concordat' was widely seen, not as a genuine repair, but as an attempt to paper over the cracks, on the part of a government which was in any case living on borrowed time.

VII THE 'SCOTTISH CROWBAR'

The issue on which the government was finally to be overthrown was not pay, but devolution. This was an issue on which the government's supporters in Parliament were divided, and on which the Conservatives, though not opposed in principle, were prepared to vote against the government's proposals. Despite numerous attempts, the government had failed to draft legislation which could command a majority in Parliament. By late 1978, the merits of the case were taking second place to the question of the government's survival. Its continuation in office depended upon the support of the Scottish Nationalist Party and of the Liberals, whose pact with the government was conditional upon progress toward devolution. The 'Scottish Crowbar' may have been used to good effect to get financial support for local industry; but for the Nationalists, this was not enough: they were impatient for devolution.

A final attempt to introduce devolution had been made when a new Bill was placed before Parliament in November 1977. But it was passed into law only after Labour Members had forced an amendment, making its implementation conditional upon the assent of 40 per cent of the electorates in referenda to be held in Scotland and in Wales.

In May 1978 the Liberals, whose standing in the opinion polls had slumped badly, had announced that the Lib-Lab Pact would not be renewed beyond the end of that parliamentary session. The Liberals seemed unlikely to oppose the government to the point of precipitating a general election, however. The scandal which had forced the resignation of their former party leader (Jeremy Thorpe), was still attracting public attention. As one Liberal put it, forcing an election under these circumstances would be 'like turkeys voting for Christmas'. And the government could, of course, count on the support of the Scottish and Welsh nationalists until the following March, when the referenda were to be held.

By mid-1978, the opinion polls had been showing a rise in the government's popularity, and it was generally assumed then that the Prime Minister would call a general election for the autumn. But in the British electoral system it is a party's support in marginal constituencies that matters; and a September poll of such constituencies showed that Labour was not doing well enough to give it a reasonable prospect of

winning a general election. The Prime Minister decided to postpone the
election until the following spring. In December, January and February,
however, the government suffered a sharp loss of popularity over its
handling of the 'Winter of Discontent'. Throughout that period, there was
every reason for the Prime Minister to put off the election.

On 1 March, 1979, the devolution referenda were held. The results
showed a four to one rejection of devolution for Wales and a narrow
majority in favour for Scotland. But the Scottish support came from only
30 per cent of the electorate, compared with the 40 per cent required by
the legislation.

Despite this result, the Scottish Nationalists gave immediate notice
that, unless the government went ahead with a Scottish assembly, they
would force an election. Labour's anti-devolution rebels were equally
adamant that they would not abandon the 40 per cent rule. The defeat of
the government had become inevitable.

The end came on 28 March, with the government losing on a Scottish
Nationalist vote of confidence by 311 votes to 310. Parliament was
dissolved on 7 April and an election fixed for 3 May.

VIII   THE 1979 ELECTION

Monetary policy was not an issue in the 1979 general election. In the
twenty-seven page Conservative election manifesto it got only a single
two-line mention, which did not appear to signal any departure from
existing practice. In the Labour manifesto, it figured only in the Prime
Minister's foreword, which attributed the 1974–6 inflation to the failure of
the previous Conservative administration to control the money supply.
Neither manifesto proposed any specific limits upon monetary growth.
The differences between the party leaderships on this issue may
understandably have been considered too subtle to explain to the electorate. In any case, Labour alone would benefit from an examination of
past achievements in this respect; and the Labour Party was by no means
united on the subject. Thus, on the basis of statements made during the
election, voters might reasonably have concluded that much the same
monetary policy would be followed whichever party came to power.

Fiscal policy, on the other hand, was central. Both parties offered
income tax cuts but only the Conservative offer was specific: a cut in the
top rate of tax from 83 per cent to 60 per cent, and in the basic rate from 33
per cent to 30 per cent. This was to be financed from reductions in public
spending and by a switch to taxes on expenditure. Public spending was, in
any case, to be progressively reduced as a proportion of national income.

Spending on defence and on law and order were to be increased immediately, however; there was to be no reduction in spending on health, and standards of education were to be improved. Specific reductions in spending were to come from reduced waste and from less support to industry. No specific commitment was put forward concerning the public sector borrowing requirement.

Both parties gave priority to the reduction of inflation but only Labour was specific: a reduction to 5 per cent over three years. This promise was made in the context of the Concordat, however, and the opinion polls suggest that the public had little faith in it. On public-sector pay, the Conservatives, like Labour, promised to carry out the recommendations of the Comparability Commission, although the Conservative manifesto said that 'settlements must take full account of supply and demand.' Elsewhere, they promised a return to free collective bargaining.

In the aftermath of the 'Winter of Discontent', the Conservative manifesto gave more space to trade union reform than to any other topic. Encouraged by opinion poll evidence of public concern about the power of the unions, the Conservatives promised to 'restore the balance', which they claimed had been tilted too far in favour of the unions. Legislation was proposed on picketing, on the closed shop, on secret ballots to reduce the influence of militants, and on the reduction of benefits to strikers' families. Labour proposed no new legislation but pointed to the code of practice in the Concordat. On this topic as on taxation, the initiative was with the Conservatives.

Unemployment figured in the opinion polls only as the second or third most important cause of concern; this was reflected in the prominence given to it in the two manifestos. Unlike the Conservatives, Labour set itself a specific aim: to achieve an economic growth rate of 3 per cent or more, and promised extended job-creation programmes. The Conservative manifesto appeared to rely mainly upon improved work incentives and better profits for the creation of jobs. But Conservative election publicity laid greater stress on this issue, and its posters captioned 'Labour isn't working' and depicting an unemployment queue, are thought by some observers to have had a significant influence upon voters.

On policy toward trade and industry, Labour promised more intervention and the Conservatives, less. But in specific terms, both were cautious. Labour promised to 'secure that imports enter our markets only within acceptable limits' – mild wording, which seemed to fall short of the comprehensive import controls envisaged by proponents of the 'Alternative Strategy'. The Conservatives rejected import controls as 'a socialist panacea' but promised to maintain existing controls upon textile imports and to oppose 'unfair foreign trade practices'. Both parties advocated reform of the European Community's Common Agricultural Policy, but both offered continued subsidies to farming. There was no reference to nationalization in the Labour programme, and the Conservatives proposed only to denationalize steel and shipbuilding, and to license private bus services. A brief reference to planning agreements 'with the necessary back-up statutory powers' was the main indication of Labour's intention to increase its control over industry.

Housing subsidies figured in different ways in both programmes; with the Conservatives offering tax reliefs on housing loans, and Labour offering more council houses. But the Conservatives gained an important initiative with their proposal for cut-price sales of council houses to their tenants. The popularity of this proposal led Labour to say that they were not opposed to such sales, except in areas of serious housing need.

The Labour manifesto reaffirmed the party's commitment to devolution for Scotland, whereas the Conservative manifesto only offered to discuss future arrangements.

The ideological differences between the moderate wings of the two major parties were presented to the voters much as they had been in the 1974 elections, and they seemed no wider than in 1974. But the much wider differences, which had developed since then between their more extreme wings, were played down.

Labour had a campaigning advantage in that James Callaghan enjoyed far greater personal popularity than Margaret Thatcher. But the Conservatives had the advantage of presenting proposals which had popular appeal even among habitual Labour supporters. According to one survey, the percentages of Labour supporters who favoured the various Conservative proposals were:

law and order: 95 per cent
picketing: 78 per cent
council house sales: 75 per cent
reduced benefits to strikers' families: 63 per cent
income tax cuts: 52 per cent.

A BBC survey in May 1979 showed 70 per cent of respondents to be in favour of keeping up government services, such as health, education and welfare, even if that meant that taxes could not be cut.

Many observers regarded Labour's association with the 'Winter of Discontent' as the decisive factor in the election, but the Conservative lead in the opinion polls which had soared to 20 per cent in February – probably on this account – had fallen to well below 10 per cent by May, suggesting that resentment was fading.

Table 4.7 The election result, 1979

	Votes	MPs
Conservative	13,697,923	339
Labour	11,532,218	269
Liberal	4,313,804	11
Welsh Nationalist	132,544	2
Scottish Nationalist	504,259	2
Northern Ireland (various)	779,488	12

In terms of seats won, the result was, as table 4.7 indicates, a decisive victory for the Conservatives. It did not, however, indicate any decisive rise in their popular support. At 33 per cent of the electorate, this was an improvement over their losing 30 per cent in February 1974, but it was the second lowest percentage secured by any party which had gained an overall majority of parliamentary seats since the Second World War. The election was not so much won by the Conservatives as lost by Labour; whose vote, at 28 per cent of the electorate, was the lowest for either of the major parties since 1935.

IX NEW BROOM: THE 1979 BUDGET

The new Chancellor of the Exchequer was Sir Geoffrey Howe, who had been a junior employment minister in the Heath government, and who had since become a convinced monetarist. The forecast presented to him as he prepared for his first budget warned of an impending resurgence of inflation and of the prospect that the economic recovery might peter out in the course of 1979.

The favourable influences, which had been present in 1978, were fast disappearing. The prices of imported commodities, which had been declining, were now rising rapidly. And – following the recent revolution in Iran which had led to a curtailment of oil supplies – oil prices were also soaring. At home, average earnings were continuing to rise by about 15 per cent a year; and might be expected to rise further when the Comparability Commission made its public sector pay awards. With costs rising faster at home than abroad, and with the exchange rate still rising, the price competitiveness of British goods in international markets was deteriorating, and exports were expected to lose their former buoyancy. Price increases at home were expected to start catching up with earnings; and the consumer spending boom, which had been the main reason for economic growth in 1978, would then fade. It was a depressing forecast. But the Chancellor was sceptical of the value of such forecasts, and it may not have had much influence on his budget decision.

The June 1979 budget was proclaimed as 'a new beginning', the keystone of which was to be a progressive reduction in income tax. As what he said was 'only the first step', the Chancellor announced the largest cut in income tax ever to be introduced in a single budget. Tax rates were cut, as had been promised, and allowances against tax were raised beyond what was required to compensate for inflation. On this occasion, the revenue's loss was to be made up by increases in value added tax (then 8 per cent on most goods and 12.5 per cent on others) to a uniform 15 per cent. Certain 'essential' goods such as food and clothing were, however, to remain exempt from tax.

Effects of the budget

The net result of these changes was to alter the incidence of taxation, rather than to make any noticeable change in its total amount. In justification, the Chancellor argued that the effect would be to stimulate economic activity by increasing the incentive to work. This implied an assumption that the 'substitution effect' – the incentive to substitute pay for leisure – would outweigh the 'income effect' – of being able to afford to work less. That assumption was questioned at the time, and its realism remains an open question.

The effects upon activity of the increase in indirect taxation received little attention, although they were probably of more immediate importance. The Chancellor acknowledged that they would produce an increase of 4 per cent in the retail price index, and he warned that any attempt to recoup this by pay increases would be self-defeating, and would cause an increase in unemployment. What he did not mention was that such an increase in prices would mean an immediate reduction in the purchasing power of people's savings; that they might save more to compensate, and that this would have a depressing effect on consumer spending. Nor did he acknowledge that, since most manufacturers would be unable to pass on all of the tax increase to their customers, another consequence would be a squeeze on company profits.

Public spending

The Chancellor also announced cuts in planned public expenditure amounting – after allowing for increased spending on defence and on law and order – to about £1.5 billion; to fall mainly on local authority and nationalized industry investment. In addition, the cash limits on public expenditure programmes, which had been set by the previous administration on the assumption of 5 per cent pay increases and 8–9 per cent price increases, would not be increased. Since much higher pay rises were by now inevitable, this meant that further arbitrary cuts would have to be made in the volume of work; amounting to an estimated £1 billion. Finally, there would be sales of public sector assets amounting to £1 billion which, under prevailing accounting conventions, would appear on the books as a further reduction of public expenditure.

Borrowing and money supply targets

The net result of these and other budget measures was a public-sector borrowing requirement for 1979–80, estimated at £8.3 billion. This was similar to the figure announced by the previous government in its January Public Expenditure White Paper. But the similarity was deceptive. Forecasts of economic growth had been cut substantially since January, depressing the revenues and increasing the borrowing requirement corresponding to the January programme. Also, large reductions in the volume of public expenditure had become necessary merely to offset public-sector pay increases above those which had then been assumed. It is impossible to say what its predecessors would have done under these changed circumstances, but the new government's first budget was to add significantly to the recessionary pressures upon British firms.

The imperative governing its public-sector borrowing requirement target had been the government's commitment to a reduction in the growth of the money supply. The Chancellor announced that monetary policy would henceforth 'rely less on curbs on the private sector and put more emphasis on fiscal restraint and curbs on the public sector'. In plain language, he intended to try to avoid interest rate increases and restrictions on bank lending; and to reduce money supply growth mainly by limiting public-sector borrowing. For the time being, however, he decided to raise the Minimum Lending Rate from 12 per cent to 14 per cent, and to continue his predecessor's 'corset' restrictions on bank lending.

At the same time, in a move which was to hamper the execution of monetary control, he announced the phasing-out of exchange control restrictions on investment overseas. For his monetary target, he retained the previous administration's choice of sterling M3, lowering their 8–12 per cent range for 1978–9 to an annual rate of 7–11 per cent for the period to April 1980.

The new broom

Thus, within six weeks of coming into office, the new government had acted upon virtually every instrument of economic management at its disposal. In retrospect, it is clear that many of its actions were based upon a conviction of their rightness in the long term rather than upon an analysis of short-term consequences, or their consistency.

Consistency between public-sector borrowing and monetary policy had certainly received attention; but here, it was hard to find a reliable guide to action. Judging by recent experience, the government could hardly expect to reduce monetary growth without holding down the public-sector borrowing, except by a considerable increase in interest rates. But there had been no previous experience of the implementation of monetary restraint during the onset of a recession. There was some evidence that bank lending tended to fall of its own accord during a recession. If this were to happen this time, there would – as Professor Terry Burns was to point out – be no need to resist the rise in public-sector borrowing which always tends to occur in a recession. The natural reduction in money supply growth would roughly offset the upward pressure upon it due to increased public-sector borrowing.[17]

There could be no assurance, however, that previous patterns would be repeated; the economy was moving again into uncharted seas.

X PRICE SHOCKS AND THE ECONOMY

During the remainder of 1979 and into 1980, the British economy – and particularly its company sector – struggled to cope with a succession of price shocks.

Oil prices doubled in the course of 1979. For most developed countries this represented, as in 1973–4, falls of several per cent in national income. British national income was not directly affected in total because the economy was by this time virtually self-sufficient in oil; but the distribtion of income was altered. The benefits to Britain of North Sea oil production went mainly to the government in the form of oil taxation. British firms had to pay the increased world price. For them, the price rise was the equivalent of an increase in company taxation. The costs of materials and fuel purchased by manufacturing industry rose by about 15 per cent, mainly because of the oil price increase.

The increase in value added tax reduced profits in domestic markets; and a combination of a rising exchange rate and accelerating labour costs, reduced profits in overseas markets. Manufacturing companies were particularly hard hit. With earnings rising by 17.5 per cent in 1979, and productivity rising by only 2.5 per cent, they suffered a 15 per cent increase in unit labour costs. The exchange rate rose on average by 13 per cent over the same period, so that in terms of the currencies of overseas markets the rise in unit labour costs was about 30 per cent. Overseas competitors in those markets experienced relatively small increases in unit labour costs, and the relative unit labour costs of British manufactured goods rose by 25 per cent. And on top of all this came the interest rate increases required to implement the government's monetary policy.

The origins of these multiple price shocks were inter-connected. The increase in the exchange rate was due in part to the increase in British interest rates. But it seems also to have owed something to the oil price increase, together with Britain's emerging position as a major oil producer. And it may have been influenced by confidence among overseas financial operators in the new government's policies. These factors in combination made Britain an attractive haven for the large surpluses, which were again accruing to the oil-exporting countries. The upward pressure on the exchange rate which they generated was only partially offset by the outflows of funds which occurred, as British financial institutions were enabled to diversify their investment portofolios into overseas assets, by the removal of exchange control restrictions.

The interactions between the causes of the various price shocks was so complex that there can be no certainty as to how much of the damage was of overseas origin and how much of it was self-inflicted.

The financial pressures which these developments imposed upon companies were exacerbated by the fact that, in rebuilding stocks which had been depleted by the strikes of the previous winter, firms had raised their stocks to historically high levels in relation to output. This increase in stocks, together with the increase in interest rates on the loans with which they were largely financed, imposed a further drain on company funds. Company liquidations started to increase, and many of the surviving firms were forced to turn to the banks for loans in order to pay their bills.

The resulting surge in bank lending put upward pressure on money supply growth, which was reinforced by what turned out to be a failure on the part of the government to reduce public-sector borrowing. These pressures pushed the growth of sterling M3 above the upper limit of its 7–11 per cent target range. It was generally recognized that the published statistics were erratic and probably distorted by temporary factors. But it was also known that the 'corset' restrictions upon bank lending were being evaded by the use of devices which by-passed the normal functions of the banks as intermediaries between borrowers and lenders (a process which was termed 'disintermediation'). It thus seemed likely that the true position was worse than that indicated by the money supply statistics.

By October, these trends had so far undermined the confidence of operators in the financial markets as to generate, once more, a reluctance to buy government bonds. In November, the government responded by raising the minimum lending rate by three percentage points to the all-time record level of 17 per cent. This restored the confidence of the financial markets, but added yet futher to the financial pressures upon companies.

By the autumn of 1979, the financial deficits of industrial and commercial companies had in any case reached an unsustainable level, and firms were trying to reduce their deficits by cutting back on employment, investment, and stocks. A classical 'inventory recession' had started, with one firm's stock reduction leading to another firm's loss of orders in the well-known snowballing pattern.

Output and employment turned down, and unemployment started a rapid rise. Britain had begun to slide into the worst recession experienced by any industrial country since before the Second World War.

NOTES

1. Larsen, Llewellyn and Potter 'International Economic Linkages', *OECD Economic Studies*, No. 1, autumn 1983.
2. Meeting of the International Monetary Fund's Committee of Twenty, Rome 1974.
3. Statement to the Annual Meeting, Manila, 1976.
4. Report of the Royal Commission on the Constitution, 1973, p. 180.
5. For unemployment rates by racial origin see *The Dept of Employment Gazette*, August 1980, p. 834.
6. W. Wells, 'Relative Pay and Employment of Young People', *Dept. of Employment Gazette*, June 1983, p. 230.
7. See D. Metcalf, 'Special employment measures', *Midland Bank Review*, autumn/winter 1982, p. 9.
8. *National Institute Economic Review*, February 1977, p. 32.
9. Treasury and Civil Service Committee, Memoranda on Monetary Policy, Session 1979–80, House of Commons, 17 July 1980, p. 56.
10. J. Barnett, *Inside the Treasury* (André Deutsch, 1982) p. 124.
11. Expenditure Committee (General Sub-Committee) 'Minutes of Evidence' (HMSO, 3 November 1978).
12. The European Monetary System (Cmnd 7405, 24 November 1978).
13. The European Monetary System (Cmnd 7419, 8 December 1978).
14. *National Institute Economic Review*, February 1978.
15. For accounts of Cabinet discussions on this issue, see Barnett, *Inside the Treasury*, p. 162; and also W. Rodgers, 'A winter's tale of discontent', *Guardian*, 7 January 1984.
16. Barnett, *Inside the Treasury*, pp. 172, 174.
17. A. Budd and T. Burns, 'The role of the PSBR in controlling the money supply', in *Economic Outlook* (The London Business School, Gower, November 1979) p. 28.

5

The British Experiment: March 1980–June 1983

I THE MEDIUM-TERM FINANCIAL STRATEGY

Until March 1980, it could not be asserted with complete confidence that the policies of economic management adopted by the new administration had differed significantly from those which its predecessor would have adopted under the same circumstances. After the Chancellor's budget statement of 26 March, the difference was beyond doubt. In this sense it can be said that the sequence of events which came to be known as 'the British experiment' dated from the announcement on that day of the government's 'Medium-Term Financial Strategy'.

The Medium-Term Financial Strategy was unique in that it set out to commit the government to a closely-defined course of action over a period of at least four years. That course of action was, in the Chancellor's words, to be 'concerned with only those things that the Government has it in their power to control'. 'Those things' were, however, defined with some precision. Money supply growth was to be halved by 1983–4. Public-sector borrowing as a percentage of national income was to be reduced by an even greater proportion (although its proposed course was not to be regarded as a target). And, for the first time ever, there was to be a progressive reduction in public expenditure over the life of a parliament.

Nothing like this had been attempted before in this or any other country. Published monetary targets had become commonplace, but elsewhere there was an understanding that they would be adjusted as seemed appropriate. In contrast, this was by implication a commitment to follow an arbitrary money supply path whatever the consequences. Policy action over a four-year period was to be directed, not to the pursuit of ultimate policy objectives, but to compliance with an intermediate target whose relation to policy objectives remained a matter of dispute.

The fact that 'the experiment' originated in Britain, and was not replicated elsewhere, is explicable in terms of the characteristics of the British political system. Had economic policy under that system been formulated by open debate, it is hardly likely that the legislature would have assented to having its hands tied for a four-year period. In Britain, however, the Prime Minister of a party which has a secure parliamentary majority is normally constrained only by the need for the consent of Cabinet colleagues. The power of dismissal over members of the Cabinet, which lies with the Prime Minister, makes that consent difficult to withhold; and economic policy proposals supported by the Chancellor and the Prime Minister are seldom rejected. It was thus possible to launch the experiment on the initiative of a handful of like-minded ministers and officials.

Expectations and estimated employment effects

Among its architects, the justification for the strategy depended strongly upon its presentational effects upon expectations. If it succeeded in lowering inflationary expectations, there were theoretical grounds for supposing that inflation could be brought down without any substantial rise in unemployment. But a decade of 'U-turns' had made the British sceptical of their politicians' ability to stay any course. To change expectations in the face of such cynicism would require the presentation of the appearance of unflinching determination to stick to its chosen course, come what may. Almost certainly it was this argument, rather than any insensitivity to the social effects of unemployment, that carried the day. But the decision to launch the experiment must also have depended upon the judgement that more weight should be placed upon these presentational considerations than upon the undoubted technical difficulties which the strategy presented.

The main difficulty arose from the lack of what control engineers term 'feed-back', that is to say, from the implication that the consequences of the strategy for output and employment were not to be allowed to influence its conduct. In engineering terms, a control system without feed-back would normally be regarded as crude and inefficient. Without feed-back through eye and brain, it would, for example, scarcely be possible to drive a car for more than a short distance. In everyday life, feed-back can be dispensed with only where control actions are precise and their consequences closely predictable – or where departures from course are of no great importance.

The Chancellor was prepared for some departure from the ideal of a reduction of inflation at no cost in terms of unemployment. In his words: 'it is not possible to reduce inflation without some early loss in employment and output.'[1] As to the magnitude of those losses, the advice of the professional economists of the day varied over a wide range.[2] The 'New Classical' economists, as represented in Britain by Professor Patrick

Minford, argued that, provided the policy was understood and believed, it would cause 'no disruption of the real economy'. Among the 'Gradualist' monetary economists, Professor Milton Friedman concluded that: 'only a modest reduction of output and employment will be the side effect of reducing inflation to single figures by 1982.' And Professor David Laidler estimated that: 'one might expect a reduction of five percentage points in inflation to be yielded as a first round effect by a one percentage point increase in unemployment.' He added, however, that: 'I would not stake much quantitative precision on this or any other estimate.'

In marked contrast, the eminent American monetary economist, Professor James Tobin, estimated that on the basis of experience in the United States: 'an extra point of unemployment for a year would reduce the outgoing rate of wage and price inflation by maybe a third of a point, or at most a half of a point.' And, for the Keynesians, Professor Lord Kaldor arged that monetary policy could bring down inflation only by engineering a recession.

The problems of monetary control

Apart from the difficulty of predicting the effect of the strategy upon the real economy, there were, at a different level, difficulties surrounding the process of controlling the money supply. Attempts to devise a new forecasting relationship for bank lending had failed, and the technique of control remained judgmental and erratic.

A futher difficulty was looming. The Chancellor's decision to abolish exchange controls had so greatly facilitated the evasion of the 'corset' restrictions on bank lending, that the corset had for practical purposes become ineffective. While it continued, however, the money supply statistics understated the true position. When, on 26 March 1980, the Chancellor announced that he was putting an end to the corset in June, he acknowledged that at that time there would be a surge in the money supply figures as the banks resumed their role as intermediaries between borrowers and lenders. As he observed, 'the scale of this exceptional increase cannot be precisely measured or predicted'. Those responsible for monetary control were thus to be faced with the additional problem of estimating and allowing for this readjustment. But the Chancellor remained optimistic: 'if as I hope, it (the monetary surge) can be accommodated within the target I have just announced, that would point to a further slowing down of monetary growth.'

The erratic nature of monetary control in practice had led to suggestions for alternative techniques, one of which was to control the 'monetary base' (mainly notes and coins). But these were seen at the time as essentially short-term difficulties. In the context of the strategy, they were put aside with the statement that:

> it goes without saying that . . . we need to have efficient methods of monetary control. We already have the means to meet our medium-term objectives. The Green Paper on monetary base control which I have laid before the House will provide a basis for public discussion of how to improve control over shorter periods.

The target path

Of the figures presented in the statement of the Medium-Term Financial Strategy,[3] the most important were as shown in table 5.1.

Table 5.1 The MTFS targets

	1980/1	1981/2	1982/3	1983/4
Growth of sterling M3 per cent	7–11	6–10	5–9	4–8
Public sector borrowing £				
billion, 1978/9 prices	6	5	3.5	2.5
per cent of GDP	3.75	3	2.25	1.5

The monetary target for 1980–1 was the same as that set in the previous budget for the last eight months of 1979–80, but was lower than the 12 per cent out-turn for that period. The 1983–4 range was presented as a firm commitment, but the other ranges were covered by the statement that 'precise targets for intermediate years will be decided at the time.'

The public-sector borrowing out-turn for 1979–80 was estimated as £9.1 billion (it later turned out to be £10.2 billion) compared with the previously planned £8.3 billion. The £6 billion (1978–9 prices) shown in the above table for 1980–1 represented a reduction of £2 billion below the estimated 1979–80 out-turn. This appeared to settle a debate on the important question of whether allowance should be made for the natural tendency for the borrowing requirement to rise during a recession. On that question, Nigel Lawson (then Financial Secretary to the Treasury) had said in January 1980 that: 'Taken together, the cycle and the medium-term trend might be expected to produce a stepped PSBR profile, with the PSBR not changing much as a proportion of GDP in recession years, but falling fairly sharply in non-recession years.'[4] But on 26 March that year the Chancellor made it clear that such was not his intention:

Despite the expection of a recession . . . it would be wrong to keep the actual PSBR at its current level as a percentage of GDP. We must not make the mistake of promising to correct the underlying weakness at some time in the future but failing to take the necessary steps today.

Tax and interest rate cuts to follow

On matters of more direct interest to companies and taxpayers, the strategy statement was cautiously optimistic.

There should over the period as a whole be a significant reduction in nominal interest rates and a steadily improving environment for investment.

There should be scope simultaneously to reduce Government borrowing and to lower taxes, including progress toward a 25 per cent rate of income tax.

But the strategy statement concluded with a passage which made its priorities clear.

. . . it may be necessary to change policies in ways not reflected in the above projections. . . . But there would be no question of departing from the money supply policy, which is essential to the success of any anti-inflation strategy.

In the budget itself, the further income tax reductions foreshadowed in the 1979 budget statement were implicitly postponed. The income tax changes were relatively small, but in real terms they amounted in total to a tax increase. The projections in the strategy statement suggested that further tax reductions would have to wait until 1982/3.

II THE FIRST YEAR OF THE STRATEGY

Within months of the launching of the Medium-Term Financial Strategy, it became evident that the Chancellor had taken the wrong advice. Judging by the money supply statistics, monetary restraint was far less severe than intended; but judging from the pressures on companies, it was a great deal more severe than had been intended. It seemed now neither feasible nor desirable to hold to the course which the Chancellor had set out in March. But an alternative had to be found. Economic policy was for years to be dominated by two problems: how to repair some of the damage which had been done, and how to restore the credibility of the government's strategy. Within the Cabinet, the priorities to be assigned to these problems were to be a source of much dissension.

By the autumn of 1980, the statistics were showing an annual growth rate of sterling M3 of 25 per cent, only four–five percentage points of which were attributable to 're-intermediation' following the ending of the corset. Public-sector borrowing over six months had been over 90 per cent of the amount targeted for the entire year. There had not, as in pevious recessions, been an offsetting fall in bank lending: companies were borrowing to survive. The short-term control of the money supply was encountering increased difficulties, and it even seemed possible that increases in interest rates would have the perverse effect of encouraging bank lending.

The crisis in company finance

Companies were in desperate difficulties, however. Profits had fallen 20 per cent in six months, giving a real rate of return estimated at 2 per cent. Company liquidations were at a record post-war level and were rising at a rate of 40 per cent a year. Surviving companies were preserving their liquidity by vigorous action to cut stocks, investment, and employment. Industrial production was down 8.5 per cent on a year ago, and manufacturing nearly 10 per cent.

Companies were suffering financial pressure mainly because of increases in labour costs which could not all be passed on into price increases. Over the year to the third quarter of 1980, average earnings had risen 21 per cent and, with output having fallen 3 per cent more than employment, labour costs per unit of output had risen 24 per cent. Labour cost increases had again been smaller in most other countries, and the relative unit labour costs of British manufactured goods in international markets had risen by 19 per cent.

On previous occasions, the effect of surging labour costs on profit margins in international markets had been offset by a falling exchange rate, which enabled firms to raise the sterling prices of exports. On this occasion, the profit squeeze had been intensified by exchange rate increases which had accounted for almost a third of the increase in relative unit labour costs.

Action on the money supply

The rise in the exchange rate was attributed by industry spokesmen to the government's action in raising interest rates, and the Confederation of British Industry clamoured for a change of policy. Treasury spokesmen argued that, on the contrary, much of the rise in the exchange rate was due to rising oil prices, and therefore beyond the government's control.[5] And, to the extent that it was a consequence of government policy, it constituted one of the ways in which monetary policy had been expected to bring down prices. It was acknowledged, however, that sterling M3 had for the time being become a misleading monetary indicator[6] and that it would not be right to attempt to curb its growth by further rises in interest rates. In July, in fact, the minimum lending rate had been reduced from 17 to 16 per cent.

The Treasury were not, however, prepared to abandon sterling M3 as a monetary target. They took the view that its surge in the course of 1980 was in the nature of a once-for-all shift, rather than a change of trend. Accordingly, they proposed to retain the target ranges set out in the Medium-Term Financial Strategy; and to take urgent steps to reduce public-sector borrowing, in order to bring money supply growth back within those target ranges. As a first step they proposed an additional £2 billion cut in public spending programmes for 1981/2.

Public spending: the revolt of the 'wets'

From newspaper accounts at the time[7] it appears that these proposals were not well received by the majority of the Cabinet. In theory the proceedings within Cabinet are highly secret, but there are occasions when unattributable press briefing by the Prime Minister's press secretary, and others, reveals something of what transpired. This seems to have been one of those occasions: the press accounts were too consistent to have been the product of uninformed speculation. Opposition to spending cuts developed which seemed to go beyond normal ministerial resistance to cuts affecting their own departments, and to amount to a co-ordinated revolt. The Prime Minister strongly supported the Treasury proposal, and used the epithet 'wets' to describe its opponents. The matter was finally settled in early November with a partial victory to the 'wets' in reducing the size of the spending cuts from £2 billion to £1 billion.

On 24 November, in what the press referred to as a 'mini-budget', the Chancellor retaliated by announcing an increase of £1 billion in oil taxation and of over £2 billion in National Insurance contributions, at least part of which were the equivalent of a tax increase. What he had been unable to get with his colleages' agreement by way of spending cuts, he got without their agreement in the form of tax increases. At the same time, he announced a further cut in interest rates by two points to 14 per cent.

Two million unemployed

By the end of the year, unemployment had topped 2 million – a 60 per cent increase on a year previously – and was growing at a rate of over one million a year. Redundancies in 1980 had been 160 per cent higher than in 1979.

Inflation, after peaking at nearly 22 per cent in April, had fallen to just over 15 per cent by December.

'The lady's not for turning'

By this time, a number of monetarist economists were expressing misgivings about the government's policy. Professor David Laidler observed that shifts in monetary relationships had occurred in a number of countries since the early 1970s, and concluded that, since such shifts seemed to be unpredictable, it no longer seemed practicable to conduct monetary policy by trying to aim at predetermined targets.[8] Professor Alan Walters, after being appointed a special adviser to the Prime Minister, is reported to have said that monetary policy was too tight, but that fiscal policy should be tightened. Professor Jurg Niehans, who had been commissioned by the Conservative Party's Centre for Policy Studies to examine British monetary policy, also argued that monetary policy was too tight; that the exclusive use of sterling M3 as a target was mistaken, and that the rise in the exchange rate had indeed been due to high interest rates.[9]

The 'British Experiment' had got off to a bad start. All of its pre-announced targets had been overshot, in spite of which the British economy was in a far steeper decline than that of any other major country. There was speculation of an impending policy change – a 'U-turn' comparable to that of the Heath administration. In fact, some changes were to take place, but the government were quick to deny that anything in the nature of a fundamental change of strategy was contemplated. The Prime Minister was particularly vehement, rejecting the speculation in punning rhetoric: 'You turn if you want to. This lady's not for turning.'[10]

III SUPPLY-SIDE POLICIES

The economic policy of the new government was not concerned exclusively with macroeconomic issues. Ministerial statements frequently emphasized the importance of improving the 'supply side' of the economy by reduction state intervention and removing obstacles to the operation of market forces. By making the economy more responsive to the needs of the market, it was intended to bring about renewed economic growth and to put an end to Britain's relative decline.

State intervention

Some moves were made in this direction in the course of the first eighteen months of the new administration. The Price Commission was abolished, restrictions upon the location of business premises were removed, and the scope of regional policy was reduced. Government holdings in British Aerospace, Cable and Wireless, and the British National Oil Corporation were put up for sale, and regulations which restricted competition in bus and coach services were lifted.

But many of the previous administration's interventionist policies were retained. The special treatment of investment in company taxation continued to favour capital-intensive, as against labour-intensive, methods of production. Intervention in the housing market continued on a massive scale, with subsidies running at over £2 billion a year and tax reliefs at well over £1 billion. Little was done to ease the restrictions which had all but put an end to the rented housing market; and local councils continued to impede labour mobility by discriminating against non-residents in the allocation of council houses. And subsidies to agriculture continued at over £1 billion a year, more than half of which was additional to the support provided under the European Community Common Agricultural Policy.

Large subventions to the nationalized industries were also continued. Their average real rate of return had fallen between 1970 and 1979 from +1 per cent to −1 per cent (without subsidies the fall would have been from 0 to −2 per cent) and the recession was depressing it further.[11] Attempts to cut output and costs were often successfully resisted by highly unionized labour forces. British Steel's losses were running at about £2 million a day in 1980, and its management tried to restrict pay increases to 2 per cent but, after a lengthy strike, settled at 17 per cent; after which the government announced a £6.6 billion 'rescue plan'. The National Coal Board tried to accelerate its programme of closures of uneconomic pits – which had been running at about a third of the rate envisaged in the 1974 'Plan for Coal'. In response to a strike threat, the attempt was abandoned, government subsidies were increased from £250 million to £575 million a year, and restrictions were placed upon the importing of coal for the generation of electricity.[12] In the motor vehicle industry, British Leyland, in which the previous administration had aquired a majority share holding, was in danger of insolvency, and the Government agreed to increase its investment by £1 billion in the course of 1981 and 1982.

It was made clear that continuing support for loss-making nationalized industries was intended as a transitional measure, pending – and in many cases, conditional upon – progress toward fully commercial operation. In that sense the increased subventions represented, not a policy of intervent-ion, but a means of avoiding the employment consequences of abrupt withdrawal.

But there were many instances of active intervention. Impressed by the ambitious French nuclear power station programme, the government decided to revive the ill-fated British nuclear construction industry. It was announced that 'the Government attach importance to the steady build-up of the NNC (National Nuclear Corporation) into a strong and independent design and construction company, fully able to supply power stations at home and abroad, efficiently.'[13] Expenditures of £15 billion over twenty years were envisaged, with the intention that – despite the very large cost advantage achieved by American companies – the work would go to the British consortium. In 1980, construction was started on two new power stations, at a time when there was already a large surplus of generating capacity and when demand for electricity was falling.[14] A similar enthusiasm was evinced for 'Information Technology' to the extent even of appointing a minister with sole responsibility for its promotion.

Trade policy

In its policy toward international trade, the government took pride in being more interventionist than its predecessor. In July 1980 the Secretary of State for Trade assured Parliament that 'we have substantially increased the number of quotas and restrictions which we inherited.' In 1981, government negotiators pressed for stricter controls upon imports of textiles and clothing under the European Community's 'Multi Fibre Agreement', and the government gave active support to negotiations initiated by British trade associations designed to restrict imports of cars, pottery, footwear and electrical goods from Far East countries. To quote a 1981 policy statement:

> The government is in favour of direct industry to industry discussions in order to resolve specific sectoral problems where possible. In appropriate cases the Government does provide support. . . . In the case of trade with Japan, regular discussions between industries in particular product areas have been important in encouraging Japanese understanding of difficulties facing UK industry and the voluntary restraint of Japan's exports. The Government fully supports these discussions and continues to watch closely their effectiveness in moderating exports to the UK.[15]

The effect of this type of import restriction was to impose higher prices upon British buyers, thus transferring wealth to the producers of selected products; a proportion, only, of which was to the benefit of British producers.[16] Government ministers and officials were also heavily engaged in the negotiation of export deals and the design of *ad hoc* support packages for particular British firms or groups of firms.

Thus, although its general policy statements indicated a more market-orientated approach to the economy than that of its predecessors, in 1982 the government's actions prompted one group of eminent economists to observe that: 'within the sphere of industrial policy the mixture remains broadly the same as before'; and: 'mercantilist ideas and practices have become more dominant.'[17]

Special employment measures

The government's interventions in the labour market followed the pattern of its predecessors but on a much larger scale. The Temporary Employment Subsidy had already been phased out, mainly because of conflicts with the Community's competition policy. The largest of the remaining programmes was a scheme designed to substitute part-time working for redundancies (the Temporary Short-Term Working Compensation Scheme). Of growing importance was a scheme to give work experience to unemployed youngsters (the Youth Opportunity Programme). A third scheme (the Job Release Scheme) encouraged the over-sixties to take early retirement. Expenditure on these and other 'special employment measures' rose from under £400 million in 1979/80 to over £1.5 billion in 1982/3.[18]

To the extent that these schemes relieved the downward pressure on pay rises created by surpluses in the labour market, they were recognized to be in conflict with the government's financial strategy. They were regarded as necessary, however, to make that strategy politically acceptable.

IV REPAIRING THE STRATEGY

As the Chancellor reviewed the first year of the Medium-Term Financial Strategy, the figures before him were as in table 5.2.

Table 5.2

	Planned	Actual
Per cent growth of sterling M3 February 1980–February 1981:	7–11	20
Public-sector borrowing 1980/1 £ billion:	8.5	13.5

For 1981/2, the strategy had envisaged a 6–10 per cent growth range for sterling M3, and a public-sector borrowing requirement of £7.5 billion (after adjustment to the current price level). Since neither of these targets was attainable, changes were unavoidable, possibly to the framework of the strategy, and certainly to the numbers to be assigned to its target variables.

Monetary policy

The Chancellor decided not to make a clear break with the existing framework. Sterling M3 was retained as the target variable, but with the qualification that 'as in the past year, the significance of short-run movements for interest rate policy will be interpreted in light of other financial developments as well.' While retaining the presentational simplicity of a predetermined path for a single target variable, this time he left the way open for discretionary departures from it.

The new path which was chosen for sterling M3 was parallel to, but well above, the path laid down in the original strategy. The growth ranges for 1981/2 to 1983/4 were to be the same percentages as before, but were to be reckoned from a higher starting point, namely the actual stock of money at February 1981. But hopes of returning to the original path were not entirely abandoned: the intention would be 'to consider clawing back some of the past year's rapid growth of sterling M3 by permitting an undershoot as and when the occasion arises'.

Borrowing

It was not obvious that the new target would require a major change of fiscal stance. The London Business School suggested that a borrowing requirement of £12 billion would be consistent with monetary growth of 8 per cent.[19] But the Chancellor – prompted, it was reported, by the Prime Minister – was anxious to avoid any return to the previous year's high interest rates. His main concern was that the borrowing requirement should be 'consistent with this announced monetary target for 1981/2, a sum which could be financed without putting undue strain on the capital markets'. The figure he chose was £10.5 billion – well below the 'unchanged policy' forecast, but still £3 billion above the figure in the original strategy.

With the recession having increased public spending, and having depressed revenues by far more than had been expected in 1980, a borrowing requirement of £10.5 billion would now require a large increase in taxation. It was estimated that it would require a reduction in the borrowing requirement of £3 billion on top of the £2 billion reduction resulting from the mini-budget of the previous November. Since the Cabinet would not agree to further spending cuts, this had to be done by tax increases.

Taxation

In his March 1981 budget, the Chancellor announced that the further £3 billion would be raised mainly by income tax increases (in fact by failing to raise tax allowances to compensate for inflation) and by increases in excise duties over and above what was required to compensate for inflation. Table 5.3 gives an estimate of the combined effects of the November and March budgets. At the same time he accounced a two-point reduction in the Minimum Lending Rate to 12 per cent.

Table 5.3 Estimated effects of the November 1980 and March 1981 budgets

	Effect on public-sector borrowing (£ billion)
National Insurance contributions:	−1.0
Oil taxes:	−1.0
Support for nationalized industries, private industries and special employment measures:	+1.8
November spending cuts:	−1.4
Income tax:	−1.9
Excise duties:	−1.2
Other:	−0.2
Total:	−4.9

In order to repair the government's strategy, while at the same time holding down interest rates, the Chancellor had introduced the largest increase in taxation ever introduced in a single year, taking British taxation as a proportion of GDP to a record level. He had done so, moreover, at a time when the economy was in the deepest recession experienced by any industrial country since the war. It could not have been more clearly demonstrated that the tax reductions, which had been the centrepiece of the election campaign, were by then taking second place to monetary policy. Above all, a demand reduction on that scale, and at that time, constituted a more extreme departure from the former Keynesian consensus than had anywhere been attempted.

March 1981 represented, in fact, the zenith of the particular form of monetary policy represented by the original Medium-Term Financial Strategy. The reduction of inflation was to remain the prime policy objective, but no further attempt was to be made to maintain a non-discretionary adherence to a predetermined path of a single monetary variable. By December of that year it had already been acknowledged that

The British Experiment

it was the exchange rate, rather than the money supply, that was for the time determining interest rate policy. An ill-judged policy change by the Federal Reserve Bank in the United States had driven interest rates there to over 20 per cent; and it had become necessary to raise British interest rates in response, in order to arrest a fall in the exchange rate which was threatening to cause the inflation rate to rise again.

Events overseas had once again forced a British government to adjust its policies.

V HITTING BOTTOM

By 1981 the British economy was at the depth of its worst recession since the war. Confidence in the authority of government was also at a low ebb, particularly among urban minorities. And government policies were under attack, even by members of the Cabinet.

Recession

The world recession which had followed the second oil price increase had been partly responsible for Britain's economic decline; but most of the other industrial countries were by 1981 in the recovery phase, following a brief reduction in growth in the course of 1980. Despite its relative immunity to oil price increases, the British economy had suffered more severely, as Table 5.4 indicates. Britain remained a comparatively high-

Table 5.4 Comparative economic performance 1980 and 1981

	GDP[a] (Index 1979=100)		Inflation rate (%)[b]		Unemployment rate (%)[c]	
	1980	1981	1980	1981	1980	1981
Britain	97.4	96.0	19.9	11.6	5.5	10.9
USA	99.7	102.2	9.2	9.6	5.7	7.5
Japan	104.8	109.0	2.8	2.7	2.1	2.2
France	101.1	101.3	12.2	12.3	5.9	7.3
West Germany	101.9	101.7	4.5	4.2	3.2	4.4
Italy	103.9	104.2	20.7	18.4	7.8	8.3
All Industrial countries	101.3	103.0	9.2	8.7		

[b] GDP deflator.
[c] Broadly comparable definitions.
Source: [a] and [b] *IMF Annual Report* 1985, [c] OECD *Main Economic Indicators,* August 1984.

inflation economy, and had become a high-unemployment economy. Its international position had deteriorated sharply.

From the peak in Britain's economic activity in the third quarter of 1979 to its trough in the second quarter of 1981, the high exchange rate and other financial pressures had produced sharp falls in exports, fixed investment, and investment in stocks. Manufacturing output had fallen by 14 per cent; industrial production by almost 11 per cent, and the output of the economy as a whole by 5 per cent. The fall in employment had been slightly less, at 4.5 per cent, productivity having fallen a little. Nearly all of the 1.1 million fall in employment had occurred in manufacturing. Unemployment had risen by about the same amount, the normal demographic rise in the labour force having been offset by reductions in the proportions – particularly of women and older men – who were seeking work. The labour market was thus even more depressed than the unemployment figures indicated.

Urban riots

The uneven incidence of unemployment created special problems. Adult unemployment averaged around 10 per cent for the country as a whole, but in many urban areas it was much higher. In the Granby ward of Liverpool, for example, it was over 33 per cent. It was also higher for young people, with a national average of over 30 per cent among those under eighteen. And, generally, it was higher than average among black people. The problems were particularly serious where these special factors coincided: for instance, the employment prospects for a young black man living in Liverpool were grim indeed.

In 1981 these problems were thrust violently upon the attention of the British people by a series of urban riots. In five widely scattered areas there was arson, looting, and attacks on the police with stones and fire bombs. The causes were complex: unemployment, racial disadvantage, bad housing, and racial discrimination by the police, all played a part. The riots could not be regarded as racial in the sense of fighting between blacks and whites. White youths frequently joined with black youths in attacks upon the police, whom they saw as an alien symbol of an authority which had betrayed them. Racial prejudice had nevertheless been an important factor in creating the sense of alienation among many of those concerned, and this was widely held to be the main influence at work.[20]

The last revolt of the 'wets'

The standing of the government in the opinion polls was by this time at its lowest level and *The Times* was able to describe Mrs Thatcher as the most

unpopular Prime Minister since records began.[21] Her authority was
further reduced by news of a revolt within the Cabinet over plans to hold
down public expenditure in 1982/3. The immediate outcome was a
victory for the 'wets', and an upward revision of some £10 billion in the
public spending plans. But the final victory was with the Prime Minister,
who used her powers to dismiss ministers and to move them to positions
of less influence.[22] By these means she strengthened the, hitherto
uncertain, influence of monetarist thinking upon her most influential
Cabinet Ministers, to the point where her own views became virtually
unchallengeable.

VI THE DIVIDED OPPOSITION

The Cabinet changes of 1981 can be seen as completing a move in the
Conservative Party away from the consensus on economic policy which
had united the two political parties throughout the post-war years until
1975. In the Labour Party since the 1979 election, there had been an
equally strong movement away from that consensus, in the opposite
direction. After the election, the policies of the Wilson/Callaghan administration came under attack from many quarters, including former members
of that administration. There were bitter recriminations about the failure
to implement policies – for instance, on planning agreements – which had
been endorsed by the party conference; about Callaghan's mistaken choice
of the election date; about the 5 per cent pay policy which was held
responsible for the 'Winter of Discontent'; and above all, about Callaghan's failure to consult the National Executive Committee when framing
the 1979 election manifesto. Groups on the left of the party had become
increasingly resentful of the degree of control over policy exerted by the
Parliamentary Labour Party and by the Cabinet; which meant that their
own success in influencing local constituency parties and – to a lesser
extent – the trade unions, was having no effect upon party policy.

The economic policies advocated by the Left varied over a wide
spectrum, but common features included an intensification of import
controls, withdrawal from the European community, controls over capital
movements abroad, and an extension of public ownership and control over
industry. There was also strong support for unilateral nuclear disarmament and for the removal of American military bases from Britain.

The controversy which raged in the Labour Party following the election
was not overtly concerned with policy, however, but rather with the
distribution of power within the party. The left wing of the party sought to
increase its influence by means of three constitutional changes:

(1) the party leadership to be elected, not by the Parliamentary Labour Party, but by an electoral college on which the constituency parties and the trade unions would be represented;
(2) selection procedures to be changed to require MPs to account for their actions to their constituency parties;
(3) the National Executive Committee to be given control over the framing of the election manifesto.

The principles of democratic accountability were appealed to in support of these demands; but alternative proposals, which would give control to the party membership on a one-man–one-vote basis, were strongly opposed by the Left. It was clear that, whatever their constitutional merits, the practical effect of the proposed changes would be to move the party's policies strongly to the left.

After a series of acrimonious public debates, the Left won their first two demands. In January 1981 a special conference decided that, in the electoral college which was to appoint the party leader, 40 per cent of the votes should go to the unions, and 30 per cent each to the Parliamentary Party, and to the constituency parties. This was seen as a humiliating defeat for the existing leadership of the party, brought about by an alliance between the Campaign for Labour Democracy and a number of groups of the 'Outside Left'.[23]

An immediate and expected consequence of this victory of the left was the departure from the Labour Party of a number of members of the previous administration, to form a new Social Democratic party. The policies of the new party included proportional representation, continued membership of the European Community and the setting up of a permanent tax-based incomes policy. A pact was made with the Liberal Party under which the two parties would fight elections together as 'The Alliance', and the by-election victories of this combination which followed, indicated that the electorate were prepared to accept it as a third force in British politics.

VII REAGANOMICS AND THE WORLD ECONOMY

A digression on United States economic policy may seem strange in a chapter on the British experiment. Despite a popular impression to the contrary, the trade linkage between the two economies was not very strong: less than 15 per cent of British exports were to the USA. But developments in US economic policy were nevertheless to have an indirect influence upon British economic policy and upon economies of its overseas customers – largely as the result of a series of accidents and misjudgements.

US monetary and fiscal policy[24]

A development which was to prove important was a tightening of monetary policy in October 1979. The Federal Reserve Bank announced that it was changing its monetary control technique from one which relied upon influencing interest rates, to a more direct system of control upon bank reserves. As in Britain, practical difficulties soon became evident. The relationships upon which control depended were uncertain; and changes in banking arrangements, which were introduced at the same time, were making it difficult to interpret the statistics.[25]

The Reagan administration, which came into power at the beginning of 1981, was strongly influenced by monetarist thinking and gave its general support to this new approach. But, like the British Conservatives, it had placed more emphasis, in its election campaign, upon tax cuts. The thinking behind the new administration's programme was a mixture of 'supply-side' economics, monetarism, and a traditional Republican aversion to budget deficits.

Supply-side thinking attached great importance to the incentive effects of tax cuts, some of its adherents even claiming that they would stimulate economic activity to the point that tax revenue would not fall when tax rates were reduced. (The official Republican platform did not go that far, but estimated that the stimulus of reduced rates would offset over 70 per cent of the initial loss of revenue by the fifth year.) This thinking rejected the Keynesian contention that tax cuts would directly raise demand. With a given money supply path, the initial fall in revenue would be made good by the sale of government bonds. Those bonds would not be seen as wealth, but merely as deferred taxation, and there would thus be no net effect upon spending. To the supply-siders, budget deficits were consequently considered to be of no importance[26] But others thought that a reduction in the budget deficit was necessary in order to reduce inflationary expectations.

From these strands, the Republican programme had acquired, as its main elements:

(1) three successive cuts, each of 10 per cent, in personal income tax, together with reductions in business taxation;
(2) a big increase in defence spending;
(3) the elimination of the budget deficit by 1984;
(4) to achieve this, a large cut in non-defence spending;
(5) a gradual reduction in money supply growth.

The burgeoning budget deficit

The first and second items of the new administration's programme were eventually put substantially into effect, but it soon became evident that the third was unattainable. The expenditure cuts adopted by Congress fell well short of what would have been necessary to meet the administration's target; the supply-side effects of the tax cuts had been overestimated; interest rates and debt service charges turned out to be higher than expected; and disappointing levels of economic activity led to higher government spending and reduced revenues.

The Federal budget deficit rose from an average of around 40 billion dollars in 1974–9 to 100 billion in 1982, and was projected to rise to 200 billion in the following few years.

The Federal Reserve Bank was also unsucessful in its attempt to bring about a gradual reduction of money supply growth. Its actions led, in early 1981, to a monetary squeeze of unexpected severity. Attempts to hold the money supply within pre-announced target ranges were then continued with varying effect. Finally, in late 1982, there was a reversion to a more relaxed and discretionary form of monetary policy.

As in Britain, these departures from programme were carried off without any explicit acknowledgement of failure.

The US recession

Having started with broadly similar intentions, the Reagan and Thatcher administrations thus followed divergent courses of policy action. Their economies also followed different courses. After falling by under 2 per cent in the early months of 1980, US GDP seemed almost back on trend when, early in 1981, its growth faltered under the impact of the monetary squeeze. Between the third quarters of 1981 and 1982, GDP again fell, this time by about 3 per cent. Compared with the deep V-shaped recession in Britain, America's recession was W-shaped, and much shallower. But the effects upon prices and jobs were similar, at least in direction. In contrast to the declining unemployment rate envisaged in the administration's 1981 scenario, US unemployment rose from 7.5 per cent in 1980 to 12.5 per cent (OECD definition) by the end of 1982. Consumer price inflation, on the other hand, fell from 12.5 per cent a year to about 4 per cent – a much faster decline than had been expected.

US interest rates and the dollar

Among the unintended consequences of the new policies was a sharp increase in interest rates, which was to persist for years, and was to affect the economies of many other countries. That increase was brought about in the first place by the adoption by the Federal Reserve Bank of policies leading to an unintentionally severe monetary contraction. It was maintained as a result of administration policies leading to an unintentional and rapid fiscal expansion. The Bank's initial misjudgement drove short-term interest rates to over 16 per cent, even before it had become evident that a large government deficit was developing. As that deficit developed, it became clear that relatively high interest rates would continue to be needed in order to finance it without a rapid monetary expansion. Short-term interest rates were held above 12 per cent throughout 1981 and for much of 1982, until fear of a deepening recession prompted a relaxation. Long-term rates continued at an historically high level after then.

The mechanism by which events in the USA came to affect the economies of other countries operated mainly through movements in the dollar exchange rate. The precedents of the 1970s suggested that a rapid fiscal expansion would lead to a fall in the exchange rate, because it would increase inflation in the country concerned, and thereby reduce the purchasing power of its currency; and because it would cause imports to rise, and thus tend to produce a balance of payments deficit. In the 1980s, this presumption ceased to hold. Without the accommodating monetary policies of the 1970s, and with unemployment exerting a bigger downward influence upon pay increases, there was no longer an expectation that fiscal expansion would lead to increased inflation.

In the USA, a very rapid fiscal expansion was accompanied by a drop in the inflation rate. And although there was a substantial substitution of imports for domestic production, the resulting balance of payments deficit on current account was more than offset by capital account inflows attracted by high US interest rates. Other forces, including the actions of other governments, were at work, but the outcome was not a fall, but a massive appreciation, of the dollar against most other currencies. By the end of 1982, the dollar had risen by nearly 40 per cent against a weighted average of world currencies.

The 1982 world recession

The rise in the dollar had both an impact effect and a more sustained effect upon other industrialized economies. The impact effect upon oil-importing countries was the equivalent of a third oil price increase. This arose from the fact that oil prices administered by the oil-producers' cartel (OPEC) were denominated in dollars; so that a rise in the dollar against a particular currency, raised the price of oil in that currency. Over a period of years this effect would be offset by reductions in demand for oil and increases in alternative sources of supply; but in the meantime, the oil price increase reduced spending, with a depressing effect upon economic growth.

The second effect arose from the reaction of governments. As high dollar interest rates pulled funds into the USA, they were faced with the choice of following suit, or else of allowing their currencies to depreciate. Depreciation might have assisted their own economic growth, but only after a long time-lag, and only if its effect on competitiveness were not offset by pay increases. And it would have contributed to inflation, which most countries were trying successfully to reduce. The response to this dilemma was in most cases a compromise: interest rates were raised, but not sufficiently to avoid a substantial depreciation of other currencies against the dollar.

Even when interest rates subsequently fell back, the falls were less than those in rates of inflation so that real (inflation-corrected) interest rates continued to rise as illustrated by table 5.5.

Table 5.5 Real bond yields 1974–82

	Annual average percentage rates[a]			
	1974–77	1980	1981	1982
Britain	−3.9	−4.5	2.1	2.9
USA	0.3	−1.6	3.2	6.5
Japan	−5.3	1.9	2.9	5.1
France	−0.6	0.6	3.1	3.0
West Germany	2.8	3.0	4.7	3.3
Italy	−5.7	−5.7	−0.2	3.6

[a] Representative long-term bond yields, deflated by six-month moving averages of percentage changes, over twelve months, in consumer prices.

Source: Bank for International Settlements *Annual Report*, 1983.

The combined effect of the US budget deficit, and of the policies pursued by the governments of the industrialized countries, was a further brief world recession in 1982. The depth of the 1982 recession varied widely: for the OECD countries as a whole GDP fell by less than 0.5 per cent; for some, output merely stagnated, and a few suffered sharp declines. Because of its self-sufficiency in oil and of its already tight monetary policies, the British economy was not directly affected. British exports must have suffered as a result of the fall which occurred in total world trade in manufactures, but they also benefited from buoyant demand in the oil-producing countries, to whom Britain was a major supplier.

The debt problem

The effect upon the developing countries was to put many of them into a sustained financial crisis. Economic collapse of the non-OPEC developing countries had been successfully averted by loans from commercial banks in Britain, the USA and elsewhere, financed largely from OPEC deposits. These loans had been used to pay for imports, and the severe restrictions upon economic activity which would otherwise have been necessary to reduce their balance of payments deficits, had thereby been avoided. At the end of 1973, the bank debts of the non-OPEC developing countries had amounted to 60 per cent of their exports. By the end of 1982 they had risen to 130 per cent. Large loans for similar purposes had also been made by Western commercial banks to the Communist governments of Eastern Europe.

The expectation among the banks had been that interest payments would be met, and that repayment of capital could be deferred, for as long as needed, by further loans. But confidence in this assumption was shaken when, in 1980, Poland found itself unable to make the payments which were then due, and its payments had to be rescheduled. The subsequent rise in the dollar exchange rates raised the debt burden in terms of the currencies of the borrowing countries (most of whose debts were denominated in dollars) and the general increase in interest rates increased the cost of further loans. To make matters even worse, the recession among the industrialized countries reduced the demand for the developing countries' exports.[27]

By 1982 it seemed that default by one of the largest borrowers such as Argentina, Brazil or Mexico, could lead to bank failures in Britain and the USA, which might reduce confidence in the banking system to the point of general collapse. This consideration may have been one of the factors which persuaded the Federal Reserve Bank to relax its monetary policy toward the end of that year.

The US deficit in perspective

The budget deficit which was the unintended product of 'Reaganomics' was by far the largest ever incurred by any government, and its international repercussions were correspondingly dramatic. This was, however, largely a reflection of the relative size and influence of the US economy. Table 5.6 shows that, viewed as a proportion of GDP, it was not particularly remarkable by international standards.

Table 5.6 Public-sector financial deficits

| | Per cent of GDP | | | |
	1979	1980	1981	1982
Britain	4.3	4.4	3.2	2.5
USA	0.4	2.6	2.2	5.1
Japan	8.0	6.8	7.4	7.1
France	0.7	−0.3	1.6	2.6
Germany	2.7	3.2	4.0	3.9
Italy	10.0	9.5	12.4	13.0

Source: Bank for International Settlement *Annual Report*, 1983.

VIII 1982: THE RETURN OF FEEDBACK

Monetary policy

The term 'Medium-Term Financial Strategy' remained in use in 1982 and beyond, but the intentions announced in the 1982 budget statement differed substantially from those of the original 1980 statement. The intention of halving money supply growth by 1983/4, which had been the central feature of the original strategy, was formally abandoned. The hope of 'clawing back' earlier overshoots which had been expressed in the 1981 statement, was forgotten. And the target path was raised substantially and modified in form.

The target range for money supply growth in 1982/3, which had originally been 5–9 per cent, was changed to 8–12 per cent of a much higher base. This represented a reduction from the actual 14.5 per cent growth for the year to February 1982, but was nevertheless higher than even the starting range of the original strategy. Targets for the years after 1982/3 were to be announced nearer the time.

The target range was no longer to apply solely to sterling M3, but was to apply also to a broader, and to a narrower, measure of the money supply. The exchange rate was formally included among the factors which were to influence monetary policy, but no exchange rate target was announced.

The Chancellor's explanation of the revised strategy contained the following passage:

The new target represents a realistic restatement of our intention to maintain
a responsible monetary policy. It should be consistent with growth of money
GDP at 10 per cent a year with continued progress against inflation, and
with a strengthening recovery of the real economy.[28]

He gave no reason for the choice of 10 per cent for the growth of money
GDP, but it can be deduced from the budget report that it was expected to
be made up of an output growth of around 1.5 per cent, together with
inflation at 8.5 to 9 per cent.

More significant than the choice of the number, was the implication that
money GDP had been adopted as a target variable; especially when taken
in conjunction with the reference to growth of the real economy. Since the
stability of the relation between money supply growth and the growth of
money GDP, which had been predicted by monetarist theory, had not
been realized, the direct use of money GDP provided a means of evading a
source of uncertainty. But the statistics of money GDP are not available
often enough, or soon enough, to serve directly as a means of control. It
would thus be necessary to act on forecasts of money GDP, and to take
corrective action when their expected path diverged from what was
desired. If, as the statement implied, growth of the real economy was to be
one of the desired objectives, this too, would have to be forecast and
corrected for.

The statement thus signalled a significant departure from the original
strategy of adhering to predetermined monetary targets regardless of the
consequences for the real economy. (Treasury spokesmen were quick to
point out that ministers had never in so many words said that this had
been their intention.) It also represented a rejection of the advice of those
economists who had maintained that monetary policy would have only a
negligible and transitory effect upon the real economy. Above all it
indicated a return to a regime in which action would be guided by its
consequences as they became apparent. Feedback had proved to be
indispensable.

Fiscal policy

Fiscal policy had been running closer to target than was realized at the
time. The £10.5 billion public-sector borrowing requirement (PSBR) for
1981/2, which had been the intention at the time of the 1981 budget,
would have been 4.25 per ent of GDP, compared with the 3 per cent of the
original strategy. At the time of the 1982 budget, it was thought that the
outcome would indeed be close to £10.5 billion. In the event, the 1981/2
PSBR turned out to be £8.5 billion, or about 3.5 per cent of GDP.

For 1982/3, the original strategy had envisaged that there would be room, both to reduce the PSBR to 2.25 per cent of GDP, and to cut taxes by about 1.5 per cent of GDP. Public expenditure had risen faster than had been expected, however, and there remained little room for tax reductions even with a PSBR as high as 3.5 per cent of GDP.

Some tax reductions were nevertheless announced. There was a partial restoration of the real value of income tax allowances, following their reduction in the 1981 budget, and the employment-related payment by companies, known as the National Insurance Surcharge, was reduced. The net cost of these reliefs to the 1982/3 PSBR was expected to be £1.3 billion, taking it to 3.5 per cent of GDP. This was thought at the time to be lower than the 1981/2 outcome.

The next steps

What remained of the original strategy was a continued determination to give priority to the reduction of inflation, but the wish to get inflation down quickly was now tempered by a fear of aborting the economic recovery. On the figures available at the time, that recovery seemed to be weak and hesitant. Profitability was recovering from a very low level, but company liquidations were breaking all records, and still rising; and confidence remained low. Renewed government action to attack inflation would require a further financial squeeze, which might well put an end to the investment and stockbuilding which was the main driving force of the recovery.

The inflation rate was in any case falling, and there was every prospect that it would fall further. Average earnings had risen by 11 per cent in the year ending the first quarter of 1982, compared with 16.5 per cent in the previous year. Productivity had picked up rapidly, and wage costs per unit of output had risen by only 3 per cent, compared with 15 per cent in the previous year. Companies were, for the time being, taking the opportunity to rebuild profit margins, but could be expected before long to pass on their lower cost increases into lower price increases. The retail prices index had risen by under 10 per cent in the year to March 1982, and was confidently expected to show smaller increases later in the year.

Action on unemployment

The topic to which the Chancellor turned first in his budget speech was unemployment. Its level was, by then, eight times higher than it had been twenty years previously, and it was still rising. It was no longer possible to regard this as a transitory problem which could be left to solve itself by the action of the self-righting forces in the economy. There was, he said, a clear case for direct action by the government. But he placed the main responsibility elsewhere:

> The key point is this. Somewhere in the gap between the levels of income which we pay those out of work and the earnings of those who have a job are rates of pay which those now out of work would be glad to take if they had a chance. But convention and a narrowness of vision prevent these bargains being struck. When jobs are in abundance, any employer will make sure that he keeps up with the market, by offering high enough pay to recruit and train the workers he needs. And trade unions will naturally encourage him. But when business is tight and jobs are scarce, the same employer owes it to the unemployed, as well as to his own employees, to react to the changed market, to pay at rates which leave room for him to earn enough for further business and further investment – and so for new jobs. In this situation too, trade unions have – or should have – exactly the same interest. That is the best service that any employer or union leader can offer to the unemployed.[29]

IX JOBS, PAY AND THE UNIONS

The Chancellor's reference to 'income which we pay those out of work' reflected what was at the time a popular cause of concern. There had been many newspaper stories about people who were better off when unemployed than they had been when working. The behaviour of people who were in, or close to, this position was referred to by the Prime Minister and others as 'the "why work?" syndrome'; and the possibility that the benefit system was contributing to unemployment received a good deal of attention. There was also much debate about the effects of union power and of pay rates upon unemployment.

The effects of benefits

Analysis of the possibility that the benefit system was contributing to unemployment was made difficult by the complexity of that system. Unemployment Benefit, under the British system, was payable during the first year of unemployment to those who remained available for work. From the beginning of 1982, this was paid at a flat rate, regardless of the receipient's circumstances. But Supplementary Benefit, related to family size and income, was also paid in order to supplement unemployment benefit and to replace it after it had run out. There was, in addition, a range of means-tested benefits which could be claimed by heads of poorer families whether they were working or unemployed.

A 1978/9 survey of unemployed men showed that:

(1) nearly 50 per cent got benefits which replaced less than half of their net earnings;

(2) 25 per cent had incomes out of work equal to at least 80 per cent of their incomes in work; and,

(3) 9 per cent appeared to have higher incomes out of work than in work.[30]

Analysis of the results of this survey indicated that a 10 per cent reduction in benefit would reduce the average duration of male unemployment by around 3 per cent. The effect was shown to be greatest for young people. Although high ratios of out-of-work to in-work incomes applied only to married men with two or more children, unemployed men in this category were the least likely to be deterred from seeking work.[31]

On the basis of this evidencce, it appeared that the direct influence of unemployment benefits upon unemployment had been relatively small. Since they had not risen faster than earnings over the previous twenty years, it seemed unlikely that they could on their own have accounted for much of the rise in unemployment over that period.

The possibility remained, that unemployment benefits had played a part, in combination with other factors. A thesis to this effect was put forward by Professor Minford of Liverpool University. His stylized model of the economy consisted of a unionized sector and a non-unionized sector. Wages in the non-unionized sector are determined by supply and demand, but in the unionized sector they are raised to a higher level by the exercise of union monopoly power. As union power increases, wages in that sector rise; and the demand for labour there, falls. The displaced labour seeks work in the non-union sector, and this puts a downward pressure on wages there. But the high level of unemployment benefits prevents wages from falling enough, and most of those displaced became unemployed.

The results of a complex econometric analysis of trends in unionization, benefits and unemployment, which Professor Minford also presented, suggested that a 10 per cent reduction in benefits could reduce unemployment by between 23 and 40 per cent.[32] But other analyses of similar data indicated a very much smaller effect.[33]

An alternative theory suggested that benefits had an effect upon collective pay bargaining in all sectors. Employees might be expected to be influenced by the risk of becoming unemployed as a result of too high a pay increase, but the weight which they attach to that risk would depend upon the loss of income which they would suffer on becoming unemployed. Thus the higher the level of unemployment benefit, the more people would become unemployed.[34] This explanation did not depend upon union power, nor upon irrational bargaining behaviour, but only upon the existence of unemployment benefits.

On a sufficiently broad view of the unemployment problem, qualitative theories about the effects of unemployment benefits could, however, be dismissed as trivial. It could hardly be doubted, after all, that the more unpleasant unemployment is made, the greater pains people will go to in order to avoid it. The non-trivial question was whether the benefits of the consequent reduction in unemployment would be sufficient to outweigh the losses which would be suffered by those who remained unemployed. Economic analysis could not answer this question, and the pointers which it provided were conflicting.

The political answer to this question soon became evident. Every move made by the government to reduce the real value of unemployment benefits, exposed it to a humiliating defeat at the hand of its own supporters in Parliament.

Union power

The political atmosphere concerning the trade unions was, however, different: opinion polls were continuing to indicate that they were regarded as too powerful, even by their own members. The policy issue was thus essentially a tactical one: how to reduce trade union power without suffering the disruption which followed previous attempts to do so. The question of the expected benefits to employment nevertheless remained relevant – if only as a guide to how fast to move and what risks to take.

Minford's results suggested that the benefits to unemployment would be very large. His econometric analysis showed a 9 per cent fall in unemployment resulting from a 1 per cent reduction in unionization. The union/non-union wage difference implied by his findings was over 25 per cent; which some others found implausibly high. A later analysis, which took account of job attributes, put the figure at 10 per cent for 1968/9;[35] and other estimates suggested that it may have risen to around 12 per cent by 1982. There were indications, moreover, that very large advantages enjoyed by union members in some industries – notably mining and printing – over non-members doing similar work elsewhere, were balanced by much smaller differentials in most industries.

Other researchers using the same data as Minford, but covering a longer period, failed to find a significant effect of union membership on unemployment.[36] There were indications from a 1980 survey, however, that firms with high union membership are less likely to expand their employment than firms with low or zero union membership.[37]

Trade union legislation

Although some ministers had favoured radical changes to trade union law, the tactics adopted had from the outset been to take a cautious step-by-step approach.

Unlike most other countries, Britain had never adopted a framework of positive legal rights for trade unions. Instead, the law afforded immunity to unions and their officials (but not to ordinary employees) against a wide range of civil actions for damages resulting from things done in furtherance of a trade dispute. One line of attack was to reduce the scope of those immunities. This had the advantage of avoiding the imposition of criminal penalties or the setting up of special courts, but the disadvantage that legal action would be at the discretion of the injured parties.

The first step was to remove immunity for 'secondary picketing'; that is to say, picketing not at an employee's own place of work; and for 'secondary industrial action', including action to induce breach of contract, if it were not against a party to the industrial dispute. This would put union funds at risk if, for example, the miners' tactics of picketing power stations were to be repeated. A further step was to remove immunity for strikes which had not been supported by a secret ballot of the union members involved.

Another move was to raise the financial penalties suffered by individual strikers. Unemployment Benefit had never been available to strikers, but Supplementary Benefit could be claimed for strikers' families. The law was changed to 'deem' that all strikers received strike pay from their unions – although this was often not the case – thus reducing their families' entitlement to benefit. Employers were free to dismiss strikers for breach of contract – although they seldom did – and the law was changed to make it more difficult for those dismissed to take legal action for unfair dismissal on the grounds of victimization. Those dismissed were in any case not entitled to unemployment benefit.[38]

A cautious attack was also made on the institution of the 'closed shop'. Over 20 per cent of the workforce were in firms in which membership of a trade union was effectively a condition of employment. This was regarded by many Conservatives as an intolerable infringment of individual liberty, but it was an arrangement which was favoured by many employers on the grounds that it facilitated negotiations with their employees. The government's tactics were to enable those dismissed for non-membership of a union to claim compensation unless the closed shop arrangement had been approved by 85 per cent of those voting in a secret ballot. Since most closed shops seemed likely to get this level of support, the effect was not expected to be very great.

These legislative changes were to alter the balance of power in the confrontations which were to follow in the next few years. However, their short-term effect upon industrial relations, pay bargaining, and employment, could not have been significant. Other influences, particularly the rise in unemployment, had in any case reduced trade union power. Union membership, which had risen from 45 per cent to 55 per cent of all employees between 1970 and 1980, was by this time falling sharply. The influence of the trade unions upon decision-making in British firms had always been small, and their power on matters other than pay had been largely restricted to that of obstructing the implementation of decisions once made. There were signs in 1982 that a less obstructive stance was being adopted, particularly in industries under threat. A few employers were following the Japanese practice of involving their employees directly in decisions concerning working methods, but in most firms the traditional division between managers and managed was preserved.[39]

Pay and employment

It had become evident, after two years of the Medium-Term Financial Strategy, that the cost in terms of unemployment of reducing the inflation rate had been very much higher than had been predicted by Professors Friedman and Laidler. Wage inflation had fallen, but it had been less responsive to unemployment than had been expected. The responsiveness of real wages to unemployment had over the years been lower in Britain than in any other OECD country[40] – a fact which some had attributed to a lower degree of social consensus.[41] In manufacturing in particular, the share of labour in value-added was higher and had risen faster, as is indicated in table 5.7.

Table 5.7 Shares of labour in manufacturing valued added (per cent)

	1969	1973	1978	1981
Britain	70.0	71.4	74.0	82.8
USA	69.1	71.6	71.6	75.6
Japan	40.3	44.5	50.2	–
France	42.0	44.8	45.6	47.4
West Germany	52.3	58.8	59.5	63.3

Source: 'Real wages and unemployment in the OECD countries', Jeffrey D. Sachs, Brookings Papers 1, 1983.

A number of investigators estimated the extent to which lower real wages would have reduced unemployment. The results suggested that employment might have been 0.5 per cent to 1 per cent (110,000–220,000) higher if real wages had been 1 per cent lower, but that even this range was subject to a substantial margin of error. The gain in employment would have come from higher market shares resulting from improved international competitiveness and from a substitution of labour for capital in production processes and products. Both effects would have taken some years to come through. In the meantime there might have been some fall in employment because of reduced personal spending, but this effect would have been offset before long by higher spending by firms.[42]

Other results suggested that the responsiveness of employment among particular groups to movements in their relative wages would have been higher. It was estimated, for example, that a fall of 1 per cent in the pay of men under twenty-one relative to the pay of men over twenty-one, would have raised employment of the under twenty-ones by at least 2 per cent.[43]

On the basis of this and other evidence, much was made of the proposition that people were 'pricing themselves out of jobs', but little by way of policy action was to follow. Close attention was for a time given to the possibility of putting an end to the setting of statutory minimum wages by Wages Councils, which regulated the pay of some 2.5 million workers. A study of their effect on the clothing industry suggested that they had been responsible for around half of the 40 per cent loss in employment in that industry between 1975 and 1978.[44] But an international agreement prevented the immediate abolition of Wages Councils, which in any case had the support of many employers. The government restricted itself to removing their powers over the pay of young people and instructing them to have regard for the employment consequences of their decisions.

Since the government was opposed in principle to any form of incomes policy, there was little else that could be done beyond repeating the Chancellor's admonitions. Even this presented some difficulty, since it implied a departure from their philosophy to the extent of suggesting that normal bargaining considerations should be put aside in the public interest. The tripartite National Economic Development Council was used as a forum for such admonitions – which were not, however, well received by the representatives of the trade unions who attended.

X   THE FALKLANDS FACTOR

In the spring of 1982, Britain fought a brief war with Argentina. The issue was the status of British settlers on the disputed territory of the Falkland Islands. A Foreign Office proposal to cede formal sovereignty to Argentina in exchange for continued British administration of the islands had been resisted by the Islanders, and was vehemently rejected by spokesmen for all three parties when put to Parliament in 1980. Neither Britain nor Argentina was disposed to submit its case to an international court. In April 1982, Argentinian troops invaded and occupied the Islands. With the support of all parties, the British government sent a task force which recaptured the islands. The war cost the lives of 225 British, and 584 Argentinian servicemen. Its result was to preserve the status of the 1,800 Islanders, and to establish a British commitment to defend the Islands against further attack. The immediate cost to the British taxpayer was probably in the region of £900 million, and the total cost, including the future commitment, was likely to reach over £3 billion by 1985/6.

The effect of the war upon the government's popularity – and particularly that of Mrs Thatcher – was decisive. Her personal support in the opinion polls, which had been 36 per cent in March, rose to 59 per cent at the end of the war. The 'Falklands factor' had become the dominant influence upon the political scene.

XI 1982–83: THE END OF TERM

In the fifteen months which followed the 1982 budget, the government was also able to lay claim to a number of victories on the domestic front. There were signs that trade union power was weakening, wage claims were moderating, productivity was growing rapidly, output was recovering, and the inflation rate was falling. On the financial side, things were at last going according to the plan laid down in the latest Medium-Term Financial Strategy; and in March 1983 the Chancellor was able to announce substantial tax reductions. It was a period which a Treasury minister of the time was later to describe as 'coasting home'.

Victory over inflation

The most notable of these developments was an unexpectedly rapid fall in inflation. At the time of the 1982 budget, retail prices were 10.4 per cent up on a year previously and the Treasury were forecasting a fall to 7.5 per cent by the second quarter of 1983. In the event, it fell by that time to under 4 per cent.

The fall in inflation owed something to a reduced growth in the prices of imported commodities under the influence of the world recession, and something to lower mortgage interest rates, following the easing of monetary policy. But the principal influence was the fall which took place in unit labour costs. With average earnings growing at around 8 per cent a year, and output per person growing at a remarkable 4 per cent a year, earnings per unit of output were rising by only about 4 per cent, compared with 15 per cent two years previously. In addition, the reduction in the National Insurance Surcharge reduced the cost of labour to employers. The happy situation had arisen in which the real wage received by employees was rising and the real wage paid by employers was falling.

Some of the factors contributing to the fall in the inflation rate were clearly temporary, and it was expected to rise again in the latter part of 1983. But the rise was expected to be modest: it could fairly be claimed that inflationary expectations had been broken.

Continuing recovery

The recovery of output, which had started in the second quarter of 1981, continued through 1982 and into 1983 at an average rate of about 2.2 per cent a year. Its main driving force was a strong growth of consumers' expenditure. This was not so much due to the rise in real earnings, as to a fall in the proportion of personal incomes which went into savings. Real personal disposable income did not in fact rise throughout the period. During the first half of 1982, the rise in earnings of those in work was more than offset by the fall in income suffered by the increasing numbers of the unemployed. The rise in spending during this period came from a reduction in the proportion of income saved, and from increased borrowing (some of it in the form of mortgages raised ostensibly for housing purposes). The fall in inflation had itself provided a stimulus because it reduced the need to add to existing savings in order to preserve their real value. After the middle of 1982, a strong rise in real personal disposable income provided a further stimulus to spending.

Although output was recovering, employment was not. Between the second quarters of 1981 and 1983, a 4.4 per cent rise in output was more than offset by a 7 per cent rise in output per employee; and employment fell 2.5 per cent, or about 530,000. There was also a small rise in the working population, and unemployment rose by 600,000 to over 3 million. From the early months of 1983, however, productivity growth slackened, employment stabilized, and unemployment ceased to rise. The Secretary of State for Employment expressed the view that a plateau had been reached. The news was bad, but it did not seem to be getting worse.

Industrial relations

There were many signs of a weakening of the power of the trade unions. By 1983, union membership had fallen by nearly two million from its 1979 peak of 13.3 million, and the numbers of working days lost in strikes had fallen to 3.75 million, compared with over 29 million in 1979, and an average of 8.7 million over the previous five years.

Several episodes had shown how the industrial relations climate had changed. An attempt by British Rail to make a pay increase for drivers conditional upon their union's acceptance of more flexible working practices led, in July 1982, to a strike which brought the entire railway system, including most of the London Underground, to a halt. British Rail's management responded with a threat to sack the strikers and close the rail network. The strike ended on terms put forward by the Trades Union Congress under which the threat of sacking was withdrawn and the drivers' union accepted 'flexible rostering' with safeguards. Later in 1982, there was an attempt by officials of the National Union of Miners to call a strike over pay and against the National Coal Board's proposals to close a number of uneconomic pits. The attempt failed because a ballot of the union's members did not give it the 55 per cent support which was required by the union's constitution. There were many other occasions on which union memberships proved to be more reluctant to strike than their leaders, and on which employers took advantage of the new mood to put an end to uneconomic working practices.

A connection was suggested by commentators between the 'new realism' among union members and the increase which seemed to have occurred in the growth rate of productivity. One government minister predicted that British firms would emerge 'leaner but fitter' from the recession, but it was not clear from the evidence whether a new productivity trend had been established or whether there had simply been a once-for-all recessional labour shake-out.

Fiscal and monetary policy

A mood of optimism was also developing among Treasury ministers. In the autumn of 1982, Treasury forecasts were indicating that the £9.5 billion public-sector borrowing target, which had been set at the time of the budget, was likely to be undershot by at least £2 billion because of increased oil revenues and reduced housing expenditure. Monetary trends were also favourable, despite a fall in bank lending rates to 10 per cent in October from the peak 16 per cent of the previous October. The various measures of the money supply (except the mainly non-interest-bearing M1) looked like falling within their new target range. There seemed to be room for immediate tax reductions.

In his Autumn Statement, the Chancellor announced a further reduction of the employment-related National Insurance Surcharge from 2.5 per cent to 1.5 per cent from April 1983, and the intention to bring part of this forward to give the effect of a 0.5 per cent reduction in 1982–3. Public-sector employers were not to benefit, and the cost was to be partly offset by an increase in the normal National Insurance contributions by employees and employers.

A threat to the Chancellor's strategy was, however, developing from the weakness in the demand for oil brought about by the world reccession, and by rumours that the oil price might collapse. Though beneficial to the economy in the long run, this could have so reduced tax revenues as to threaten the government's borrowing target. Under the influence of these rumours, and of uncertainties about American interest rate prospects, the sterling exchange rate fell 14 per cent between November 1982 and March 1983. In March 1983 the OPEC cartel reached an agreement to reduce the reference oil price by $5 a barrel to $29 a barrel, and to stabilize it at that level by restricting output. Britain was not a member of the cartel but was widely believed to have colluded in that agreement.

With that threat removed, the Chancellor was able, in his March budget, to make some substantial tax reductions. Income tax allowances and thresholds were raised by 14 per cent, compared with the 5.5 per cent needed to keep pace with inflation. There was also an assortment of other tax reductions, mainly intended to stimulate business. The borrowing target for 1983–4 was set at £8 billion – 2.75 per cent of GDP, compared with the previous year's target of 3.5 per cent. It was believed at the time of the budget that the 1982–3 target had been undershot by £2 billion, however. The contingency reserve in the 1982–3 budget had been set at £2.5 billion and the undershoot was taken to indicate that a reserve of that size was no longer necessary. In the 1983–4 budget, the contingency reserve was reduced to £1.1 billion, and this had enabled the tax reductions to be pitched about £1.4 billion higher than would otherwise have been consistent with the borrowing target. It was only later discovered that the 1982–3 target had not been undershot by £2 billion, but only by less than £0.5 billion. A substantial part of the 1983 tax reductions could thus be attributed to estimating errors.

The 1983 general election campaign

By mid-April the opinion polls were giving the Conservatives a five-point lead over Labour, and the Liberal/SDP Alliance was less of a threat than it had been. The results of local government elections confirmed these trends, and in early May the Prime Minister called a general election for 9 June – some eleven months before she was constitutionally required to do so.

The Conservative election manifesto spoke with pride of past achievements and with confidence for the future:

In the past four years, Britain had recovered her confidence and self-respect. We have regained the regard and admiration of other nations. . . . The bravery, skill and determination with which Britain's task force recaptured the Falklands reverberated around the world. . . . Prices are rising more slowly than at any time in the past fifteen years. . . . Output is rising. . . . We have laid the fundations for a dynamic and prosperous future.

On economic policy the manifesto was brief and not very specific:

We shall maintain firm control of public spending and borrowing. . . . We shall continue to set out a responsible financial strategy which will gradually reduce the growth of the money supply. . . .

The remainder of the Conservative programme included further trade union legislation, a major programme of denationalization, improved discounts for the sale of council houses and continued subsidies for agriculture.

The Labour manifesto spoke of four years of Tory failure:

unemployment and industrial decline . . . the damage done to our social services . . . the dangerous commitment to nuclear weapons . . . the deep sense of bitterness and despair felt among so many sections of the community.

The task confronting Labour was to:

heal these wounds and rekindle among the British people a new sense of unity and common purpose. . . . [and to] bring about a fundamental and irreversible shift in the balance of power and wealth in favour of working people and their families.

The Labour Party's economic proposals were highly specific. The aim would be to reduce unemployment below one million in five years. This would be done by a massive programme of public expenditure supported by controls on imports, prices, and foreign exchange (but not on pay). It was also proposed to end council house sales at a discount, to renationalize industries which had been denationalized, and to repeal the Conservatives' employment legislation. On international policy, Britain would withdraw from the European Community, US nuclear bases (together with the planned deployment of cruise missiles) would be scrapped, and the British independent nuclear deterrent, Polaris, would be phased out.

The Liberal/SDP Alliance proposed a modest reflation together with powers to introduce a tax-based incomes policy. The voting system would be changed to one of proportional representation. Membership of the European Community would continue, and disarmament would be multilateral.

The election result

In terms of popular support, the result was a further setback for the two major parties. The Conservative Party got 700,000 fewer votes than in 1979, its support falling from 33 per cent to 31 per cent of the electorate. Such a result could have signalled defeat – as had an only slightly better percentage in 1974 – but for the Labour Party's disastrous loss of support, from 28 per cent to 20 per cent of the electorate. The votes lost by those two parties went to the Liberal/SDP Alliance; but its support was too widely spread to secure many seats in Parliament. In terms of seats, the result was, as shown in table 5.8, a landslide victory for the Conservatives, who gained an unassailable majority of 144 over all other parties combined.

Table 5.8 The election result, 1983

	Votes	MPs
Conservative	13,010,782	397
Labour	8,456,504	209
Liberal/SDP Alliance	7,781,764	23
Scottish and Welsh Nationalists	457,284	4
Northern Ireland (various)	962,940	17

The experiment continues

Thus the British Experiment did not end with the 1983 general election but was to continue for another parliamentary term. The story of the experiment breaks off here, however, for an overview of the decade as a whole.

NOTES

1. Budget Statement, 26 March 1980.
2. 'Monetary Policy', Third Report from the Treasury and Civil Service Committee, Sesssion 1980–1, House of Commons, 24 February 1981, paras 4.33 – 4.57.

3. *Financial Statement and Budget Report* (HMSO, 26 March 1980).
4. Speech to the *Financial Times* 1980 Euromarkets' conference in London, on 21 January 1980 (as reported in HM Treasury Economic Progress Report March 1980).
5 'Monetary Policy', para. 7.30.
6. *Financial statement and Budget Report 1981–2*, (HMSO,.10 March 1981), p. 16.
7. Later confirmed in: J. Bruce-Gardyne, *Mrs Thatcher's First Administration* (MacMillan, 1984), p. 89.
8. D. Laidler, 'Monetarism: an interpretation and an assessment', *Economic Journal*, March 1981, pp. 4, 25.
9. Reported in: W. Keegan, *Mrs Thatcher's Economic Experiment* (Penguin, 1984), p. 159; – and confirmed in A. Walters, *Britain's Economic Renaissance* (Oxford University Press, 1986), p. 145, footnote.
10. Speech at the Conservative Party Conference, Brighton, October 1980.
11. 'Financing of the Nationalised Industries' (Eighth Report from the Treasury and Civil Service Committee, Session 1980–1), para. 2.1.
12. See 'The Department of Energy's Estimates' (Second Report from the Select Committee on Energy, Session 1981–2), para. 33.
13. Statement to the House of Commons by the Secretary of State for Energy, 18 December 1981.
14. 'The Government's Statement on the new Nuclear Power Programme' (First Report from the Select Committee on Energy, Session 1980–1, 13 February 1981), paras 65–117.
15. The Government's Reply to the First Report of the Select Committee on Industry and Trade, Session 1980–1 (Cmnd 8247, May 1981).
16. K. Clements and L. Sjaastad, 'How Protection Taxes Exporters' (Trade Policy Research Centre, 1985).
17. A. Cairncross, P. D. Henderson and Z. A. Silberston, 'Problems of Industrial Recovery', *Midland Bank Review*, spring 1982.
18. See D. Metcalf, 'Special employment measures', *Midland Bank Review*, autumn/winter 1982.
19. A. Budd and M. Beenstock, 'Economic viewpoint', *London Business School Economic Outlook*, February 1981, p. 23.
20. See Lord Scarman, *The Scarman Report: The Brixton Disorders, April 10 to 12* (Penguin, 1982).
21. *The Times*, leader, 9 October 1981.
22. See P. Whitehead, *The Writing on the Wall* (Michael Joseph, 1985), p. 382.
23. For a detailed account of these happenings, see D. Kogan and M. Kogan, *The Battle for the Labour Party* (Fontana, 1982).
24. For a concise analysis see OECD Economic Surveys 1981–82, the United States (OECD, June 1982).
25. See S. H. Axilrod, 'US monetary policy in recent years: an overview', *Federal Reserve Bulletin*, January 1985, p. 14.
26. For a summary, see B. Bartlett, 'Supply-side economics: theory and evidence', *National Westminster Bank Quarterly Review*, February 1985 – and for an inside story see P. C. Roberts, *The Supply Side Revolution* (Harvard University Press, 1984).
27. For an account of the world debt problem see Bank for International Settlements 53rd Annual Report (Basle, June 1983).

28. Budget Statement, 9 March 1982 (Hansard Col. 733).
29. Ibid., Col. 731.
30. D. Wood, 'Men Registering as Unemployed in 1978 – a Longitudinal Study' (Department of Health and Social Security, Working Paper No. 1, 1982); see also B. Davies, L. Hamill, S. Moylan and C. H. Smee, 'Incomes in and out of work', *Dept. of Employment Gazette*, June 1982, p. 237.
31. W. Naredranathan, S. Nickell, and J. Stern, 'Unemployment benefits revisited' *Economic Journal*, June 1983.
32. P. Minford, *Unemployment, Cause and Cure*, (Martin Robertson, 1983).
33. See the review by Nickell and the response by Minford in the *Economic Journal*, December 1984.
34. J. Oswald, 'The microeconomic theory of the trade union', *Economic Journal*, December 1984.
35. A. Shah, 'Job attributes and the size of the union/non-union wage differential', *Economica*, November 1984.
36. S. Nickell and M. Andrews, 'Unions, Real Wages and Employment in Britain 1951–79' (Oxford Economic Papers, 1983).
37. N. Millward, 'Trade Unions and Employment Growth: an Establishment-level Analysis' (unpublished paper, based on data from *Workplace Industrial Relations in Britain*, by W. W. Daniel and N. Millward, (Heinemann, 1983).
38. For a concise summary of the legislative changes see Minford, *Unemployment*, appendix D.
39. For case studies see D. A. Buchanan and D. Boddy, *Organisation in the Computer Age* (Gower, 1983).
40. D. Grubb, R. Jackman and R. Layard, 'Wage rigidity and unemployment in OECD countries', *European Economic Review* (North Holland, 1983).
41. J. McCallum, 'Inflation and social consensus in the seventies', *Economic Journal*, December 1983.
42. For a review of the evidence see *The Relationship between Employment and Wages – Empirical Evidence for the United Kingdom* (HM Treasury, 1985).
43. Wells, 'Relative pay and employment of young people', *Dept of Employment Gazette* August 1980, p. 230.
44. P. Morgan, D. Patterson and R. Barrie, 'Wage Floors in the Clothing Industry 1950–81' (Department of Employment Research Paper No. 52).

6

Decade of Discontent: an Overview of the Period 1973–83

I INTRODUCTION

Chapter 1 began with a brief speculation about the changes which would have been observed by a traveller returning to Britain in 1983 after a ten-year absence. It went on to look at the trends and ideas which had been established before he left. Chapters 2–5 recounted events as they occurred during the intervening period, together with the attitudes and ideas which shaped them. In this chapter, those events and ideas are reconsidered from a later perspective.

The returning traveller would view those events and ideas from a perspective which for several reasons would be different from that of a person who had stayed in Britain. Obvious, tangible changes which had occured gradually (such as the increase in litter) would be evident to him but might have escaped the notice of the stay-at-home. He could be presumed to have missed the misleading statistics and mistaken forecasts which had so often distorted the perceptions of observers at the time. Above all, his view of events would not be influenced by the reports which had appeared in the media at the time. In the spheres, particularly of economic and social policy, these were usually coloured by the impressions which the politicians of the time attempted to create. Objective measures of trends affecting such matters as public expenditure, crime, education and the social services thus frequently conflicted with popular perceptions.

Even a ten-year perspective does not, however, remove the difficulty of distinguishing underlying trends from transitory variations. On the evidence so far presented it might, for example, be concluded that the problem of conforming to monetary targets had at last been solved. By the autumn of 1985 it had become clear that this was not the case. Thus it would be foolish not to make use of all the hindsight which is available. This and the following chapter are written from the perspective of autumn 1986 and, where it seems necessary, use is made in this chapter of the statistics available at that time concerning events after mid-1983. On past experience, substantial revisions to those statistics can be expected over the next few years.

It is not possible to review the trends of the decade without inviting comparisons with what 'might have been.' The difficulty of making such comparisons can hardly be overstated. It is tempting, for example, to attribute the world-wide setback in economic growth solely to the rise in the price of oil, but to do so is to assume that growth would otherwise have continued as before. The task of reconstructing such a hypothetical 'might-have-been' world is, in fact, an immensely complex one. It requires an understanding of what otherwise would have happened to exchange rates, trade flows, the policies of governments, and a host of other interacting factors. It also requires an accurate interpretation of the signs of change which were evident before the oil price increased. Justice could not be done to such a task without the use of a large forecasting model – and experience suggests that, even then, the result would be very much open to question. The comparisons which are made with previous post-war trends in what follows do not, therefore, imply an assumption that those trends were sustainable: indeed there are grounds for regarding the post-war period up to 1972 as historically atypical.

The interpretation of comparisons with overseas trends presents similar diffiulties. The accuracy of such comparisons is in any case open to a certain amount of doubt. The collection of economic statistics requires the adoption of arbitrary distinctions, and there is no guarantee that such distinctions are similarly drawn in different countries.

While these difficulties prompt caution in drawing conclusions, they do not mean that nothing can be learned from a scrutiny of past trends. History may be an imperfect guide, but it is better than mythology.

A review of the decade should, in particular, throw some light on the conduct of economic policy. What follows is, however, influenced by a presumption that the influence of policy upon events is smaller and more uncertain than is popularly supposed; that the room for manoeuvre is more closely limited; and that imperfect understanding of human behaviour is a greater obstacle to effective policy design. Accordingly, after a summary of the main trends affecting life in Britain, the influences, first of overseas events, and then of other domestic developments are examined below, before turning to the influence of government policies.

II THE MAIN TRENDS

Output and productive capacity

The growth rate of British GDP between 1973 and 1983 averaged 0.9 per cent a year, compared with 2.8 per cent a year over the previous post-war period. This is believed to be the lowest growth rate over any comparable period since 1856 – except for 1913–24, which included the severe depression following the First World War. Of that 0.9 per cent a year growth, 0.6 per cent a year was accounted for by oil and gas production from the North Sea; a capital-intensive activity which contributed little to British employment. The output of the remainder of the economy thus grew at an average rate of only 0.3 per cent a year.

Average figures of this sort do not, however, convey a very useful impression of the true course of events. (Besides being sometimes rather sensitive to the choice of period.) Since 1973 was a peak year, the choice, instead, of 1972 would have raised the average. A graphical presentation,

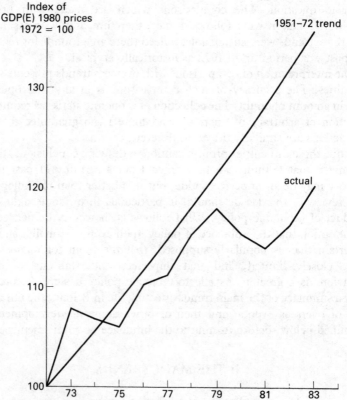

Figure 6.1   **GDP 1973–83 compared with 1951–72 trend**
Source: CSO *Economic Trends* 1985

such as figure 6.1, gives a fairer and more illuminating impression. This shows the brief output surge which followed the unprecedented fiscal and monetary expansion of 1972, and the fall in output which followed the oil price increase of 1973. During the four years of recovery from 1975 to 1979, output can be seen to rise at almost the 1951/72 trend rate. A full recovery from a recession is normally taken to have occurred when output itself (and not just its growth rate) has returned to its previous trend. In this sense, the economy had not fully recovered when it was again plunged into recession in 1980. As the graph shows, the recovery which started in 1981 brought the growth rate back to roughly its previous trend, but there was not, by 1983, any sign that the gap between current and trend output was being closed.

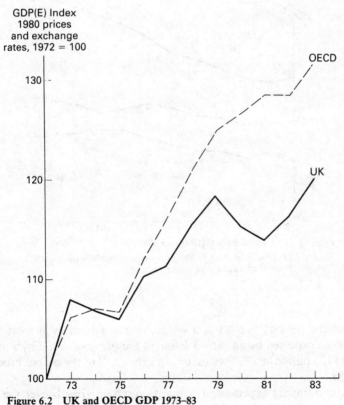

Figure 6.2   UK and OECD GDP 1973–83

Sources: CSO *Economic Trends* 1985
OECD *National Accounts* 1985

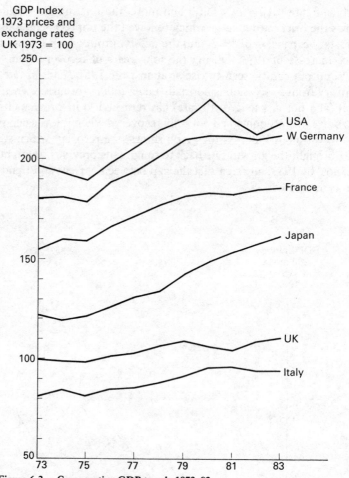

GDP Index
1973 prices and
exchange rates
UK 1973 = 100

Figure 6.3. Comparative GDP trends 1973–83
Source: Derived from OECD National Accounts 1985 taking 1973
figures of Table 1.14 as a baseline

Over the period 1973–83 as a whole, output fell short of what might
have been expected by an extrapolation of the previous trend by a total of
about £125 billion at 1980 prices, or just over a half of the output produced
in 1983.

Other countries experienced reduced economic growth over the same
period but, as figure 6.2 shows, the OECD countries as a whole
maintained a faster growth than Britain's. The 1975 recesssion was milder

for them – and the 1981 recession very much milder – than for Britain; but they suffered a further brief recession in 1982, which Britain escaped. Figure 6.3 shows how output of five of the major economies was affected, and how Britain's relative position declined.

In Britain, the 3 per cent growth in output (excluding North Sea output) which occurred between 1973 and 1983 was made up of falls of over 15 per cent in the output of the manufacturing and construction industries, and of 2 per cent in the output of distribution, hotels and catering; more than offset by a 22 per cent increase in agricultural output, a 9 per cent increase in output of transport and communications, and a 28 per cent increase in the output of other services. A major change had thus occurred in the structure of the economy. Britain's traditional role as an exporter of manufactures and an importer of food and fuels had been reversed: by 1983 the country was a net exporter of fuels, was self-sufficient in most of those agricultural products which can be produced in temperate climates, and was a net importer of manufactures. A particularly dramatic example of the decline in manufacturing output was passenger car production, which fell by 40 per cent, despite a 10 per cent increase in domestic demand (and despite restrictions upon imports from Japan).

It seems possible that part of the fall in output below its previous trend (depicted in figure 6.1) was accounted for by a similar setback in productive capacity. Whether this is so cannot be established, because no measurement of the country's productive capacity has been made. Estimates are available of net additions to the stock of fixed capital, but these are based upon arbitrary (though reasonable) assumptions about obsolescence and scrapping. These estimates indicate that the rate of addition to capital stock in 1983 was just over half what it had been in 1973.[1] In the manufacturing and construction industries, scrapping and obsolescence are estimated to have outweighed new investment after 1980, so that there was acually a reduction in capital stock over the following three years.

The gross addition to the stock of capital (before allowing for scrapping and obsolescence) for the economy as a whole in 1983 was only slightly below its 1973 level; growths of 17 per cent and 10 per cent for the private sector and for the nationalized industries respectively, being roughly offset by a fall in government investment of 65 per cent (the latter figure being somewhat inflated by the treatment of council house sales as negative investment). Routine maintenance of the public sector's capital stock had frequently been postponed, as evidenced by a backlog of repairs to hospitals, schools, roads, drainage and housing running into many billions of pounds. A 1981 survey had shown that of the country's 21.7 million dwellings (housing 20.8 million households), 1.1 million were unfit for habitation and a further 574,000 were in a state of serious disrepair.[2]

The labour market

In round figures, the working population (employed plus unemployed)
rose by one million between 1973 and 1983, employment fell by one and a
half million, and unemployment consequently rose by two and a half
million. Here again, an examination of trends within the period, as
depicted in figure 6.4, is more illuminating than the overall numbers. In

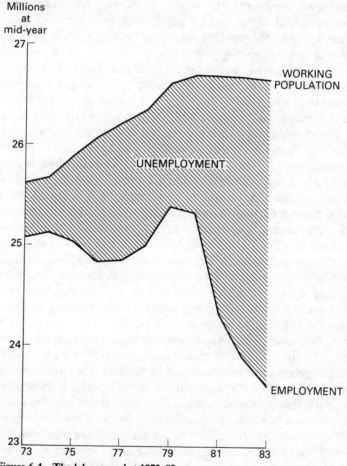

Figure 6.4 The labour market 1973–83
Source: *Employment Gazette* April 1985 Historical Statistics No 1

the period from 1973 to around 1979, the increase in the population of working age was augmented by an increase in activity rates (the proportion working or seeking work) to produce a rapid increase in the working population. After 1979, the population of working age continued to increase at about the same rate, but this was offset by a decline in activity rates, so that the working population remained broadly stable. This was because, before 1979, the increase in female activity rates outweighed the downward trend in male activity rates; and after 1979, female activity rates ceased to rise, and male activity rates continued their downward trend.

In 1973 and 1974, employment was close to the post-war maximum, and after falling by about 300,000 in the subsequent recession, it rose by 500,000 to reach a new peak in 1979. The rise in unemployment between 1973 and 1979 was not due to a fall in employment, but to the failure of employment to rise as fast as the working population. After 1979, its rise can be accounted for almost entirely by the fall in employment.

Of the two million reduction between 1979 and 1983 in employees in employment, all but 100,000 or so occurred in the production and construction industries; over one and a half million of which occurred in manufacturing, which thus lost almost a quarter of its labour force. There was a slight rise in employees in employment in the service industries, which accounted on average for over 60 per cent of all employment. There was also an increase of about 300,000 in the numbers of the self-employed (which are included in the definition of employment used in figure 6.4, but are excluded from the figures of 'employees in employment' quoted above).

Female unemployment rose from 3.7 per cent in 1979 to 9 per cent in 1983: a smaller rise than in male unemployment, which increased from 6.5 per cent to 15.8 per cent. There is reason to suppose, however, that female unemployment was understated by these figures: British unemployment statistics count only those who claim benefits, to which many women are not entitled. It seems likely that the flattening-out of the working population numbers after 1979 (shown in figure 6.4) was largely due to the apparent departure of women from the labour force because they could not find work and had no reason to claim benefit, or otherwise to register as unemployed.[3] Those engaged on special employment measures were mostly regarded for statistical purposes as being neither employed nor unemployed, and thus were also excluded from the total of the working population.

A major development during the period was the rapid increase which occurred in long-term unemployment after 1979. The numbers of those who had been unemployed for more than a year doubled from 170,000 in 1973 to around 340,000 in 1979, and then increased to 1.1 million in 1983.

The increase in unemployment between 1980 and 1983 was, in fact, accounted for entirely by the increase in those unemployed for more than a year. Rates of male long-term unemployment were highest among those aged over sixty, and among those aged between eighteen and twenty-four. The unskilled, semi-skilled and disabled were also over-represented among the long-term unemployed. The extent of the problem was again understated by the published figures, which did not take account of spells of unemployment which lasted more than a year, but which were briefly interrupted by spells of employment or of sickness. All the evidence suggests that the longer the period of unemployment, the more difficult was it to get a job, or to hold on to it, once it was obtained.[4]

Prices and earnings

Prices (as measured by the Retail Prices Index) increased by 260 per cent between 1973 and 1983: an average annual increase of 13.6 per cent, and the fastest rise over such a period for over a hundred years.

Figure 6.5 traces out the path of the annual increases in prices and earnings. Over the period as a whole, the annual price increase fell from around 9 per cent to below 5 per cent. Within the period, however, there

Table 6.1 Contributions to inflation 1973–83[a]

Year	Employment costs	Non-employment costs	Import costs	Indirect taxes	Residual	Total
1972/3	2.7	2.6	5.0	−0.1	−1.6	8.6
1973/4	7.2	0.8	9.0	−0.3	0.6	17.3
1974/5	11.2	4.3	3.0	3.8	1.3	23.6
1975/6	3.5	5.0	4.7	3.1	−0.6	15.7
1976/7	3.2	7.4	3.0	4.4	−2.8	15.2
1977/8	3.9	3.4	0.6	1.6	−0.7	8.8
1978/9	5.6	2.6	1.6	4.7	−1.7	12.9
1979/80	7.6	3.0	2.0	3.8	0.1	16.5
1980/1	3.8	2.5	1.1	3.1	0.4	10.9
1981/2	1.5	2.8	1.6	1.8	0.8	8.5
1982/3	1.2	2.7	1.7	0.2	−0.4	5.4

[a] (Contributions to increases in the consumers' expenditure deflator, per cent.)

Source: M. Lewis 'Money and the control of inflation in the UK', *Midland Bank Review*, Summer 1985.

were peaks of over 26 per cent and over 21 per cent (taking monthly figures) in 1975 and 1980. The growth of earnings can be seen to have exceeded the growth of prices in every year except 1976 and 1977.

Table 6.1 gives estimates of the contributions of employment costs, selling margins, import costs and indirect taxes to annual price increases (as measured by the consumers' expenditure deflator) throughout the period. A steep rise in import costs can be seen to be the major contributor in 1972/3 and 1973/4; followed, in 1974/5, by an even more rapid rise in unit labour costs. Between 1973 and 1975 the effect of pay increases upon unit labour costs was augumented by a fall in output per employee: after 1975 there was a progressive increase in output per employee, which partially offset the effects of pay increases. Reduced growth in unit labour costs contributed to lower price increases after 1975, but the oil price increase and the increase in indirect taxes in 1979 led to another surge of price and wage inflation. After 1980, falling pay increases, rapidly rising

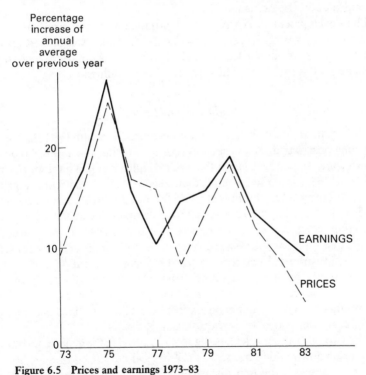

Figure 6.5 Prices and earnings 1973–83

Source: Calculated from data in CSO *Economic Trends* 1985 Prices 1973–83: Retail Price Index Earnings 1973–80 Average Earnings Older Series 1981–83 New Earnings Survey

productivity, and low increases in import prices, all contributed to a rapid fall in inflation.

(It should be noted that the pattern shown in the last column of table 6.1 differs from that of figure 6.5 because of the different composition of the price index.)

III EXTERNAL INFLUENCES

No hard and fast line can be drawn between external and domestic influences upon the events described above, because in some cases they interacted. The change which took place in the course of world trade can clearly be regarded as an external influence, as can the trend of world commodity prices. But exchange rate movements were influenced by – as well as influencing – domestic events. The policies of other industrial countries, and of the United States in particular, were the other major influence upon the exchange rate.

The development of North Sea oil production was a major influence, which might properly be regarded as domestic. But it was so tied up with matters which lay outside the normal working of the domestic economy as to make it convenient to treat it as an external influence.

World trade and prices

World trade grew much less rapidly between 1973 and 1983 than in the previous post-war decades (see figure 6.6). During the 1960s, trade had grown some 40 per cent faster than world industrial production. Between 1973 and 1983, it did little better than keep pace with the reduced growth of world output. The volume of trade fell briefly during the recessions of 1975 and 1982, but there was nothing comparable to the 25 per cent reduction which had occurred between 1930 and 1932. In this sense, the institutions (such as the General Agreement on Tariffs and Trade) set up by the industrialized countries after the Second World War to avoid a repetition of the inter-war trade collapse, can be said to have been successful. Nevertheless, a substantial increase took place after 1974 in the use of import controls and export subsidies. This may have played a part in reducing the buoyancy of world trade.[5]

The two oil price shocks (see figure 6.7) provided a major contribution to the slowdown which occurred in industrial output and trade, but – as figure 6.8 shows – the first oil price increase was preceded by, and then reinforced by, a surge in the prices of commodities such as metals, sugar, rubber and cotton. Thus 1972 saw the abrupt ending of what had been a

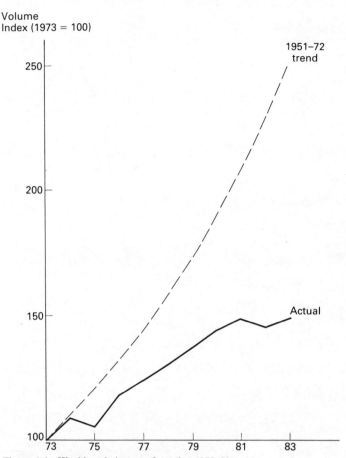

Volume
Index (1973 = 100)

Figure 6.6   World trade in manufacturing 1973–83
Source: United Nations Monthly Bulletins of Statistics

trend decline in the real prices of such commodities. The 1972 surge was brought about mainly by a strong and synchonized boom in the industrialized economies. Over the whole period to 1983, however, commodity prices were very volatile, but they rose no faster than those of manufactures.

The predominant influence upon prices in the industrialized countries was the sharp increase in unit labour costs which occurred in the years immediately following the first oil shock. Inflation in all of the industrialized countries rose substantially above previous post-war levels, and as

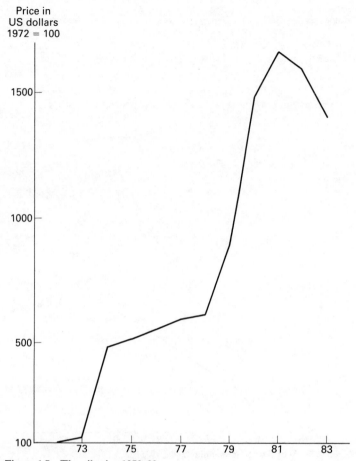

Figure 6.7   The oil price 1972–83
Source: Calculated from data in *Petroleum Economics*

figure 6.9 shows, it did not on average subside to anything approaching previous levels until after 1981.

Exchange rates and competitiveness

Because of its high degree of dependence upon international trade, the British economy was strongly influenced, as regards both output and prices, by overseas developments. To the the extent that external influ-

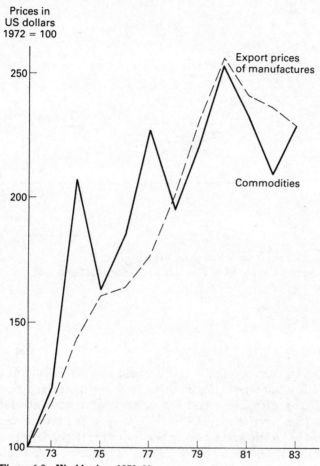

Figure 6.8 World prices 1972–83
Source: United Nations Monthly Bulletins of Statistics

ences account for the difference which has been noted between British and overseas experience, the major factor was, however, the behaviour of the exchange rate.

It had been expected by advocates of floating exchange rates that exchange rates would then move in such a way as to compensate for any differences between national inflation rates. It was argued that an increase in the costs of a country's products relative to those of its competitors would bring about a reduction in demand for its products, and conse-

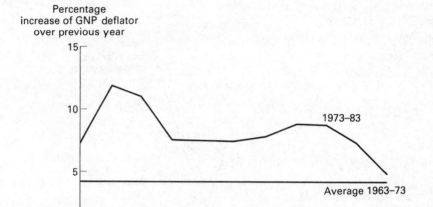

Figure 6.9   Inflation in the industrialised countries 1973–83
Source: International Monetary Fund Annual Reports 1982 and 1985

quently for its currency; and that this would lead to a fall in its exchange rate, which would tend to remove the cost difference in international markets. The exchange rate movements which occurred after fixed exchange rates were abandoned in 1973, were in fact often unrelated to differences in inflation rates. Partly because of the large trading surpluses obtained by the OPEC countries, capital movements, rather than trade flows, came to dominate the determination of exchange rates. The transactions in foreign exchange markets involved amounts said to be as high as a hundred billion dollars a day – amounts which were certainly many times what was needed to finance trade. The volatility of exchange rates which developed after 1973 introduced uncertainties which may have contributed to the reduction which has been observed in the growth of world trade. For Britain, however, the effects of exchange rate movements upon the cost competitiveness of its products in international markets were of greater importance.

Figure 6.10 shows the large swings which occurred in the rate of exchange of sterling against some other currencies, and figure 6.11 relates them to movements in competitiveness, taking labour costs in manufacturing as a convenient measure. (The lower line in each figure traces

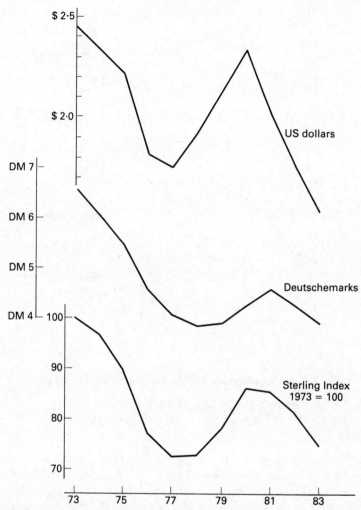

Figure 6.10 Sterling exchange rates 1973–83
Source: CSO *Economic Trends*, 1985

sterling's 'effective exchange rate', which is its rate against a trade-weighted mean of other currencies.)

The upper line of figure 6.11 indicates that unit labour costs in British manufacturing rose between 1973 and 1981 in relation to a weighted average of those of its overseas competitors, when all are measured in terms of their national currencies. Between 1973 and 1977, the effect of

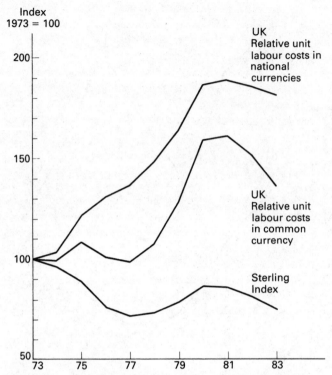

Figure 6.11   Manufacturing cost competitiveness and the exchange rate 1973–83

Source: CSO *Economic Trends* 1985

these relative increases upon international competitiveness was roughly offset by a fall in the effective exchange rate. Relative unit labour costs measured in a common trading currency were thus roughly stable over that period, as indicated by the middle line. In 1979 and 1980, however, sharp and unexpected increases in the effective exchange rate combined with a continuing increase in relative domestic costs to produce a dramatic rise in the common currency measure of relative costs – and hence a rapid reduction in the international cost competitiveness of British manufactures. The consequences of this were described by an eminent international banker in the following terms:

> This is by far the most excessive overvaluation which any major currency has experienced in recent history. . . . The large real appreciation of sterling from 1979 to 1981 was probably the most important single element in that

period's British economic policy, as concerns its effects both on domestic inflation as well as on British trade, production and unemployment.[6]

The 60 per cent increase in relative unit labour costs in common currency terms, which occurred between 1977 and 1981, was a (multiplicative) combination of a 37 per cent increase in unit labour costs in domestic currency terms, and a 17 per cent increase in the exchange rate. The movement of the exchange rate was, however, influenced in turn by the development of North Sea oil production.

North Sea oil and gas

By the beginning of 1973, virtually the whole of the country's gas requirements were being met from domestic sources in the North Sea, and the existence there had been established of large oil deposits. The price of oil at that time was, however, barely sufficient to cover the costs of developing and operating those deposits. Between 1973 and 1981, the world price of oil rose to £120 a tonne, while the cost of North Sea oil remained at around £45 a tonne (both at 1980 prices). Over that period, some £30 billion (1980 prices) went into exploration development and operation, much of it financed from abroad. It was not until 1977 that substantial quantities of oil started to be landed, and sales revenues started to cover current and capital costs. From then on, output grew rapidly, reaching 115 million tonnes (over 3 per cent of world production) by 1983, and making Britain a substantial net exporter of oil.

The contribution of oil and gas production to GDP rose steadily from about 1 per cent in 1977 to 5 per cent in 1983, but its direct effect upon domestic activity was small: at no time did employment in the North Sea oil sector exceed 25,000. Its indirect effects were, however, substantial. It enabled Britain to avoid the reduction in consumption which would otherwise have been necessary to meet the second oil price rise, and it turned what otherwise would initially have been a substantial balance of payments deficit into a surplus. But in doing so, it brought about a rise in the exchange rate which reduced the competitiveness in international markets of other British products. It was widely assumed at the time that North Sea oil had thus contributed to the growth of unemployment, and there were some who suggested that the country would have been better off had the oil been 'left in the ground'. However, the balance of the effects upon non-oil activity is not obvious. An estimate which used the National Institute's economic model suggests that the reduction in consumption which would have been necessary in absence of North Sea oil would have outweighed the effects of higher competitiveness, so that non-oil output (including manufacturing output) and employment would have been lower.[7]

The importance of the debate which developed in the 1980s about the contribution of North Sea oil to the 1979–81 appreciation of sterling lay in the presumption that, what could not be explained in that way, should be laid at the door of government policy. Professor Alan Walters, who was the Prime Minister's economic adviser at the time, has since written that: 'There is no reason to dispute Niehans's conjecture that not more than 20 per cent of the appreciation of sterling can be explained by the oil factor.'[8] There were other economists who reached a similar conclusion, but some who disagreed.[9] (The conclusion of the National Institute study referred to above, that manufacturing output had benefited from North Sea oil, was reached despite an assumption that its effect upon the exchange rate had been very substantial.) Professor Walters has pointed out that the loss which followed in Britain's share of world exports of manufactures, was in any case relatively small. This does not, of course, remove the possibility that British exporters had to reduce their selling margins to avoid a worse loss. There was also a large incursion of manufactured imports into the domestic market. As regards the contribution of North Sea oil to these developments, the word 'conjecture' in the above quotation appears well chosen.

There was no doubt, however, that North Seal oil made an important contribution to government revenues. As sales revenues increased, so did the proportion taken in taxation, and the Exchequer benefited by amounts which rose from £2.3 billion in 1979/80 to £7.8 billion in 1980/2. Set against total receipts in the latter year of £122 billion, this may not seem dramatic, but public-sector borrowing that year was only £9.2 billion. To maintain it at that level in the absence of oil revenues would have required a tax increase corresponding to eight to ten pence in the pound on the basic rate of income tax. Moreover, this is to take account only of direct effects. The indirect effects upon tax revenues of the reduction in national income, which would have occurred in the absence of North Sea oil, might have been even greater.

Interest rates

External, as well as domestic, influences affected interest rates in the 1973–83 period, particularly the influence of developments in the United States. The British authorities had from time to time felt it necessary to adjust interest rates to influence the exchange rate, either to move it down in order to maintain competitiveness, or to move it up in order to avoid the inflationary impact of increased import prices. The differences between interest rates in Britain and the United States were allowed to vary from time to time, but only within modest limits. External influences thus played a part in the rise which took place over the period in real (inflation-corrected) interest rates, with the conflict which developed in the United States between a loose fiscal policy and a tight monetary policy exerting an upward influence after 1980. Real post-tax rates to corporate borrowers were not, however, significantly higher in the 1980s than in the 1960s: it was the period of negative real rates in the 1970s which distinguished the 1973–83 period from previous experience.[10]

The possibility thus has to be considered that some of the interest rate changes made by the British authorities in pursuance of domestic policy might in any case have been necessary, in part at least, for external reasons.

IV DOMESTIC INFLUENCES

The domestic influences which concern us here are those related to productivity, industrial relations, industrial performance and the labour market. In keeping with the intention of treating it as residual, the influence of domestic policy is later considered under a separate heading.

Productivity growth

In common with most other industrial countries, Britain experienced a marked reduction in productivity growth after 1973, compared with previous post-war trends. Figures 6.12 and 6.13 show the paths of output per employee for the whole economy and for manufacturing (for which more reliable measures of productivity are available). The fall in productivity which normally occurs in a recession, as employers hold on to labour in the hope of a recovery, is noticeable in 1975, and again in 1980. The productivity increase which correspondingly occurs as output picks up was, however, less rapid after 1975 than would have been expected from the experience of previous recessions, and productivity in 1979 was thus markedly below trend. The pattern in the following recession was different again, with productivity starting to rise before the increase in output, and then growing much faster than the previous trend.

The rapid growth in productivity which began in 1980 received a good deal of attention from commentators and analysts at the time. One view was that there had dawned a new era of industrial relations, in which power had shifted towards management, and workers and trade unions were less able to engage in restrictive practices or resist the introduction of new technology. On this view, the future rate of productivity growth

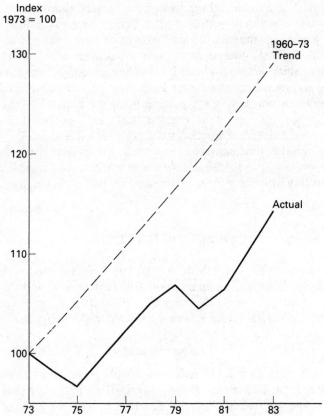

Fig 6.12   **Output per person employed, Whole Economy 1973–83**
Source: CSO *Economic Trends* 1985

would be permanently higher. It was a view which was to gain support
from accounts of change at British Steel and British Leyland where
aggressive new managements had used the threat of the end of government
support – and hence of closures – to reduce overmanning. (Some 40 per
cent of the productivity improvement in manufacturing was estimated to
be accounted for by the metals and vehicles industries.) Government
supporters were inclined to attribute these developments to a 'Thatcher
Factor' of macroeconomic stability and microeconomic reform.[11] There
were some, however, who feared an industrial relations 'backlash', with
concessions yielded under duress being reversed as order books improved.

An alternative view emerged from a 1983 study which indicated that
most of the improvement of manufacturing productivity above its

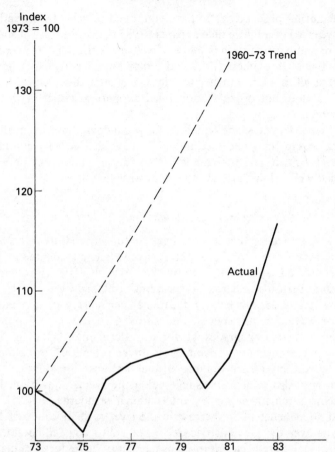

Fig 6.13 **Output per person employed, Manufacturing 1973–83**
Source: CSO *Economic Trends* 1986

previous trend could be accounted for by a statistical correction for low-labour utilization in the trough of the recession (which depressed the measurement baseline), and by the closure of the more labour-intensive of manufacturing plants (which would raise average productivity without implying any improvement among the survivors). The implication of this study was that productivity growth would revert before long to somewhat above its 1970s trend, but that only if rates of investment recovered to pre-1973 levels would future productivity growth be sustained at the trend rate of the 1960s.[12]

A footnote to this controversy is provided by later figures which show manufacturing productivity to have continued to grow by around 5 per cent a year (a lower figure than appars in 1983 studies because of statistical revisions and reclassifications, but still well above the 3.5–4 per cent trend of the 1960s) throughout 1983 and 1984; but then to have shown no growth at all in 1985. Further revisions may alter this picture, but as it stands, it does not provide unqualified support to either of the above explanations.

Very considerable scope remained for productivity improvement using existing equipment and technology, as evidenced by comparative studies.[13] British productivity levels in all sectors except agriculture remained well below those in other industrial countries.[14]

Training, management and industrial relations

The comparative studies which have been referred to indicate that Britain's inferior industrial performance could not be accounted for by the use of outdated equipment, nor by the devotion of fewer resources to education. British standards of vocational training were low by international standards, however. Educational curricula gave generally less attention to job requirements, and firms gave less attention to skill training. Supervisory grades at foreman level and below in British factories were normally appointed by direct promotion from the shop floor, without any formal training or qualifications.

There was also evidence to suggest that the average quality of British management remained low by international standards. A 1983 study showed no evidence of an increase in the level of qualification of British managers over the previous decade.[15] The status and self-confidence of managers may have been improved as a result of the reduced militancy of the workforces in the 1980s, but this is as likely to have damaged as to have improved communications. Elaborate consultation machinery remained in place, but there was little to indicate that it was used to involve employees in decisions which affected them. A popular dictum of the early 1980s was 'it is the function of management to manage', but its users seemed to interpret that slogan more in terms of machismo than of understanding.

On the basis of official strike statistics, the state of British industrial relations improved greatly in the course of the early 1980s, with days lost in industrial disputes in 1983 at their lowest level since 1976. The structure of industrial relations had also changed, to throw more responsibility upon local officials, and less upon national trade union officials – a very marked change since the days of incomes policies.[16] Trade union membership showed a marked decline, even allowing for the decline in employment: as a percentage of total numbers employed, it had risen from under 50 per cent in 1973 to over 55 per cent in 1980, but had then fallen to 46 per cent by 1983.

Pay bargaining

A puzzling feature of the British scene in the 1973–83 period was the absence of a fall in real wages in the face of soaring unemployment. As figure 6.5 shows, earnings growth remained above inflation throughout the period, except for the 1976–7 period of wage restraint; so that real earnings rose by 14 per cent while unemployment trebled. Even in 1983, with unemployment over three million and the inflation rate below 5 per cent, money earnings were growing at an underlying rate of 9 per cent a year – and were to continue to grow at close to that rate over the following two years.

Chapter 5 included a discussion of the part played by trade unions in holding up real wages. Some evidence not presented there suggests that the earnings differential between union members and non-members among male manual workers had risen from around 5 per cent in the early 1960s to 8 per cent by 1973, and, after remaining at about that level during the incomes policies of the 1970s, had risen again to about 12 per cent by 1983.[17] But it is also the case that the earnings of the substantially less unionized non-manual male workforce rose more rapidly. Non-manual employment was displacing manual employment over the period, and this suggests some influence of demand upon pay. The decline in the relative position of manual workers in the rapidly contracting vehicles industry, from an 11 per cent pay advantage over the average for manufacturing, to a 4 per cent disadvantage between 1973 and 1983, conveys a similar impression.

However, the effect of the general level of demand upon earnings seems uncertain. A 1985 paper[18] reports no measurable effect (although an earlier Treasury study[19] had suggested that output has a strong influence, with long time-lags). The results of the 1985 study indicate that proportionate, not absolute, increases in unemployment affect earnings, and the hypothesis emerged that the long-term unemployed exert relatively little influence upon pay bargaining. Since – as was noted earlier in this chapter – the rise in unemployment between 1980 and 1983 was accounted for entirely by the increase in long-term unemployment, this offers a possible explanation of the absence of a downward pressure on real wages during that period.

The low responsiveness of real earnings to unemployment in Britain compared with other countries over the period as a whole requires a broader explanation. The movement (already noted) away from national multi-employer pay bargaining, toward local or single-employer negotiations, seems to have played a part. There is no doubt that it contributed to the difficulty of administering incomes policies in the 1970s. There were at least two occasions when the relatively successful, but strike-prone, Ford Motor Company negotiated pay increases in breach of existing pay norms. The loss of moral authority of national trade union officials over their members, which became so painfully evident in the late 1970s, owed something to this development, and may well have contributed to it. The importance which was attached to the preservation of pay differentials between various groups, and the emergence of the concept of an annual 'going rate' for pay increases, were factors which contributed to the collapse of a pay policy, once breached.

With the return in 1979 to 'free collective bargaining', the move to single-employer bargaining made for greater sensitivity to the employer's financial position, particularly where stocks of unsold goods could be seen by employees. Employers, for their part, had by then become more conscious of the importance of labour costs for the prospects of survival, and their boards of directors had become accustomed to supervising pay bargaining, rather than leaving it to the industrial relations manager. Company profitability and liquidity thus came, for a time, to be an important influence upon bargaining. Even at a time of rapidly increasing unemployment there is no reason, however, to suppose that even well-informed collective bargaining of this sort will lead to 'market-clearing' pay rates. As has been noted, employees would rationally weigh the benefits of a pay increase against the risks and penalties of unemployment, and the existence of unemployment benefit would affect the balance. As the financial pressures on companies eased, the downward pressure upon pay settlements was correspondingly eased.

Explanations of labour market responsiveness in terms of bargaining institutions and behaviour, rather than in terms of trade union power alone, receive support from international comparisons. It has been noted that Sweden, Norway and Austria, which have centralized bargaining with powerful trade unions, were able to escape very lightly from the two oil price shocks and to experience comparatively minor effects upon inflation and unemployment. This was probably due to the considerable degree of social consensus which exists in those countries.[20]

The company sector

Company profitability fluctuated sharply between 1973 and 1983, following the pattern of the economic cycle. Real rates of return for non-North Sea industrial and commercial companies averaged about 9 per cent in 1973 (having fallen from 12 per cent in 1963) and, after falling to around 4 per cent in 1975 and again in 1981, recovered to 6 per cent in 1983. Their financial deficit (capital expenditure less retained income) was much lower, however, in the second recession than in the first, and by 1983 it had been turned into a substantial surplus. Between the two recessions, many companies had learned to avoid large deficits by restricting investment on stocks and capital equipment, and by shedding labour. The average figures conceal a wide variety of experience and behaviour, however, and there were many company failures. Company liquidations rose continuously throughout the decade, to reach five times their 1973 level by 1983. The majority of the employmnt loss was due to redundancies and plant closures by multi-plant firms, rather than to company failure. Reported redundancies reached over 530,000 in 1981 – three-quarters of them in manufacturing – and fell back to 326,000 in 1983.

V THE INFLUENCE OF ECONOMIC POLICY

A tidy way of examining the influence of economic policy is first to consider policy objectives and priorities, and then to assess the effectiveness of policy design and implementation in pursuing them. Indeed, to adopt any other sequence would be unthinkably confusing. Nevertheless, this procedure will be misleading if it is taken to imply that the sequence of determining priorities, formulating policy and carrying it out was – or could have been – a logical progression in which each successive step followed from its predecessor.

The conflict which arose between the wish to control inflation and the wish to avoid mass unemployment, illustrates one of the dangers of adopting an over-simple logical framework. In pursuit of its inflation objective a government might logically respond to the danger that pay levels might rise in response to an external price shock, by threatening action which would raise unemployment. If the fear of unemployment then averted the pay rises, an objective would have been gained. If it did not, there would seem to be no logical reason to carry out the threat: to do so, when the price shock was over and the pay rises could no longer be averted, would unnecessarily sacrifice the other objective. The defect in that logic lies, of course, in the loss of credibility which the government would then suffer, and the sacrifice of the effectiveness of future threats. The abandonment of that logic may, however, lead to policy decisions which are inconsistent with previously determined priorities; the more so if unforeseen setbacks intervene.

The importance of credibility for the effectiveness of economic policy goes deeper, moreover, than is indicated by any threat parable. Expectations have turned out to have an important influence upon economic behaviour, and it has become clear that policies which people expect to be reversed, are likely to be relatively ineffective in influencing behaviour. Against this background, Mrs Thatcher's repeated and apparently foolish assertion that 'there is no alternative' (shortened to 'Tina' by the journalists of the day) can be seen as fulfilling the purpose of raising the political cost of a policy change, and so making it appear less likely. It is also understandable that greater confidence was often expressed in forecasts of the consequences of policy actions than the supporting evidence available at the time appeared to justify. Whether such expressions of confidence were genuine – and if not, whether plausible alternative consequences were considered – can only be guessed at. Open debate about the conduct of economic policy is not a feature of the British system.

Comparisons with 'what might have been' are of course of particular interest in connection with policy. It is legitimte to make use of hindsight for this purpose, but it is not legitimate to expect the decision-makers of the time to have taken account of information which only subsequently became available. 'Murphy's Law'[21] plays a part in our story, and some policy decisions were based upon economic statistics – or upon widely-held assumptions – which we now know to have been false. Risks of that sort must be regarded as unavoidable – although this again raises the question whether their existence was recognized in general terms at the time.

Policy Objectives

Both the Heath and Thatcher governments were elected on pledges to give over-riding priority to the reduction of inflation. Similarly, the Labour Party's claim to be able to reduce inflation by means of the 'Social Contract' was an important plank in its successful 1974 campaign. Also, it was a Labour Chancellor who, in 1975, was the first to adopt a deflationary policy in the face of rising unemployment. At almost every stage of the story, there seems to have been a ruling consensus that inflation was so serious an evil as to justify sacrifices – or at least, risks – to overcome it.

The reasons for that consensus are not entirely obvious. Some economists had argued that, given the appropriate institutional arrangements, inflation need not be disruptive. Wages, pensions and taxes could be indexed; interest rates would adjust; and a floating exchange rate would in due course take care of any trade problems. The setting up of such arrangements would involve some initial costs, and on these grounds an absence of inflation would be preferable; but those costs were not thought to be high enough to justify any great sacrifice in order to avoid it.[22] Professor Friedman, on the other hand, suggested that inflation increases the volatility of prices; adding to uncertainty and reducing the clarity of price signals; so reducing economic efficiency, and probably raising unemployment.[23] The evidence suggests, however, that this link between inflation and unemployment is weak. The purely economic damage done by inflation seems, on the evidence, not to be great enough to justify really major sacrifices to avoid it.

The general feeling of insecurity generated by rising inflation was, nevertheless, sufficiently unpleasant to many people to make an undertaking to bring it under control electorally appealing. And it was not in any case thought that bringing inflation under control would involve any great cost in terms of unemployment.

A decisive factor, which enabled governments to continue to attempt to reduce inflation despite rising unemployment, was the change which took place in attitudes to unemployment. In 1972, the prospect that the numbers unemployed might exceed a million was sufficiently alarming to prompt a major policy reversal and produce a record fiscal expansion (which, however, many then thought had not gone far enough). By 1983, the prospect that unemployment would remain over three million was regarded as electorally damaging; but not decisively so. It had by then been discovered that the threat that it posed to law and order, and to the fabric of society, was far smaller than had been supposed. The characteristic attitude of those worst affected had turned out to be one of dejection and apathy, rather than of militancy. The riots of 1981 had been the product of a number of local factors – of which unemployment may not have been the most important – and they were not repeated on any scale in the short term.

It was not that people had come to regard unemployment as unimportant, or less important than inflation. Two-thirds of those questioned in an opinion poll in 1983 thought that if the government had to choose between keeping down inflation and keeping down unemployment, it should give priority to unemployment.[24] But there were other indications that many thought that choice not to be open: that no government, of whatever persuasion, had the power to do much to reduce unemployment. Some credence may also have been given to the claim that once inflation had been conquered, unemployment would in due course fall, by the normal action of market forces.

The priorities assigned to policy objectives were not in any case the only influence on policy. Uncertain perceptions of the effects of various policy measures upon inflation and upon unemployment were probably more important. Politically acceptable measures which would reduce the 'non-accelerating inflation rate of unemployment' (NAIRU) by reducing unemployment without raising inflation were hard to find, and were in any case likely to be slow-acting. Little was done, for example, to improve labour mobility by altering the rules of tenure of council houses, or of private rented accommodation. Faster-acting schemes such as special employment measures, many of which had a small or doubtful impact upon NAIRU, were adopted, probably mainly in order to make other policies more palatable; and some undoubtedly damaging measures, such as import restrictions, were presumably adopted solely for that purpose.

In the operation of monetary and fiscal policy, however, a conflict – at least in the short term – between the unemployment and inflation objectives was unavoidable. The only major escape from this dilemma seemed for a time to be offered by incomes policies.

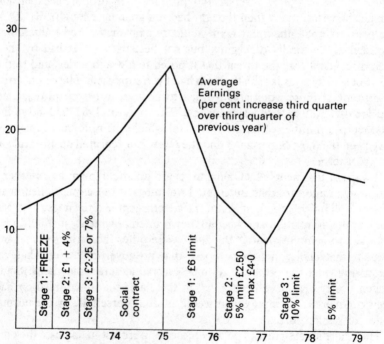

Fig 6.14 **Earnings growth and pay policies 1973–79**
Source: CSO *Economic Trends* 1985

Pay policies

Figure 6.14 summarizes the experience of pay policies between 1973 and 1979. A 1978 study has shown that the effects of such policies over the period 1961–75 had been, at best, to place a temporary restraint upon pay increases which was subsequently fully offset by later catching-up,[25] and it has been argued that this was true also of the period 1975–9. By way of qualification, it has to be said that there has been no example in Britain of a pay policy which was legitimized by the normal political processes. On very nearly every occasion, the government which introduced them had in fact been elected on an implicit or explicit undertaking not to do so. Moreover, the policies which were adopted were devised in haste and in secrecy, and were administered by people who were ill-suited to the task. This is not, however, to question the difficulty of devising and implementing a politically acceptable policy which would control inflation without producing distortions which would actually increase NAIRU in the long run. The 'thresholds' provision of the Heath government's pay policy, and the imbalance between public-sector and private-sector pay which developed under the Callaghan administration (leading to the 'comparability' undertakings which were implemented by the Thatcher administration), provide examples of the damage which can be done.

In any case, from 1979 onward, incomes policies had for different reasons disappeared from the policy agendas of both the major political parties.

Monetary policy

It may seem surprising that although policies of monetary constraint were in operation over most of the period, 1973–83 was a decade of historically high monetary growth. The comparative figures are shown in table 6.2.

Table 6.2 Growth rates of sterling M3 1963–83

Period	Compound annual rate of growth of sterling M3 (%)
1963–73	9.7
1973–83	12.8
1976–83	13.0
1979–83	14.2

Figure 6.15 shows the path of growth of sterling M3 and of the retail price

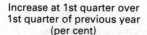

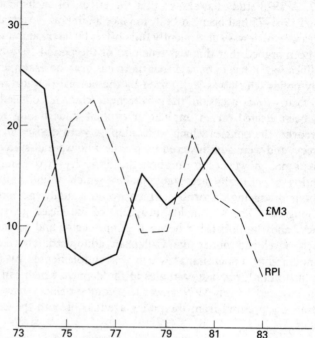

Figure 6.15   Money supply growth and inflation 1975–83
Source: CSO *Economic Trends*

index over the decade, starting with the explosive growth which occurred under the Heath administration, and table 6.3 sets out money supply projections and outcomes, from the time that targets were first announced in 1976, to the latest period for which outcome figures are available. It would appear from table 6.3 that the authorities' success in 1982/3 and 1983/4 in bringing M3 sterling within the much relaxed target ranges for those years, was transitory. In all save two of the remaining periods, the target ranges were overshot.

It has been pointed out that narrower measures of money supply showed a sharp contraction from the late summer of 1979 and that the growth rate of MO, in particular, has been much lower since then than that of sterling M3.[26] This has been taken to indicate that monetary conditions were exceptionally severe in 1980 and have not been very

Table 6.3 Sterling M3 projections and outcomes, 1976–85

	1976/7	1977/8	1978/9	1979/80	1980/1	1981/2	1982/3	1983/4	1984/5	1985/6
Budget Projections										
1976	9–13									
1977		9–13								
1978			8–12							
1979				7–11						
1980					7–11	6–10	5–9	4–8		
1981						6–10	5–9	4–8		
1982							8–12	7–11	6–10	
1983								7–11	6–10	5–9
1984									6–10	5–9
1985										5–9
Actuals	7.8	14.9	10.9	16.2	19.4	12.8	11.2	9.4	11.9	16.5

greatly relaxed since. It cannot, however, be taken to indicate that had MO been the target variable, the targets would have been met. The probability is that it, too, would have fallen victim to 'Goodhart's Law' (that any observed statistical regularity will tend to collapse once pressure is placed upon it for control purposes). As has been noted, the authorities ceased after 1981 to place exclusive reliance upon sterling M3 as a guide, and have since taken account of narrower and broader measures, and of the exchange rate. The management of the money supply had come to be guided by discretion rather than by rules, and its rationale ceased to be open to inspection.

The intention throughout had been to adopt a 'gradualist' monetary policy. What appears to have been overlooked in 1980 was the possibility that foreign exchange dealers would take the Medium-Term Financial Strategy, then announced, to presage a regime of high interest rates – and, possibly, of low inflation – making sterling an attractive investment, and provoking a rise in the exchange rate. The extent to which this, as against external factors, contributed to the rise in the exchange rate, remains a matter of dispute (as has been noted) but the outcome was a regime which was anything but gradualist.

A declared objective of the Medium-Term Financial Strategy had been to present business with an environment of financial stability, reducing the uncertainties facing it, and enabling it to plan for expansion. As regards domestic prices, impressive progress was made in this direction. Exchange rates showed great volatility, however, as figure 6.10 has indicated. Figure 6.16 shows that this was true also of interest rates. Real interest rates (indicated in figure 6.16 by the gap between the broken line and the solid line) showed even greater volatility. The extent to which this, too, was due to external influences remains open to question.

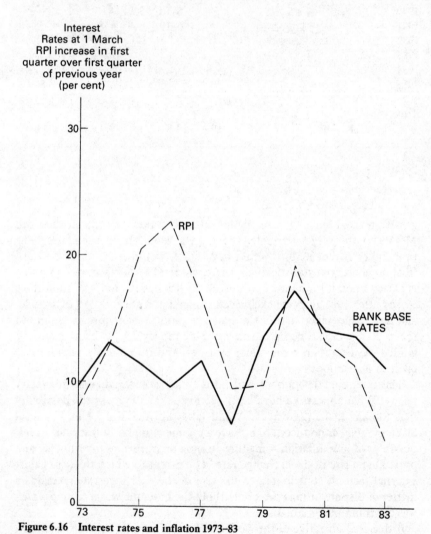

Figure 6.16   Interest rates and inflation 1973–83

Fiscal policy

Another feature of the period 1973–83 was an historically high level of public-sector borrowing as a percentage of GDP – an average of 4.8 per cent, compared with 2.2 per cent in the period 1963–72. (Even more dramatic was the change from −1.1 per cent in 1969/70 to +9.6 per cent in 1975/6.)

Table 6.4 compares budgetary projections with outcomes over the 1973–83 period. Both projections and outcomes show very substantial falls from the peak in 1975/6. By 1982/3 the borrowing out-turn was down to a level only some 50 per cent above the average of the previous decade. Large discrepancies between projections and outcomes are apparent, but some of these are due partly to policy changes announced after the budget in question. The bottom row of the table shows the forecasting errors after allowing for those budgetary changes. Particularly noticeable is the very large error, amounting to over 150 per cent of the projection, for 1975/6, which led to fears at that time that public expenditure was out of control.

Table 6.4 PSBR as percentage of GDP, projections and outcomes, 1973–83

	1973/4	1974/5	1975/6	1976/7	1977/8	1978/9	1979/80	1980/1	1981/2	1982/3
Budget projections										
1973	5.9									
1974		3.0								
1975			8.2							
1976				9.3						
1977					5.8					
1978						5.0				
1979							4.5			
1980								3.75	3.0	2.25
1981									4.25	3.25
1982										3.5
Actuals										
	6.0	8.9	9.6	6.6	3.8	5.4	4.8	5.6	3.4	3.2
Forecasting errors after allowing for policy changes										
	0	+4.7	+1.4	−2.7	−2.6	+0.4	+1.1	+2.0	−0.7	−0.5

Source: Financial Statements and Budget Reports, and Treasury Economic Progress Report, September 1983.

Table 6.5 Public expenditure as percentage of GDP 1973–83

Year	Total goods and services[a]	Grants to personal sector	Total transfers[b]	Total public expenditure[c]
1973	22.5	8.7	12.4	39.3
1974	24.4	9.4	14.6	44.0
1975	25.7	9.7	14.6	45.0
1976	24.9	10.1	14.5	44.4
1977	22.8	10.3	14.4	42.3
1978	21.9	10.6	15.1	42.0
1979	21.7	10.7	14.9	41.9
1980	22.9	11.1	15.1	43.7
1981	22.8	12.2	16.2	45.0
1982	22.7	13.1	16.8	45.4
1983	23.1	13.1	17.0	45.6

[a] The first column includes (as negative public expenditure) net sales of land and buildings, rising to 0.8 per cent in 1983.
[b] The third column includes subsidies and grants to other sectors, as well as grants to the personal sector.
[c] The final column includes debt interest (which rose from 3.7 per cent in 1973 to around 5 per cent in 1980–3).

Source: United Kingdom Annual Accounts, 1984 edn (CSO, 1984).

Tables 6.5 and 6.6 demonstrate that the reduction in borrowing between 1975/6 and 1982/3 was brought about, not by a reduction in public expenditure, but by an increase in taxation: which, incidentally, took taxation as a proportion of GDP to well above its 1975 post-war peak. It has been estimated that, for a person on average earnings, the proportion of any increase in earnings taken in direct and indirect taxation rose from 54.6 per cent in 1978 to 57.5 per cent in 1983.[27]

Table 6.5 shows that the bulk of the increase in public expenditure between 1973 and 1983 was due to an increase in grants (such as unemployment benefit and supplementary benefit) to the personal sector, resulting from the increase in unemployment. The revenue under a given tax regime would also have been depressed by the recession, but additional revenues from oil made a significant contribution.

Changes in the public-sector borrowing requirement are, however, for a number of reasons, an inadequate measure of the impact of fiscal policy upon economic activity. One reason is that different components of

Table 6.6 Taxes as percentage of GDP, 1973–83

	Income tax	Taxes on income +NIC[a]	Taxes on expenditure	Total tax[b]
1973	9.5	17.8	13.7	32.6
1974	11.4	21.0	13.6	35.7
1975	13.5	22.2	13.3	36.2
1976	13.2	21.6	13.0	35.2
1977	11.9	20.5	13.7	34.8
1978	11.2	19.4	13.7	33.6
1979	10.4	18.7	15.2	34.4
1980	10.5	19.4	15.7	35.7
1981	10.9	20.4	16.6	37.5
1982	10.9	21.1	16.9	38.6
1983	10.4	21.2	16.5	38.2

[a] The second column includes company taxation, oil revenues (which rose from 0.1 per cent in 1978 to 2 per cent in 1983) and National Insurance Contributions.
[b] The final column includes taxes on capital (which fell from 1.1 per cent in 1973 to 0.5 per cent in 1983).

Source: United Kingdom National Accounts, 1984 edn (CSO, 1984).

expenditure and taxation have different effects. Increases in social security payments to low-income families have a greater effect than cuts in the higher rates of income-tax, because less of the benefits go into increased savings. Government expenditure on construction, which tends to have a low import content, has a greater effect than overseas aid. Some trans-actions, such as the sale of council houses or of public-sector assets, may have little or no effect upon economic activity, and changes of North Sea revenues would have had only minor effects. Adjustments for the composition of expenditure and taxation tend to reduce the effective levels of the deficits incurred after 1979.[28]

An important distinction can also be drawn between 'structural' deficits, and those due to the reductions in receipts and increases in expenditure, which occur automatically in a recession. The former can be expected to persist after the recession is over; while the latter act temporarily as 'automatic stabilizers', which tend to reduce the fluctuation in economic activity. By correcting for cyclical variations in activity, estimates can be made of the extent to which the government added to or offset the effects of the automatic stabilizers. Estimates which include

cyclical corrections of this type, together with the compositional adjustments mentioned above, indicate a change in fiscal stance in the direction
of surplus between 1978/9 and 1982/3, which was more than sufficient to
offset the effects of the automatic stabilizers.[29] Such estimates do,
however, depend upon arbitrary assumptions concerning 'what might
have been', and it has been argued that the postulated alternative would
not have been sustainable.[30]

VI ASSESSMENT

In 1973, the prospect that unemployment might reach one million was
regarded by many as unthinkable: by 1984 the prospect that it might fall
to as low as twice that level seemed remote. That change alone, is
sufficient to justify the then Governor of the Bank of England (Lord
Richardson) in describing the period as 'our decade of discontent', in a
speech given in 1983 to an international audience.[31] Other industrialized
countries had suffered an increase in unemployment and had tackled a
surge in inflation. In 1973, the British unemployment and inflation rates
had been close to the OECD average. In 1983, the British inflation rate
was again close to the OECD average, but its unemployment rate was
nearly 50 per cent higher. Thus, to the question: 'why did the British
economy perform so badly?' has to be added the question: 'why did the
British fare so much worse than others?'

The unprecedented surges in price and wage inflation which occurred in
the 1970s have been an important feature of the story, and they have a
large part to play in any explanation of what happened to unemployment.
The economic linkages between pay and employment were described in
chapter 5, but a simpler linkage was also operating. No government could,
in practice, refrain from taking action in face of the prospect of accelerating inflation. There might, in principle, have been the option of
accepting inflation and learning to live with it, but there were sound
political and practical reasons for rejecting that option.[32] The remaining
options were to attempt to restrain pay increases, either directly by
incomes policies, or indirectly by means which involved an increase in
unemployment.

Most of the actions taken by governments over the period can thus be
seen largely as being in response to external and domestic influences. This
could be regarded as a trivial point, but it has to be set against the natural
temptation to assign prime responsibility to governments for everything
that happened. It is of course possible that governments reacted from time
to time in such a way as to make matters worse, or introduced a cure which

was worse than the disease. In what follows, an attempt will be made to identify some such episodes – treating each, however, as a response to a perceived problem, rather than as an initiative in its own right.

The Heath legacy

The inflationary surge of 1972–5 had its origins in the world-wide rise in labour costs which started in 1968, and the boom in commodity prices which began in 1972. It was then powerfully reinforced by the first major oil price rise in 1974. None of these influences was unique to Britain, but the British government's response to them seems in retrospect to have made matters worse in every way.

It has since come to be generally accepted that the fiscal and monetary expansion initiated in 1972 was ill-timed, as well as being vastly over-done.[33] With hindsight, it is clear that it gave unnecessary reinforcement to a recovery which was already under way. At the time, however, the fiscal expansion received support and encouragement from most commentators. The monetary expansion was mainly the unexpected consequence of 'Competition and Credit Control', rather than a deliberate act of policy. The sharp fall in the exchange rate (brought about by the 1972 budget) then combined with the increase in commodity prices to raise the costs of the surge of imports which followed. As table 6.1 shows, it was the rise in import prices which provided most of the initial impulse to the following burst of inflation. To a large extent, this can be attributed to external influences, but the government's contribution to it was substantial.

The failure of the 'thresholds' gamble of the last stage of the Heath government's pay policy ensured that those import price rises – exacerbated by the oil price rise – were to be reinforced by pay increases. The absurdity of an attempt to compensate for import price rises by pay increases was not understood by Mr Heath at the time,[34] and the further inflationary impetus which the thresholds system generated, must be put down to a remarkable ignorance of economics, combined with a seriously mistaken forecast that import prices would rise no further. The OPEC cartel was making its first moves at the time that the thresholds system was due to be announced, but these were presumably not taken seriously at the time.

The Social Contract

Desperate measures would have been necessary to counteract the inflationary consequences of the combination of the Heath legacy and the first OPEC price rise, but it was a year or more before the problem was faced.

A strategy of borrowing, rather than of deflation, was adopted to meet the balance of payments consequences of the oil price rise; but nothing was effectively done to counter inflationary pressures. This, if ever, would have been the time to introduce a pay freeze: the fall in real incomes which it would have engendered would have been temporary, and, in any case, a reduction of national income below trend was unavoidable. Instead the government was preoccupied with the redistribution of income (including social benefits) in favour of wage-earners. Whatever can be said in favour of such a policy it was, at that stage, ill-timed. In party-political terms it might, however, have been regarded as unavoidable.

1974 and 1975 saw unprecedented rises in wage inflation and in public-sector borrowing. The extent to which the latter was due to a failure of control – as against deliberate ministerial action – is difficult to discern, but the size of the borrowing requirement (and its enormous overshoot in 1974/5), together with the surge of inflation, damaged the confidence of potential lenders to an extent which was to prove difficult to repair. These were problems which the government had no choice but to tackle. It was acknowledged that their solution would involve a price in terms of unemployment, but by this time it was a question, not of policy priorities, but of imperatives for survival.

The sense of crisis which prevailed in 1975 led to policies which were to be effective in stemming the growth of the inflation rate and of public-sector borrowing. Union leaders were persuaded to agree to measures which would produce temporary falls in their members' real incomes, and a reluctant Cabinet agreed to measures designed to reduce the growth of public expenditure.

By 1976, output had started to rise, employment was no longer falling, and the inflation rate was decreasing. But British inflation still remained high by international standards. The sterling crisis, which led the government to seek the help of the International Monetary Fund, can be regarded mainly as a consequence of Britain's relative failure to deal with inflation.

After the IMF

The story of the years 1977 and 1978 is one of paradox. The statistics now available suggest success, but attitudes at the time spoke of failure. Output and employment grew fairly strongly, the inflation rate fell to below its 1973 level, and real earnings increased rapidly. The fact that the government found itself in an increasingly beleagured position owed something to the misleadingly gloomy forecasts and statistics of the time. This can only be put down to the operation of Murphy's Law. Changes in attitudes in the labour market and in the financial markets were, however, the decisive factors. Economic policy options were confined within close limits by the need, on the one hand to hold together the crumbling Social Contract, and the support of Parliament, and on the other, to maintain financial confidence. The meticulous attention then given by the financial markets to small month-by-month movements in the money supply and borrowing figures may seem bizarre from the perspective of 1986 and beyond, but its influence was real enough at the time. The government had a fair measure of success – as tables 6.3 and 6.4 indicate – in meeting its financial targets, but little success in maintaining support for its incomes policies. Poor communications between ministers and the government's supporters may explain some of the misjudgements and misunderstandings which made matters worse, and led to the final breakdown in 'the winter of discontent'.

The period between the end of 1976 and the beginning of 1979 must thus be seen as one in which the government could do little but react within closely drawn limits to influences – largely domestic – which it was unable to control.

The 'British Experiment'

The 'rebound' in pay claims which followed the breakdown of pay policy faced the incoming Thatcher government with problems similar to those encountered by their predecessors. Just as the Labour government had implemented the Heath government's 'thresholds' undertaking, so the new Conservative government had chosen to implement its predecessor's 'comparability' undertaking. Ministers appeared at the time to hold to a naïve version of monetarism under which nothing but the money supply could influence inflation, and thus professed indifference to the conduct of pay bargaining.[35] The steep increase in indirect taxation, which they immediately introduced, was similarly not expected to affect inflation. Its first round effect was of course upon the price level, not its rate of increase; and second-round effects – via its effect upon pay bargaining – were discounted. A multiple new impetus was thus given to inflation, all of it of domestic origin.

Rising import prices made a further contribution, but the second oil price rise had a much smaller effect than the first, because Britain was, by this time, virtually self-sufficient in oil. As table 6.1 indicates, wage costs and indirect taxes made the major contributions to the surge in retail prices in 1979/80.

The fall in output in the following years owed something to the fall in the growth of world trade brought about by the world recession, and something to domestic (including domestic policy) influences. Because of its greater openness, the British economy was more vulnerable than most to the influence of world trade, but it is reasonable to suppose that the greater part of the very large difference between the depth of the recession in Britain and in other countries, which is illustrated in figures 6.2 and 6.3, was due to domestic influences.

The controversial decision to over-rule the normal 'automatic stabilizers', and to take no account of the tendency of public-sector borrowing to rise during a recession, would appear to have been a major factor. As table 6.3 indicates, the attempt to reduce the borrowing requirement in 1980/1 was unsuccessful. This was because of the unexpected severity of the recession – an output fall of 4 per cent instead of the forecast fall of 2 per cent. In 1981/2, the attempt was repeated with success. Estimates by the International Monetary Fund showed the effective 'fiscal impulses' which these represented to have been very much more contractionary than those of any other of the seven major industrial countries.[36] In 1982, however, the Treasury acknowledged that 'it would be possible to raise the PSBR relative to its declining path without threatening the monetary targets.' Subsequent moves appear – after allowing for the low economic impact of revenues from North Sea oil and from council house sales – to have been in the direction of fiscal relaxation.

Table 6.3 gives little indication of a significant reduction of monetary growth after 1978–9, and it seems that any account of the influence of monetary policy must be in terms of its interaction with the exchange rate. The initial intention of reducing monetary growth mainly by cutting public expenditure was frustrated by the effects of the recession, and the Treasury turned instead to interest rates. Although interest rate increases did not have the desired effect upon the money supply, it might be supposed that they had a part in the rise in the exchange rate which occurred between 1979 and 1981. However, it would appear that the explanation is not so simple. In fact, the one thing upon which the experts seem to be unanimous is their inability to explain the exchange rate movements of that time. From early 1981 onward, monetary policy was in any case not concerned solely with the money supply The evidence suggests a series of compromises in which the money supply was allowed to over-run its target when the strength of the exchange rate appeared to be achieving the effect upon inflation that a tight domestic monetary policy had been intended to achieve. This, and other evidence, suggests that the steep rise in the exchange rate which occurred in 1980 had been unintended, and that policy was thereafter adjusted to avoid a repetition.

All this makes it very difficult to assess the relative contributions of demestic policy and of other domestic and external influences. The results of simulations done in 1983, using the National Institute and the Treasury economic models, suggest that the effect of domestic economic policy was much more important than the effect of world trade, and that these two factors accounted for the bulk of the shortfall of GDP growth below trend between the fourth quarters of 1979 and 1982.[37] As the authors themselves acknowledge, such estimates are subject to very wide margins of error. Domestic policy is not, in any case, conducted independently of external and domestic influences. One indication of the relative importance of domestic influences is provided by the estimate, referred to above, that the increase in British unit labour costs relative to those in other countries was the dominant factor in the massive loss of international competitiveness of British manufactures which occurred between 1977 and 1981 – contributing to it more than twice the effect of the rise in the exchange rate.

Summary

The story, as recounted in earlier chapters and summarized in this, has been largely one of mishaps, misunderstandings and misjudgements. There can be little doubt that the majority of the damage which was done to the British economy was self-inflicted. But this cannot be ascribed to any single agency.

A substantial part of the rise in unemployment, which is the story's most depressing aspect, must be attributed to a lack of responsiveness of pay to market conditions; or to what has been termed 'a lack of social cohesion'. But the origins of this are, in turn, unclear. They may well have a great deal to do with human relations at the workplace – a realm which, however, outside observers have seldom penetrated, and about which there is little objective information to call upon. Economic analysis can make only a limited contribution to the questions of communication and co-operation which are at the heart of the workings of a firm; and when it brings the model of competitive market behaviour to bear upon them, the results are generally depressing. Whatever the internal reasons, the external evidence indicates that British firms tend to be relatively poorly adapted to the management of change. The indications are that this may be a characteristic as much of British management as of its workforce.

Economic analysis has more to contribute to policy evaluation; but on the record of the period, it is hard to defend from the familiar criticism that it is much better at explaining the past than at predicting the future. In view of the unusually strong influence which it had on macroeconomic policy in the course of our story, this would seem to be a matter of some importance. There is little to suggest that this in itself was an especially British failing. The lack of open debate on economic policy, which is a feature of the British system, may, however, have made it easier for decision-makers to fail to appreciate – or deliberately to overlook – the known limitations behind the advice which they were given.

Outside commentators have remarked also upon the British tendency to go to extremes.

> Other countries have fine tuned their economies or have moved towards more monetarist positions – none seems to have pursued either doctrine as wholeheartedly as Britain. No European country would have indulged in the saga of nationalisation and denationalisation . . . none would probably have introduced fairly major and radical reforms almost solely on the basis of economic theorising, as in the case of the Selective Employment Tax or Competition and Credit Control. . . . For a country which prides itself on a pragmatic and commonsense approach to policy making, this strong belief in the power of economic theory seems surprising. . . .[38]

The greater tendency on the part of policy-makers to gamble and to go to extremes, combined with the lower degree of adaptability in industry may have some part in the explanation of the differences between the performance of the British and other economies.

Much of what had been believed was subsequently discarded, and the effects of policy differed frequently from expectation. Also, there were episodes which, with hindsight, would better have been avoided. Examples are the legacy of the Heath administration's failed gamble; the Wilson government's delay in tackling the problems of adjustment; and the temporary – and probably accidental – 'overkill' of the fiscal and monetary policies of the Thatcher administration. Whether, in the light of the circumstances of the time, and of the knowledge then available, they were in practice avoidable, it is more difficult to judge. Such episodes apart, it is not easy to envisage alternative policies which would have yielded a significantly different outcome.

NOTES

1. United Kingdom National Accounts 1984 edn (CSO, 1984) p. 85.
2. See the results of a survey by the National Economic Development Office reported in the *Guardian*, 11 July 1985; and also the report of the Audit Commission for Local Authorities entitled 'Capital Expenditure Controls in Local Government in England' (HMSO, 1985).
3. The same reasoning applies broadly to the pre-1982 statistics of unemployment, which were a count of those registering as unemployed.
4. See 'Long-term Unemployment' (Manpower Services Commission, HMSO, 1982).

5. See S. Page, 'The increased use of trade controls by the industrialised countries', *International Economics*, May/June 1980; and P. D. Henderson, 'Trade policies: trends, issues and influences', *Midland Bank Review*, winter 1983.
6. Dr O. Emminger, former President of the Deutsche Bundesbank, in evidence to the Treasury and Civil Service Committee (5th Report from the Treasury and Civil Service Committee, Session 1983–4, HMSO, 1984).
7. F. J. Arkinson, S. J. Brooks and S. G. F. Hall, 'The economic effects of North Sea oil', *National Institute Economic Review*, May 1983, p. 38.
8. A. Walters, *Britain's Economic Renaissance* (Oxford University Press, 1986) p. 163.
9. See F. A. Forsythe, and J. A. Kay, 'The economic implications of North Sea oil revenues', *Fiscal Studies*, July 1980; see also W. H. Buiter and M. Miller, 'The Thatcher Experiment: the First Two Years' (Brookings Papers on Economic Activity, 1981) p. 315.
10. See 'A note on short term interest rates', *Bank of England Quarterly Bulletin*, December 1983.
11. See Walters, *Britain's Economic Renaissance*, p. 176.
12. L. Mendis and J. Muellbauer, 'British Manufacturing Productivity 1955–1983: Measurement Problems Oil Shocks and Thatcher Effects' (Centre for Economic Policy Research Discussion Paper No. 32, November 1984).
13. See a series of papers in the National Institute's special issue on comparative productivity, *National Institute Economic Review*, August 1982.
14. A. Daly, D. M. W. N. Hitchens and K. Wagner, 'Productivity machinery and skills in a sample of British and German manufacturing plants', *National Institute Economic Review*, February 1985.
15. G. Crockett and P. Elias, 'British managers: a study of their education training mobility and earnings', *British Journal of Industrial Relations*, March 1984.
16. K. Sisson and W. Brown, 'Industrial Relations in the Private Sector: Donovan Revisited' in G. Bain, (ed.) *'Industrial Relations in Britain* (Basil Blackwell, 1983).
17. D. Metcalf and S. J. Nickell, 'Jobs and Pay', *Midland Bank Review*, spring 1985.
18. R. Layard and S. J. Nickell, 'The causes of British unemployment', *National Institute Economic Review*, February 1985.
19. S. Wren-Lewis, 'A Model of Private Sector Earnings Behaviour', Treasury Working Paper No. 23, HMSO.
20. M. Bruno and G. J. Sachs, 'Labour Markets and Comparative Macroeconomic Performance' (Harvard, Mimeo, 1983); Metcalf and Nickell 'Jobs and Pay'.
21. One of the many versions of Murphy's Law is that 'if anything can go wrong, it will.'
22. For a survey of the evidence on the costs of inflation, see D. Higham and J. Tomlinson, 'Why do Governments worry about inflation?' *National Westminster Bank Quarterly Review*, May 1982.
23. M. Friedman, 'Inflation and unemployment', *Journal of Political Economy*, Vol. 85, No. 3. 1977).
24. R. Jowell and C. Airey (eds), *British Social Attitudes – the 1984 Report* (Social and Community Planning Research, 1984).

25. S. G. B. Henry and P. A. Ormerod, 'Incomes Policy and Wage Inflation: Empirical Evidence for the UK 1961–1977', *National Institute Economic Review*, August 1978.

26. Walters, *Britain's Economic Renaissance*.

27. A. Dilmot and C. N. Morris, 'The tax system and distribution 1978–83', *Fiscal Studies*, May 1983, p. 59.

28. Corrections to allow for the effect of inflation upon public-sector debt convert post-war deficits into surpluses. They have little effect, however, upon the trend of deficits over the period considered.

29. See D. Savage, 'Fiscal policy 1974/5–1980/1: description and measurement', *National Institute Economic Review*, February 1982; and updated estimates in the February 1984 issue. See also the IMF's Annual Report 1985, p. 5; and the OECD Economic Survey of the UK, 1984.

30. Walters, *Britain's Economic Renaissance*, p. 59.

31. Lord Richardson in an address to the Italian Senate on 12 April 1983 (reported in the *Bank of England Quarterly Bulletin*, June 1983, p. 197).

32. Those who thought so seem to have been right. The British accounting profession has struggled unsuccessfully for over a decade to devise an acceptable way of correcting company accounts for inflation. The problem of devising a system of indexation which excludes (as it must) the effects of import prices looks at least as difficult.

33. By even – to some extent – the then Chancellor. See: P. Whitehead, *The Writing on the Wall* (Michael Joseph 1985), p. 84.

34. Heath is reported as saying that he considered it right that people should be given an additional safeguard against the possibility that the prices of world imports might rise exceptionally fast in the following year. See: D. Hurd, *An End to Promises* (Collins, 1979), p. 114; and Whitehead, *The Writing on the Wall*, p. 101.

35. *David Steel*: 'Is the Chief Secretary seriously telling the House that the income increases that have taken place over the past twelve months have not been a contributory factor to inflation?'
John Biffen: 'Broadly speaking, yes.'
(*Hansard*, 1 July 1980, col. 1397).

36. IMF Annual Report, 1985, p. 5. See also *OECD Economic Outlook* December 1982, p. 24; and, for a somewhat different picture, The Commission for The European Communities' *Annual Economic Review*, 1983–4.

37. M.J. Artis, et al. 'The effects of economic policy: 1979–82', *National Institute Economic Review*, May 1984, p. 54.

38. Andrea Boltho, in a discussion of a paper entitled 'Are the British so Different?' by Guido Carli, reported in F. Cairncross (ed.) *Changing Perceptions of Economic Policy* (Methuen, 1981), p. 246.

7

Postscript: Consequences and Prospects

I CONSEQUENCES

What happened between 1973 and 1983 was to have consequences for the British economy in the years to follow, and the story would be incomplete without a brief account of subsequent developments.

In 1983 the majority of people were better off and better equipped than ever before. Consumers' expenditure – especially on consumer durables – had suffered comparatively little in the recessions. Over the ten years since 1973, the percentage of families with refrigerators had risen from 78 to 94 per cent; with washing machines, from 67 to 80 per cent; with central heating, from 39 to 64 per cent; with telephones from 45 to 77 per cent; and with a second car, from 11 to 16 per cent.[1] Most people did not, however, feel themselves to be better off than five years previously. There were signs of an increasingly divided society, with the majority of low earners feeling worse off and relatively insecure, and the more affluent feeling better off and relatively secure.[2]

The main reason for the continuing sense of discontent and insecurity was the high level of unemployment, and its differential impact. The average male unemployment rate was nearly 17 per cent, and it was more than four times as high among unskilled or semi-skilled manual workers, as among non-manual workers. The average duration of unemployment for those becoming unemployed had risen to about a year.

A sense of insecurity of a different sort was prompted by a rise in the reported crime rate, which had doubled since 1973 – although some of that increase had been due to an increase in the proportion of burglaries which were reported to the police.

Survey evidence from a variety of sources suggests that Britain in 1983 was more divided, more violent, more racially prejudiced (but not more class-conscious) than it had been. In most respects, however, this can be seen as a continuation of historical trends rather than a direct consequence of any particular developments during the previous ten years.

Output, employment and costs, 1983–85

A number of favourable trends were apparent, in the first half of 1983. Output was growing (see figure 6.1, p. 178) at close to its pre-1972 trend, productivity was rising strongly, and the growth of unit labour costs had fallen. Company profitability was increasing, business confidence was returning, and investment intentions were strong. Most of these trends continued through 1983 and 1984, and into 1985. Output growth strengthened to exceed 3 per cent, and employment started to pick up.

After falling from a peak of 25.5 million in 1979 to 23.5 million in the first quarter of 1983, the numbers employed rose by some 800,000 over the following two years. The number of part-time workers increased considerably during this period, as it did during the period of strong employment growth between 1976 and 1979, so that despite the rapid growth in numbers employed, employment in terms of full-time equivalents remained below the levels of the 1950s.[3] The increase in employment was strongly concentrated upon the service sector and upon female employment. The numbers seeking work increased even more rapidly than the numbers employed, so that unemployment continued to rise. The rising trend in the working population which was interrupted between 1979 and 1983, resumed at an even more rapid rate thereafter (see figure 6.4, p. 182). This was due not to a more rapid growth in the population of working age, but rather to a surge in female participation rates. Thus the temporary departure of large numbers of women from the working population had served to reduce the numbers counted as unemployed between 1979 and 1983 and their subsequent return prevented the numbers from falling between 1983 and 1985. Unemployment rose from 3.2 million at the beginning of 1983 to 3.3 million at the beginning of 1985.

It was after the 1983 election that it became evident that legislation designed to reduce the power of trade unions was beginning to have the desired effect. In a few well-publicized cases, starting with the closed shop dispute between the National Graphical Association and the *Stockport Messenger*, employers began to show a willingness to make use of the new laws. The sequence of a court injunction; a fine for contempt of court when the injunction was disobeyed; and sequestration of union funds when, at first, the fine was not paid, proved an effective way of convincing union leaders that the new laws should be respected. In particular, the requirement to hold a ballot of members before calling a strike gained general acceptance. Failure to hold a ballot in defiance of the spirit of their own rule book, played an important part in the humiliation of the leaders of the National Union of Mineworkers, at the end – in March 1985 – of a violent, damaging and abortive year-long action against pit closures. The government's victory in that long-awaited showdown with the miners' union leadership, greatly enhanced its popularity, and the 'Scargill Factor' (named after the hapless union president) came to be compared with the Falklands Factor of its previous term.

While most people felt that an improvement had been brought about in industrial relations law, the signs were that labour relations on the shopfloor had continued to deteriorate. A 1985 survey showed that shopfloor workers felt themselves to be less well informed by management than in 1976, and that they were less inclined to believe such information as they were given. Significantly, it also showed that, whereas job security had been given priority over pay by the majority of shopfloor workers in 1976, pay was being given top priority in 1985.[4]

There were few signs, too, that the change in the industrial relations climate was continuing to be reflected in pay bargaining. The steep downward trend in the growth of average earnings between 1980 and 1983 (see figure 6.5, p. 185) did not persist thereafter. Despite a fall in the inflation rate, the underlying growth rate of earnings continued throughout 1984 and 1985 at, or above, the 7.5 per cent level which it had reached in 1983. In manufacturing, it continued at between 8.5 and 9 per cent. At first, the effect of earnings growth in manufacturing was substantially offset by productivity growth, so that unit labour costs rose less rapidly than prices. In the course of 1985, however, wages and salaries per unit of output in manufacturing grew by over 6 per cent. This was above the inflation rate, and well above the growth rates of labour costs in most industrial countries. The downward pressure on pay increases appeared to have been relieved by the slower growth of unemployment, and by the increase in company profitability.

Real rates of return for non-North Sea industrial and commercial companies continued the recovery which started in 1981. By 1985 they were estimated to be at their highest level since 1973. Companies at first responded strongly to the lifting of the financial pressures which had been placed upon them. Business investment grew by 10 per cent between 1983 and 1984, but then by only 2 per cent in the following year.

Monetary and fiscal policy

It has already been noted that the authorities' success in bringing sterling M3 within its target range in 1982/3 turned out to be temporary (see table 6.2, p. 205). After the 1983 election, the authorities attempted to offset the effects of a rapid growth of bank lending by sales of government bonds and savings certificates which were well in excess of the public-sector

borrowing requirement – an expedient known as 'overfunding'. At the
same time they attempted to relieve the resulting pressures upon company
liquidity by Bank of England purchases of commercial bills held by the
banking system. The resulting 'bill mountain' at the Bank of England
reached about £17 billion by the spring of 1985. The financial markets
regarded these devices with suspicion, and when, despite them, the money
supply looked like overshooting its target, there was a precipitous fall in
the exchange rate against European currencies as well as the dollar in
January 1985. This was thought to be due also to uncertainties about the
oil price, and to developments in the United States. The Chancellor
responded by raising interest rates from 9.5 per cent to 14 per cent in the
course of the month, and expressing a determination to bring money
supply growth 'well within' the target range. In October 1985, however,
he announced that no further attempt would be made to bring sterling M3
within its target range for the remainder of the financial year; but that a
new target range would be set in the following budget. He also announced
that systematic overfunding would no longer be used to control the money
supply.[5] In March 1986, a new target range was set at 11–15 per cent: a
higher range than had ever previously been set.

At the time of the 1983 budget, the intention had been announced of
reducing the public-sector borrowing requirement to 2.5 per cent of GDP
in 1984/5, and 2 per cent in 1985/6, compared with an estimated 2.75 per
cent in 1982/3 (it later turned out to be 3.1 per cent). In the event, the
percentages for 1983/4 and 1984/5 were close to that for 1982/3. By then
they were, however, increasingly dominated by receipts from sales of
public-sector assets and from council house sales. The 'underlying'
borrowing requirement, after deducting these items, showed a slightly
rising trend.[6] In 1985/6, the target of 2 per cent was met, representing a
reduction of the underlying percentage to somewhat below its 1982/3
level.

The fact that the credibility of the government's strategy was not
seriously damaged by these developments seems to have been due mainly
to continued success in holding down inflation, and to forecasts that it was
likely to fall further. Financial commentators seem also to have accepted
that sterling M3 is frequently a misleading measure. (Few of them were
prepared, however, to take seriously any attempt to divert attention
toward the slow growth of cash in circulation and in bank tills – which
they were inclined to attribute to the growth of cash dispensers, rather
than to any act of policy.) The further falls in the exchange rate which
occurred in 1986 appeared to owe much more to external developments
than to any further concern about monetary policy.

External influences

The dominant influences upon the world economy, and upon the British economy in particular, after 1983, were the threatened collapse of the OPEC oil cartel and the massive US budget deficit.

Since the 1979 oil price rise, the demand for oil had fallen because of the recession, and because of measures taken to economize in consumption. Non-OPEC sources of oil were also developed on a large scale. OPEC's pricing policy made it effectively the residual source of supply, and the demand for OPEC oil nearly halved between 1979 and 1985. Saudi Arabia's production fell particularly sharply.

The sterling exchange rate proved to be sensitive to these developments, tending to fall in response to even a rumour of an impending fall in the oil price. An appreciable part of the 6.5 per cent fall in its trade-weighted index between 1983 and 1985 is thought to be attributable to that factor. That fall in the exchange rate roughly offset the relative increase in British labour costs, so that the competitiveness of British manufactured goods in international markets remained broadly constant between 1983 and 1985.

Towards the end of 1985, Saudi Arabia indicated that it was no longer prepared to hold its oil production at very low levels in order to maintain the existing level of prices. Between November 1985 and the beginning of August 1986, oil prices dropped from $28 a barrel to $8 a barrel, to recover to $14 on the news of a temporary OPEC production agreement, reached in August. Sterling fell further in the first nine months of 1986. By September, its trade-weighted index was down 15 per cent, and its rate against the Deutschmark decreased 20 per cent, on its 1983 average.

Exchange rates over the period 1983–6, were strongly influenced also by developments in the United States. The enormous budgetary and trade deficits, which were the accidental result of the Reagan administration's fiscal policies, together with swings in the Federal Reserve Bank's monetary policies, had powerful effects upon foreign exchange markets and upon the real world economy.

The compromise reached between the administration and the Congress led to tax cuts combined with public spending increases, which produced a powerful fiscal stimulus. After the brief recession (described in chapter 5) United States GDP grew by 11 per cent between 1982 and 1984, and the volume of its imports grew by an astonishing 34 per cent, leading to a current account deficit of over $100 billion. Largely as a result of this, world trade picked up rapidly, to grow in volume by 10 per cent between 1983 and 1984, bringing it back to the pre-1982 trend (shown in figure 6.6, p. 187). This produced a stimulus to output in the other industrial countries, especially Germany and Japan, and the output of the seven major economies grew by some 4.5 per cent. After the middle of 1984, US economic growth slowed sharply to about 2.5 per cent a year, the growth in the volume of world trade between 1984 and 1985 slowed to about 3 per cent, and GDP growth in the major seven economies to about 2.5 per cent. The episode had been a graphic demonstration of the importance of the United States to the world economy.

The rapid rise of the dollar exchange rate (described in chapter 5), continued through 1983 and 1984 taking its trade-weighted index in early 1985 to a peak some 65 per cent higher than its value in 1980. The growing current account deficit on the balance of payments continued to be more than offset by net inflows on the capital account, made up of the repatriation of US funds invested abroad, and – to a lesser extent – of an inflow of overseas money.[7] A lifting of Japanese restrictions upon institutional investment abroad led, in particular, to substantial inflows from Japan. The Federal Reserve Bank had reduced interest rates from their 1981 peak of over 16 per cent, but was then for a time reluctant – in view of the size of the budget deficit – to reduce them below 10–12 per cent, for fear of a surge in money supply growth. The reduction in the inflation rate, and the fear of provoking a recession, subsequently prompted a reduced preoccupation with the money supply and increased concern with the exchange rate. In September 1985 the United States Treasury announced that it was seeking the co-operation of other countries to engineer a fall in the dollar exchange rate. By the summer of 1986 the Federal Reserve Bank brought its discount rate down to 5.5 per cent – the lowest for nine years – and by September the trade-weighted dollar exchange rate index had fallen by some 30 per cent from its 1985 peak.

A summary and a footnote

The deliberately sketchy account which has been given of events since mid-1983 serves to dispose of some possibilities which could not entirely be dismissed on the basis of events up to that time. The possibility then appeared to remain that the obstacles in the way of adherence to a simple money supply rule were technical and temporary, and would in due course be overcome It certainly seemed possible that, with inflationary expectations substantially broken, pay increases would continue their downward trend. The stable financial environment, in which business could plan confidently for expansion, might then have seemed to be not far distant. A continuing reduction, and finally the virtual elimination of inflation, did not seem too much to hope for.

As regards the last of those possibilities, what has been achieved since 1983 would appear to owe more to the continued weakness of world commodity prices than to domestic policies. The prospect of a continuing downward trend in inflation without a reduction in domestic labour costs must at best be uncertain. The collapse of the OPEC oil cartel should eventually make for greater stability and faster economic expansion. However, even negative price shocks impose adjustment costs, and for Britain, a major adaptation to the resulting reduction in revenues from North Sea oil would be required. In the meantime, there is little to indicate that the trade imbalances, which have made for such violent fluctuations in the world financial environment since 1983, are likely to disappear.

Above all, as the concluding section of this chapter sets out to demonstrate, there seems little prospect that the 'self-righting' capacity of the economy will produce a return to the unemployment levels of the early 1970s by the end of the decade.

(The footnote referred to in the above heading is an acknowledgement that no account has been taken in the above summary, of the 'pause' or 'plateau', which appears to have developed in the growth of output since the first quarter of 1985. The statistics which are available at the time of writing do not tell an entirely consistent story, and they are likely to be subject to considerable revision. Its relevance to the story of the 1973–83 period seems in any case to be doubtful.)

II PROSPECTS

The rise in unemployment between 1973 and 1983 amounted to 9 per cent of the labour force, or about 2.4 million people, and the bulk of that increase occurred in the last three years of the period. The full extent of the damage which that implies depends upon whether it will turn out historically to have been merely a transitory surge of unemployment, or something more persistent. To bring unemployment back to its 1973 level in another ten years – or to bring it substantially below two million over a five-year period – would, for example, imply a fall averaging 240,000 a year. Is the outcome likely to be better or worse than that?

A 1984 Treasury study provides a broad framework for considering such prospects.[8] That study formed part of a Green Paper which set out the implications of the Chancellor's undertaking (since abandoned) to hold public expenditure broadly constant in real terms over the following ten years. The Treasury does not publish its forecasts of unemployment, but something can be gleaned from the assumptions which it used for long-term projections of public expenditure. The approach adopted concentrated upon long-term trends, taking no account of the cyclical fluctuations which occur in recessions and recoveries – and the post-1983 developments described above were, of course, not then known.

The Treasury study made use of the definitionally true statement that employment growth is equal to output growth, less the growth of labour productivity; and then of the statement that the decline in unemployment will be made up of employment growth, less the growth of the working population. Output growth was projected to average 2.5 per cent a year, excluding North Sea oil. On a plausible interpretation of what was said in the study, this was taken to be associated with productivity growth averaging 1.75 per cent a year on the same basis. Those projections implied employment growth averaging 0.75 per cent a year, or about 180,000. Labour force projections, combining demographic trends with expected activity rate changes, put the growth of the working population at about 120,000 a year up to 1988, with virtually no change thereafter.[9] Put together, those projections implied a decline in unemployment averaging 60,000 a year up to 1988 and 180,000 a year thereafter. The benefit-related unemployment count would fall rather more slowly because some of those gaining employment would not have been entitled to benefit. Thus unemployment was effectively projected to remain at over two million, well into the 1990s.

Small changes in the assumptions underlying those projections would

Table 7.1 Rates of sustained growth of output and labour productivity[a]

Period	Annual output growth rate (%)	Annual growth rate of labour productivity (%)
1951–55	3.0	1.9
1955–60	2.6	2.1
1960–64	3.2	2.3
1964–68	2.7	2.8
1968–73	3.2	2.6
1973–79	1.3	1.0
1979–83	0.1	1.3

[a] Pre-war growth rates tended to be lower. The growth rate between most cyclical peaks from the 1850s to the Second World War was within the range 1.5 per cent to 2.5 per cent a year, and productivity growth was nearly always within the range 0.5 per cent to 1.5 per cent a year.

Source: Economic Trends, Annual Supplement (HM Treasury, 1984).

have made a substantial difference to the outcome. If output had been taken to grow by an extra 0.25 per cent, the employment projection would have been 60,000 a year higher, and a reduction of 0.25 per cent in productivity growth would have the same effect. But high output growth has historically been associated with high productivity growth, as table 7.1 indicates. If past experience is to be taken as a guide, a sustained annual growth rate much in excess of 3 per cent a year, accompanied by productivity growth of less than 2 per cent a year, must be regarded as unlikely. This suggests an upper limit to sustained employment growth of 240,000 a year. At that rate, and assuming the labour supply projections to be correct, unemployment would still not have been projected to fall below two million until 1990.

(Employment growth in 1983 and 1984 was, in fact, over 350,000; but this must be regarded as a cyclical effect. The large proportion of part-time jobs which were created would have depressed the productivity trend, and artificially widened the gap between output growth and productivity growth. There was, correspondingly, an above-trend growth in the working population, which more than offset the growth in employment, leading to a rise in unemployment. Between the first quarters of 1985 and 1986, employment growth fell back to a more normal 230,000. These aberrations do not in themselves throw doubt upon the plausibility of what has been said about sustainable trends.)

The prospects of a more rapid fall in unemployment depend in principle upon three possibilities:

(1) a faster sustained increase in output than is suggested by historical experience – not accompanied by a fully offsetting increase in productivity growth;
(2) the substitution of labour for capital in the production of given levels of output;
(3) a slower growth in the labour supply, such as might result from reductions in the numbers of hours worked per week, in the number of weeks worked per year, or the number of years worked per lifetime.

The last of these possibilities amounts, in effect, to learning to live with a lower demand for labour. Provided that economic growth continues, it does not appear to be an altogether unlikely development. It would not, after all, be surprising if an increasing number of people decided to take the benefits of increasing prosperity in the form of increased leisure rather than of increased earnings. It is possible that the downward trends – already observable for males – in hours worked per week, weeks worked per year, and years worked per lifetime might be steeper than assumed in the projections. If those trends were faster on average by only 1 per cent a year, unemployment would fall by around one million in five years – provided that there were no consequent increase in productivity or of unit costs. Institutionally bargained reductions in the length of the working week in the early 1980s did not usually yield employment gains, however, because there were offsetting effects upon productivity and costs.

The substitution of labour for capital could result from a change of production methods, or from a change in the patterns of spending. The former presupposes a change in relative costs: unless labour became cheaper relative to capital, the change could not take place without an increase in costs and a consequent fall in sales. The latter could result from a change in tastes in favour of labour-intensive products, such as consumer services, and away from the more capital-intensive consumer durables. But again, the economic motive for such a change would be lacking if there were no change in relative costs. Government action to reduce tax relief on capital investment, and to reduce taxes on employment, could produce benefits to employment through these routes, as could a reduced growth rate of earnings.

A lower-than-expected earnings growth could lead to greater employment growth also through lower unit costs, increased international competitiveness, and a greater share in world trade. One estimate[10] suggests that a 3 per cent reduction in the trend of real earnings over a three-year period would lead to employment gains from all sources of 500,000 a year, accumulating eventually to 1.5 million. This would require an even larger reduction in the trend of money earnings, because there would be a partially offsetting fall in inflation. In view of the relatively low price-sensitivity of British trade shares, an improvement in non-price competitiveness through product improvements might be even more effective.

The fastest and surest way of producing a short-term reduction in unemployment would nevertheless be the traditional Keynesian remedy of a stimulus to domestic demand through tax reductions or increases in public expenditure. The experience recounted in the preceding chapters suggests that such a remedy could not, however, be carried very far without encountering financing difficulties. Even within that constraint, its effectivenesss and acceptability would be narrowly limited by the dangers of a surge of inflation, unless it were accompanied by an effective measure of pay restraint. A further recourse to a stringent monetary policy for that purpose seems, on recent experience, to be unlikely. Whether an acceptable and effective incomes policy could be devised, remains open to question. If it could, the prospects would look a great deal better.

Without some successful policy innovation or some favourable departure of economic behaviour from past trends, the prospect of even a modest rate of reduction of unemployment appears remote.

NOTES

1. *Social Trends*, CSO, 1985.
2. R. Jowell and C. Airey (eds) 'British Social Attitudes – the 1984 Report' (Social and Community Planning Research, 1984).
3. On OECD estimates (*OECD Economic Survey, the United Kingdom* (1985) p. 19.
4. Survey by Market and Opinion Research International, reported in the *Sunday Times*, 5 January 1986, p. 17.
5. Speech at the Mansion House, 17 October 1985.
6. See estimates in *Barclays Bank Economic Review*, May 1986, p. 49.
7. See 'The United States economy: an overview' in *Midland Bank Review*, Autumn 1985, p. 7.
8. 'The Next Ten Years: Public Expenditure and Taxation into the 1990s' Annex 3, HM Treasury, March 1984 (Cmnd 9189), p. 27.
9. 'Labour force outlook for Great Britain' (*Dept of Employment Gazette*, February 1984, p. 56.
10. An estimate put forward by the Chancellor on the basis of a review by Treasury officials, 'The Relationship between Employment and Wages' (HM Treasury, 1985).

Index

Index by
Caryl Sutcliffe